Families with a Difference

Varieties of surrogate parenthood

Michael *and* Heather Humphrey

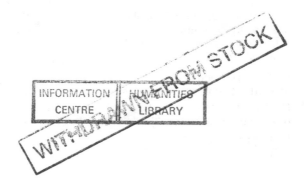
ROUTLEDGE
London and New York

First published in 1988 by
Routledge
a division of Routledge, Chapman and Hall
11 New Fetter Lane, London EC4P 4EE

Published in the USA by
Routledge
a division of Routledge, Chapman and Hall, Inc.
29 West 35th Street, New York NY 10001

Printed in Great Britain by Biddles Ltd, Guildford

British Library Cataloguing in Publication Data

Humphrey, Michael
   Families with a difference: varieties of
   surrogate parenthood.
   1. Family   2. Interpersonal relations
   3. Surrogate mothers
   I. Title   II. Humphrey, Heather
   306.8'7   HQ728

ISBN 0 415 00689 9
     0 415 00690 2 Pbk

Library of Congress Cataloging in Publication Data

Humphrey, Michael.
   Families with a difference.
   Bibliography: p.
   Includes index.
   1. Parenthood. 2. Childlessness. 3. Surrogate
mothers. 4. Adoption. 5. Foster parents.
6. Stepparents. I. Humphrey, Heather. II. Title.
III. Title: Surrogate parenthood.
HQ518.H86 1988   306.8'743   87-33608
ISBN 0 415 00689 9
    0 415 00690 2 (pbk.)

Contents

List of tables

Foreword

Since the publication of the Warnock Report in 1984 there has been increasing public interest and debate over infertility and the problems associated with it. On a different level from many of the issues raised for society, but equally important, are the emotional and practical problems as they affect individuals. Michael and Heather Humphrey have many years of experience of counselling childless couples, and working with families.

In this book they consider families where the children have been adopted or fostered, or where there are other non-genetic relationships between a parent and child. Many different family make-ups are considered. The book combines a review of previous studies from the scientific literature of relevance to each topic, together with the authors' own contributions and insights. Also included are the results of a new survey of adopted persons in search of the identity of their biological parents.

The rewards and problems of the many variant forms of surrogate parenting, including adoption, fostering, step-parenthood, and donor insemination are dealt with individually, and the book brings together a wealth of experience and knowledge, in a lucid and readable form.

The book can be recommended to all who work professionally with children, parents or families, and those who counsel individuals concerned about their origins. Readers will gain new understanding of how families work, and the particular problems that may be encountered where there is surrogate parenthood. I learnt much on reading it that is of relevance to my own work as a practising paediatrician, and I am sure it will be of equal benefit to many others from the caring professions.

Richard West, MD, FRCP
Dean, St George's Hospital, and Medical School
August 1987

Prologue

A convenient way of launching this book is to quote the opening paragraph of our preliminary statement to the publishers. This will not only help to explain our reasons for wanting to write it, but possibly also their reasons for hoping that it would be worth publishing.

A surrogate family for our purposes is one where the usual genetic linkage between parents and children is absent or incomplete, whether or not this situation is openly acknowledged. Are there any disadvantages to growing up in such a family? In particular circumstances there may be, but the extra stresses are not always easy to identify. On the whole it has been left to the helping professions and the judiciary to try to sort out the muddle after something has gone wrong. Preventive action calls for both effective guidelines and better opportunities for family counselling.

We have chosen the word 'surrogate' for our title in preference to some of the more prosaic alternatives, such as 'substitute' or 'reconstituted'. In its more specialized sense, 'surrogate' refers to the deputy of a bishop or his chancellor appointed to grant marriage licences without banns (*Concise Oxford Dictionary*), which is doubtless an important function but not one that need concern us here. We shall be using the term far more generally to encompass any situation where one or more adults in a household are acting *in loco parentis*. Much has been written about adoption and foster care, which typically involve two surrogate parents; much less about families created by remarriage or by donor insemination, where only one care-taker is genetically unrelated to the child(ren). We saw the need for an attempt to bring these various departures from the norm within the compass of a brief monograph, possibly for the first time in Britain. New trends in human reproduction, such as *in vitro* fertilization, were also thought to deserve inclusion. Surrogacy in its more sensational aspects, where a woman agrees to use her womb as an incubator (to quote from the Warnock Report of 1984), will also be discussed. However, we would emphasize at this point that dramatic stories of this nature are not our main preoccupation, and in any case nothing is known of the consequences for family life.

We are well aware of an element of risk in our venture, which is certainly not without its difficulties. No authors could hope to be equally expert in all these diverse fields, and we would never claim to be. We have personal experience of adoptive parenthood, and one of us at an earlier period of his career was also professionally involved. More recently we have devoted a good many hours to the co-operative venture of counselling candidates for donor insemination, now that a flourishing service has been established at our place of work. But our contact with stepfamilies, personally or professionally, has been distinctly limited; whilst couples in search of the latest techniques on offer from gynaecologists have for the most part eluded us. Thus, although every chapter bar one has been written by Michael Humphrey, any semblance of stylistic unity is liable to be offset by differences between chapters in the content and manner of presentation. For example, Chapters 2 and 6 are straight surveys of the literature (ample and growing in the case of foster care, tantalizingly meagre on step-parenthood), whereas Chapters 3 and 4 are amplified versions of our own previously published work. Chapter 5, written by Heather Humphrey, is the only one to report new empirical data. In the final chapter we shall do our best to allay some of the doubts raised at the outset, when we enquire whether there are adequate grounds for suspecting that the nuclear family as we know it is on the way out. Some commentators (for example, Cooper 1970) have been willing to write it off without due ceremony, yet we ourselves are less easily persuaded. And even if it should turn out that we are mistaken in our view, and the family is indeed already moribund, we anticipate that its terminal phase will be protracted – like Charles II, it will be an unconscionable time dying!

What is the basis of our incorrigible faith, if not sheer wishful thinking? Other social historians besides Laslett (1972) have reminded us that the nuclear family is no modern invention, having existed in Britain well before the industrial revolution. And, even if the extended family (outside little enclaves such as

Bethnal Green[1]) has become more dispersed in the twentieth century, the valued link between grandparents and their grandchildren shows no signs of diminishing. From an extraordinarily wide-ranging survey of 250 different societies, both agricultural and industrial, Murdock (1949) concluded that the nuclear family was not only flourishing but well-nigh universal. What varied from one society to another was not the nuclear element itself but the kinship network. True, alternative modes of living have appeared since Murdock's contribution, notably the Jewish kibbutz, the Chinese commune and the hippie communes of the 1960s. Yet in one form or another the family as a basic social unit has shown what is almost a built-in capacity for survival. Whatever its inherent drawbacks it must surely serve some kind of a useful purpose. For an up-to-date account of sociological aspects the reader may wish to consult Harris (1983) or Wilson (1985).

One way of exploring such a hardy social institution is to look at some of the more ubiquitous variants, what Goody (1971) has entitled 'forms of pro-parenthood'. It was partly with a view to highlighting the importance of the nuclear family that we were ready to embark on our self-appointed task. But above all, of course, we hope that our material will be of interest in its own right.

Acknowledgements

Many people over the years have helped to clarify our thinking on surrogate families, far too many to acknowledge individually. In the course of writing this book we have received specific help from Jane Rowe, John Triseliotis, and Michael Rutter, to whom we extend our thanks.

We are particularly grateful to Linda Savell of NORCAP (National Organization for Counselling Adoptees and their Parents) for her indispensable aid in launching the survey reported in Chapter 5. Some ninety members of that organization took the trouble to complete and return our postal questionnaire, of whom more than twenty offered further contact. We were delighted to take advantage of their generous offer, and hope that our findings will filter through to them in due course.

Although it is fast becoming fashionable for authors to process their own words, we have pleasure in thanking Sue Arnold and Sue Stevens for relieving us of that task. It was thanks to their efficiency that we were almost on time in delivering the goods. Finally we thank Caroline Lane of Tavistock for coaxing us through the gestation period, and her successor Rosemary Nixon for acting as midwife.

Michael and Heather Humphrey, September 1987

1 The nuclear family as an endangered species

'A Runaway World?' was the title given by Sir Edmund Leach to his 1967 Reith Lectures. Were he to repeat these lectures today he might wish to dispense with the question mark, for the rate of change has continued to escalate. As an anthropologist he set out to be provocative, and was duly rewarded with a spate of misunderstanding (or a *succès de scandale*, as he has put it in a postscript to the published version). Writing ten years later, Rapoport *et al* (1977), on the basis of their massive literature survey commissioned by the DHSS, accused Leach and other family 'doomwatchers' of nostalgia for the 'world we have lost' (Laslett 1972). So let us recall what he actually said:

> In the past, kinsfolk and neighbours gave the individual continuous moral support throughout his life. Today the domestic household is isolated. The family looks inward upon itself; there is an intensification of emotional stress between husband and wife, and parents and children. The strain is greater than most of us can bear. Far from being the basis of a good society, the family, with its narrow privacy and tawdry secrets, is the source of all our discontents.
>
> (Leach 1968: 44)

Strong words, to be sure, but despite that detectable middle-class bias to which academics (apart from a few left-wing sociologists) are notoriously prone, they ring truer today than at the time of utterance. The nuclear family, for all its remarkable capacity to cushion its members in times of stress, is really not in a particularly healthy state. We shall begin by considering the extent to which families are *intact*.

In the mid-1960s, when the first report on the famous 1958 cohort[1] was being prepared for the Central Advisory Council on Education (Pringle, Butler, and Davie 1966), all but 6 per cent of a national sample of 11,000 children were found to be living with both natural parents. This means that only a small minority were

either living with an unsupported parent by reason of illegitimacy, desertion, or mutual separation, divorce or death; or were
being brought up by a parent and a step-parent, foster parents or
adoptive parents; or were in care of a local authority. (The small
number who were more or less permanently confined to a hospital or other institution were excluded from the survey.) In stress-
ing how hard it can be to assess the significance of abnormal
factors in a child's home life, the authors pointed out that:

> A child living with his own parents, one of whom may be
> mentally or physically seriously ill, may well be growing up in
> an atmosphere of much greater strain than another child who
> has been successfully adopted or fostered. Nevertheless, a child
> not living with both his parents will in many cases have experi-
> enced a period of separation which may have been prolonged;
> in others, for example, one-parent families, the child may be
> permanently deprived of a normal home life. Thus at one time
> or another he will probably have undergone an upsetting, if
> not seriously traumatic, experience.
>
> (Pringle, Butler, and Davie 1966: 86)

Fewer than 10 per cent of these 7-year-olds were only children,
and more than 50 per cent had at least two siblings. So *prima facie*,
it does not look as if their parents were doing too badly, at least
in terms of providing a supportive structure for the children's
development. Admittedly a large-scale exercise of this kind
allows only superficial judgements as to the quality of family life.
Intelligence, progress in the basic subjects such as reading and
arithmetic, and even social adjustment, can all be measured with
acceptable accuracy; however, concepts such as 'narrow privacy'
and 'tawdry secrets' are much less open to evaluation, let alone
measurement. Self-sufficiency has its virtues, yet to function
at its best a family needs to become at least partially integrated
with the local community. The efficiency of the state schools, the
friendliness of the neighbourhood, access to parks and playing
fields, plus a host of other factors in the immediate environment
will interact with family influences in promoting healthy progress
towards maturity. We have no means of judging how many of
these relentlessly monitored children (who are now just turned
29) would have reason to agree with the celebrated Reith lec-

turer's view of the family as 'the source of all our discontents', but it would scarcely go unchallenged.[2]

THE INSTABILITY OF MARRIAGE TODAY

But what of the declining stability of the family? Chester (1985), in a useful summary of recent data from national sources, appears to accept current projections suggesting that one in three of today's marriages may end in divorce. The possibility cannot be denied, but it is indeed no more than a projection based on a life table analysis by the Office of Population Census and Surveys (Haskey 1982). This is inevitably a hazardous exercise, since there is no way of forecasting whether divorce rates will continue at their current levels. Nothing short of a longitudinal follow-up of a marriage cohort can be expected to yield a reliable figure in respect of today's marriages. Obviously we shall have to wait many years before marriages contracted in the 1980s can be compared with those of the early inter-war years, of which Rowntree and Carrier (1958) reported only 3 per cent as ending in divorce. Even by 1950 the estimated current rate had crept up to only a little over 7 per cent (Fletcher 1966).

As Chester aptly points out, most western countries have exhibited broadly similar divorce trends since 1945. A brief period in which hasty war-time unions were given a decent burial was followed by a plateau throughout the 1950s, and then a strongly rising trend from 1960 onwards. This has recently shown signs of levelling out, but Chester thinks it would be mistaken to attach too much weight to the Divorce Reform Act of 1969 which replaced specific matrimonial offences (such as adultery and cruelty) with the concept of irretrievable breakdown. Certainly it has become easier to obtain a divorce by mutual consent, or against the wishes of one party after five years. But the significant rise had begun a decade or so earlier, and changes in the law may well have had a less dramatic effect than is commonly supposed. In fact it would be reasonable to suggest that the main influence was upon the timing rather than the occurrence of divorce. However that may be, it seems doubtful whether we ought to pay too much attention to demographers, who always have trouble with their interpretation of current trends. And although a longitudinal perspective can be helpful, the difficulty remains that divorce is in any case not the most sensitive index of marital failure – it is merely 'the tip of the iceberg'.

However, we shall stay with divorce for a while longer on the grounds that it does at least carry the implication of something seriously wrong with a marriage. It has long been the case that about one in three broken marriages are childless, although this is not the same as saying that childlessness drives couples apart – it may do, but it also makes the decision to separate much easier. Another one divorcing couple in ten have independent children only, and we would expect such couples to be relatively few since marital breakdown is known to be commonest in the early years. It is only quite recently, however, that we have gained new understanding of the relationship between fertility and divorce from General Household Survey data on over 5,000 ever-married women (Murphy 1984). This intricate analysis suggests that greater risk of divorce is associated with the birth of several children in quick succession as well as with childlessness. It would appear that the carefully regulated two-child family is least at risk – although forward planning and living within one's resources are no guarantee of marital happiness, they may be able to prevent downright failure. But studies of this kind are of more academic interest than practical value, since people have a habit of marrying when they feel like it and having children when they feel like it – or not, as the case may be. And meanwhile the sad truth is that about 160,000 children annually are hit by divorce, and hit very hard indeed. As we shall discover in Chapter 6, the last thing most children want is their parents to split up. Again, Chester (1985) quotes recent projections to the effect that almost one child in five will suffer parental divorce before the age of 16. This is surely a far more sobering prospect than the one in three figure assigned to marital breakdown. But obviously these disturbing trends are interrelated, with the miseries of the parents likely to be visited upon the children over a much longer time span.

And for children of divorced parents the most immediate and often inescapable aftermath is the one-parent family. This may be no more than a transitory phase giving way to the complexities of life in a step-family, to be discussed in a later chapter. But it is tough while it lasts, and the numbers involved have risen from 570,000 in 1971 to 940,000 in 1984, an increase of 65 per cent in

the space of fifteen years. About one in eight of all families with
dependent children are now headed by lone parents, of whom 87
per cent are mothers, and altogether something like 1.5 million
children are affected. The comparable figure from the 1961
census, when the divorce rate was only just beginning to creep
up, was approximately one family in twelve. A much higher proportion of one-parent families arise from separation and divorce
than from bereavement, which has become increasingly rare as a
cause of family disruption in the twentieth century. The Finer
Commission on one-parent families (1974) was both preceded
and followed by well-documented studies of the problems they
experience (Marsden 1969; George and Wilding 1972; Ferri
1976). As can be readily imagined, these problems are not exclu-
sively financial, even if the Finer report gave most weight to this
aspect. Although we originally planned to include a chapter on
single parenthood, this was abandoned when we realized that
the element of surrogacy in such families is hard to discern until a
step-parent figure enters the picture.

To return to Leach's diatribe against the nuclear family, we
have already suggested that it was launched from a middle-class
perspective. It is therefore worth remembering that youthful
working-class marriages are especially vulnerable, as has been
known for a long time. Granted that pre-marital conception as a
reason for early marriage is now less common than it used to be,
whilst the interval between marriage and first childbirth has
lengthened even among working-class couples, the fact remains
that the annual divorce rate for unskilled working-class men is
more than four times higher than for professional men (Chester
1985). Youthful inexperience and adverse social circumstances –
what Ineichen (1977) has referred to as the 'vortex of disadvantage' – go hand in hand as a basis of marital failure and family
disruption. Hence the emotional pressures of middle-class family
life may be more intense simply because they have to be contained over a much longer period.

THE BIRTH OF THE FIRST CHILD

The scrupulously planned two-child family has always been essentially a middle-class phenomenon. Even before the recent trend
towards cohabitation as a prelude to marriage, well-educated

young women and (more especially) young men were typically
two or three years older on their wedding day than their working-class contemporaries who had left school at the earliest possible age. And since fertility (like sexual activity) is at its peak in the
late teens and early twenties, it calls for self-discipline as well as
long-term goals to postpone parenthood during the years of emotional immaturity and financial insecurity. Ineichen's study of
179 young couples in Bristol marrying for the first time in early
1974 was focused on housing, a major aspect of marriage at
any age that is sometimes conveniently ignored by comfortably
housed social scientists. He found that teenage marriage was
predominantly a working-class event, with three times as many
older brides (45 per cent versus 15 per cent) having husbands in
non-manual occupations. His couples were interviewed two or
three times during the first eighteen months of married life, and
their expressed intentions of family size were initially very similar
across the social spectrum: for example, a little over 60 per cent
of both teenage and older brides were reckoning on not more
than two children (compare Dunnell 1979). However, it comes as
no surprise to learn that four times as many teenage brides had
conceived before marriage (40 per cent versus 10 per cent).
Fewer than half of the group as a whole were expecting to wait
more than two years for their first child, whilst a mere 4 per cent
were intending to remain childless; and here older brides predo-
minated, especially in the last category.

It is of course youthful parents rather than youthful marriers
who are most in need of help, whether from their own parents
(as in the average middle-class family) or from the state. It is just
unfortunate that these two major sources of marital vulnerability
are so often interwoven. Both Gavron (1966) and Woolf (1971)
had already drawn attention to the level of awareness among
some young couples – for instance, a third of Woolf's large
sample of teenage brides thought they had married too young.
And pregnancy does not last long enough to afford a gradual
period of adjustment. As Ineichen wittily observes: 'Not only is it
like advancing from a novice apprentice just signed on at the
factory to works manager in one day, but it is a 24-hour-job with
no guaranteed tea-breaks and no paid annual holidays, and it is
difficult to hand in your notice until the first fifteen years are up.'
(1977: 67) Small wonder that Cobb (1980) chose 'Babyshock' for

the title of his edited contributions on the transition to parenthood.

But perhaps things have changed in the ten years since Ineichen's survey was published? Oral contraception has been with us for a quarter of a century now; and whilst it may have taken some years to percolate through all strata of society, by the early 1970s it was already the most popular method in overall current use. Thus Dunnell (1979: Appendix 4), from an analysis of well over 3,000 women aged 16−49 in England, Wales, and Scotland, reported that nearly four times as many were using the Pill (59 per cent) as the condom (15 per cent), whilst only 3 per cent were relying on the notoriously risky method of withdrawal. Although her contraceptive data were not analysed by social class, it seems reasonable to assume that any young couple with sufficient motivation to postpone parenthood until other more pressing goals have been realized are in a strong position to do so. It is sexually inexperienced teenagers (not necessarily virgins) who are most likely to take chances, either deliberately or because they are caught unawares in their search for a stable partnership (Skinner 1986). Dunnell's interview survey did not go beyond 1975, and we are aware of no published data on more recent marriage cohorts; yet Skinner's survey (again by interview) suggests that little change has occurred over the past ten years in the sexual behaviour of adolescent girls. Table 1.1, however, shows that even within marriage the realities of fertility control lag behind the opportunities. Between 1975 and 1985 all four social groups demonstrated the same fertility trends, an initial decline followed by a rise to the original value (or even above it in the case of skilled non-manual workers); the gap between semi-skilled/unskilled and professional couples remains, with the latter waiting twice as long to become parents. They also continued to wait longer before marrying, as may be inferred from Table 1.2. The difference of four years between the two mean ages at first childbirth is more than twice as long as the difference between the two median intervals between marriage and parenthood. Evidently it still requires a certain level of education and occupation to instil a due sense of priorities for living, in that parenthood can wait (up to a point anyway), whereas other significant aims relating to work or leisure activities may be compromised if children arrive too soon.

Table 1.1   *Median interval from first marriage to first birth, by social class of husband*

	Median interval in months (legitimate births only)				
Year	All social classes	I–II	IIIN	IIIM	IV–V
1975	28	37	35	25	18
1977	29	40	36	27	19
1980	29	41	37	25	18
1983	29	39	34	27	20
1984	29	38	34	27	20
1985	28	37	33	26	18
Mean (s.d.)	28.7 (0.52)	38.7 (1.63)	34.8 (1.47)	26.2 (0.98)	18.8 (0.98)

Source: Adapted from Table 11, *OPCS Monitor* FMI 86/2, 15 July 1986

Table 1.2   *Mean ages of women at first childbirth within marriage, by social class of husband*

Social class of husband	Mean ages in years (legitimate births only)		
	1975	1984	1985
I–II	26.7	27.8	28.0
IIIN	25.6	26.4	26.5
IIIM	24.0	25.1	25.2
IV–V	23.0	23.8	24.0
All classes	24.7	25.8	26.0

Source: Adapted from Table 12, *OPCS Monitor* FMI 86/2, 15 July 1986

LIVING IN WHAT USED TO BE CALLED SIN

But how long is it safe to delay trying for a child? The *Sunday Express Magazine* of 22 March 1987 carried an article about an international model turned TV presenter. At 36 she has all the trappings of success: new career, new love affair, new home – but what about the patter of tiny human feet?

'I do want to have children eventually', she muses. 'I have been thinking about it more and more lately. But if I'm going to be a mother I'll give everything to that for as long as it takes. The thing that fulfils me now is my career, and for the moment that's what I'm going to put first.'

The next *Sunday Express* carried an article about a female consultant, one of only five women in Britain to have reached the summit in general surgery, who had produced her first child at 36 and then another three children, the youngest at about 43. 'Once I had become a consultant surgeon, I could organize my day rather better than when I was climbing the ladder and had to put in so many hours' work', she is quoted as saying.[3]

These are striking examples of procrastination over motherhood, in one case planned to fit in with a woman's awe-inspiring dedication to her chosen career, in the other case suggestive of a more *dilettante* approach. Readers will be familiar enough with this dilemma facing gifted − and indeed not so gifted − women today, even if they do not move in the world of show business or hospital medicine. And it really is rather a cruel dilemma for women who wish to pursue higher qualifications without losing out on the maternity stakes. As one of the author's students remarked when forced to extend her clinical training as a result of an untimely pregnancy, if only she could have waited until after the menopause for her family, there would have been no need to jeopardize her career! There is no easy answer, and there are obvious hazards however a woman decides to balance her priorities.

The rapidly growing trend since the 1970s towards cohabitation (known to demographers as consensual unions, and more popularly as LTR, living-together relationships) has to be seen in the context of planned procrastination. Of women marrying in the early sixties, only 2 per cent reported having previously lived with their husbands, and by the early seventies this figure had grown to a still-modest 7 per cent. By 1979 the figure was approaching 20 per cent; and though Chester (1985) does not quote a more recent figure, it could well be nearer 25−30 per cent at the time of writing. For remarriage it is naturally much higher, at least 60 per cent, since one or other if not both partners may not even be free to marry (let alone willing to commit themselves) until their divorce is finalized. It would appear that in 1980–81, divorced and separated women accounted for 44 per cent of all cohabiting women; and in Britain at least there has been no suggestion of a flight from marriage on the part of those not previously married. A more secular view of marriage may indeed prevail nowadays, and the concept of 'holy matrimony' is wearing thin; nevertheless in our own society we can still safely regard cohabitation as no more than a staging post along the route to a more public, if not also more permanent, destination.

In Scandinavia, notably Denmark and Sweden, it has been a different story. There the fall in legitimate births is almost entirely due to the rise in offspring of consensual unions, which currently amount to a third of all Swedish births. In France and West Germany, as in Britain, the decision to have a child is usually a stimulus to marriage; not so for couples living in Copenhagen or Stockholm, who are apparently quite content to leave the knot untied even after they have become parents. They may marry eventually if they do not split up, but prolonged cohabitation does have the presumably desirable effect of reducing the incidence of divorce. It is only as the ageing process gathers momentum, and sexual attractiveness wanes, that couples the world over may be tempted to settle for the staid comforts of marriage. Yet in Sweden as elsewhere the mating game has never been more popular (Trost 1987).[4]

CONFLICTS OVER PARENTHOOD

To set up home with an apparently congenial partner has become quite an easy decision over the past decade or two. It is when it comes to deciding whether to test the partnership with a child that difficulties may arise. For just as marriage is a more public commitment than cohabitation, so parenthood is a much deeper commitment than any childless relationship, inside or outside marriage. For some years now we have been wondering how far reliable contraception has contributed to the rising divorce rate. Couples with all the advantages of a dual income can so easily become hooked on the child-free life, so that the moment for throwing contraceptive caution to the winds of chance somehow never arrives. And if Jackson (1983) was correct in maintaining, on the basis of his disarmingly informal meetings with 100 new fathers, that it was usually the wife who decided when that moment had come, we are left with the question of whether prolonged hormonal intervention in the female partner's cycle may have reinforced the male partner's reluctance to accept family responsibilities. Are women on the Pill less liable to become broody than women whose cycles are allowed to pursue their natural course? We do not know the answer to this question, which remains ripe for investigation. It could even become urgent if there were reason to suspect that well-educated couples were opting out of parenthood in disproportionate numbers, although so far there is no satisfactory evidence of such a trend (Veevers 1980; Humphrey 1987).

Only a small minority of men or women are familiar with published research on the impact of parenthood on the marriage relationship, and perhaps that is just as well. As pro-natalist propaganda it leaves much to be desired. Jessie Bernard, an emeritus professor of sociology in an American university and herself a mother of three, takes an uncompromisingly bleak view:

> Parenthood expands marriage into a family, and everything changes. And the changes are not all for the better, for although having children may do a great deal for the character of parents, schooling them in unselfishness and sacrifice, it does not always do much for their marriage.
>
> (Bernard 1976: 69)

It is not unrealistic to think of parenthood as a training in self-sacrifice for women and in coping behaviour for both sexes, and emotionally there can be no doubt that it takes its toll. The sexual relationship is one aspect of marriage that is almost bound to change after the birth of a child, and not always for the better during the first post-natal year (Kumar, Brant, and Robson 1981; Elliott and Watson 1985). In our experience of childless couples seeking donor insemination (see Chapter 7) sexual problems are seldom of any serious magnitude, yet couples asking for sex therapy will often date the onset of symptoms to the birth of their first child. For most couples – given that the marriage is basically sound – such problems are likely to resolve quickly enough with or without help, but it is a testing time in any marriage. It has to be added, unfortunately, that the mainly transatlantic literature on marriage and parenthood goes way beyond transient sexual disturbance. Loss of marital satisfaction increases during the pre-school and early school years to reach a peak in adolescence, reverting towards its pre-parental level only after the children have left home – always assuming that the marriage has sur-vived (Lupri and Frideres 1981)! There is simply no escaping the universal truth that babies are unflagging competitors for mater-nal love, and mothers – especially new mothers – are pro-grammed to respond to their babies' needs. Any emotionally greedy and sexually demanding young father is in for a rough time.

There must be many young and some not-so-young couples today who find themselves year after year trembling on the brink of parenthood, as if waiting for some mysterious signal which may or may not be intercepted. How long dare they wait before taking the plunge? Obviously it is the female partner's age that counts, for the complacent male can expect to have little or no difficulty in launching a family by a new and younger partner at the age of 40 or beyond. It has long been thought that women's fertility begins to decline after the age of 30 and more sharply after 35, when the risk of an abnormal child is underlined by the offer of amniocentesis. However, the mechanism of this biologi-cal decline remains obscure, and indeed it is only quite recently that the possible contribution of lower coital frequency has been virtually ruled out. A study of over 2,000 women with sterile husbands undergoing donor insemination with frozen sperm in France (Schwarz and Mayaux 1982) showed that the conception rate over twelve months' follow-up went down from almost 75 per cent up to the age of 30, to not much over 60 per cent from age 31–35, with a further decline to about 55 per cent from age 36 onwards.[5] Since the quality of the donors was uniform across maternal age groups we can confidently infer that biological factors were involved, whereas a similar study with married couples would leave other potentially relevant factors besides coital frequency uncontrolled.

What of the relationship between fertility and marital break-down? Dunnell (1979: Table 7.7) presents evidence of progress-ively more rapid divorce among women separating from their original husbands between 1961 and 1975: the proportion di-vorcing within a year of separation rose from 8 per cent in 1961–

65 to 23 per cent in 1974−75. However, this may partly reflect the more immediate effects of the Divorce Reform Act, which was implemented in 1971. A more interesting calculation for our purposes is the proportion of couples in successive marriage cohorts who separated within different periods. This information can be extracted from Dunnell's Table 7.6, and is summarized in our own Table 1.3. The gradual erosion of early marital stability emerges clearly enough, and would doubtless stand out with even more startling clarity if the data could be extended to include more recent marriage cohorts. Of crucial significance is the question of parental status in broken versus intact marriages, and here Dunnell offers a more guarded interpretation of her findings:

> How did the fertility of the marriages that had broken down compare with those that continued? Table 3.4 showed that at two years' marriage duration, just over one half of women had started childbearing. By five years' duration four-fifths had, and by ten years' duration nine-tenths had a child. Table 7.9 suggests that there are no great differences in the proportions of separated and non-separated women who had children at different marriage durations.

However, to make exact comparisons, the proportions that separated and the numbers of children born to women married

Table 1.3   *Cumulative proportions of women whose first marriage had ended, by given marriage durations*

Cumulative proportions separated by:	Year of marriage			
	pre-1956	1956−60	1961−65	1966−70
2 years	1.3	1.3	2.3	4.4
5 years	2.0	2.5	5.0	9.1
10 years	4.9	6.8	11.3	—
Number of ever-married women (100%)	1147	916	888	1006

Source: Adapted from Dunnell (1979: 38)

at similar ages in the same years should be compared at yearly marriage durations. But even in a large survey such as this the number of separated women was small; 572 of the 5083 first marriages had ended in separation, which precludes this type of analysis.

(Dunnell 1979: 39)

Social enquiry is a tantalizing exercise, and we can but sympathize with Dunnell's honest disclaimer. We have already acknowledged that childless couples are freer to part, the more so when they are not even legally tied. It would be rather remarkable if the absence of children – whether fully intended, half intended, or completely involuntary – had nothing whatever to do with marital stability. On the contrary, it seems much more likely that the added commitment of parenthood creates an extra incentive to nurture and sustain a marriage through periods of stress. Our own Table 1.3 showed that separation within five years of marriage became three to four times more common over a period of only ten years, during which contraception became increasingly efficient. The relevance of more frequent and prolonged cohabitation from 1970 onwards, with consequent deferment of parenthood, is not beyond dispute, but it invites speculation and further research.

Meanwhile marriage retains its popularity, and remarriage is on the increase again after a brief decline during the 1970s. There is evidence to suggest that some two-thirds of divorced persons succumb, sooner or later, to Dr. Johnson's 'triumph of hope over experience', and we know that currently a third of all marriages are remarriages for at least one partner (36 per cent in 1983, as against 14 per cent in 1961). Furthermore, in 1983 one divorce in five was a second or subsequent divorce for one or both partners (Chester 1985). Can it be that people expect too much of marriage nowadays? We are inclined to agree with Bernard (1976) that in its traditional form it is probably less beneficial to women than to men. She saw more role sharing and less emphasis on sexual fidelity as the most promising way forward. Of the first there are already clear indications, even if men are apt to withdraw from housework when the first child arrives – a tendency recognized not only by Bernard but by another feminist writer, Oakley (1974). The second is happily much less open to inspection, but it is far from self-evident that sexual freedom would enhance the stability of marriage. If marriage and parenthood represent a curious form of sublimation, so be it!

In this opening chapter we have not set out to convey a pessimistic view of marriage and parenthood. If the nuclear family can realistically be seen as an 'endangered species', this is for two quite distinct reasons: firstly because it has become more fragile through marital disruption, and secondly because of the ever-present threat that more and more couples will succeed in remaining childless. However, if voluntary childlessness had already become the norm there would be much less point in writing about surrogate families. It is precisely because today's children, for better or for worse, are more often exposed to family changes that we think this book was clamouring to be written. In exploring the main varieties of surrogate family in some detail we shall hope to discover that parenthood in all its forms is alive and well. We may even gather enough material for a convincing final chapter, in which we pose the question: will the nuclear family survive?

2 Foster care

Fostering is a time-honoured practice, going back at least to the rescue of Moses from the bulrushes (*Exodus*: ch.2). The adjective 'foster' is defined by the *Concise Oxford Dictionary* as 'having a specified relationship not by blood, but in virtue of nursing or bringing up'. Fostering is thus a more generic concept than adoption, and adoptive/foster parents (or adopted/foster children) have not always been sharply distinguished in the literature. It will probably make sense to deal with foster families first, especially as there have been fewer scientific studies of the fostering process and hardly any by psychologists. There is also the fact that our own work has been predominantly concerned with adoption, which will occupy the next three chapters. A brief historical overview may serve to launch the topic.

The plight of children deprived of family life has impinged on British society for several centuries. Prior to the twentieth century such children were typically orphans. The provision of foster care, then as now, was seen as a humane alternative to the bleakness of institutional life. Declining adult mortality and improved contraception have meant that parents have gradually become more capable of seeing their fewer children through to maturity. Simultaneously the shrinkage and dispersal of the extended family has made caring relatives less readily available. The growth of the welfare state over the past forty years has made it easier for parents to hand over their responsibilities at times of crisis, whether through illness or marital breakdown. The philosophy of substitute care has largely evolved from the failure of the kinship system.

Boarding out had become an accepted feature of social policy in the seventeenth century, when 'poor law' children were made apprentices and younger children were placed with wet nurses in the London suburbs. With the Poor Law Amendment Act of 1834 it became recognized as a passport to a more effective training than could usually be achieved at either a workhouse or a school.

Foster parents were required to provide evidence of their health, moral character, and material circumstances. They were actuated by either charitable or pecuniary motives, allowances being based on the cost of maintenance within the poor law institution. The primary aim of supervision was to ensure that children were not neglected or ill treated, and its overall quality left much to be desired (DHSS 1976).

In the early years of the twentieth century substitute care of this kind was taking place on a modest scale. After the First World War the Ministry of Pensions established a system of boarding out large numbers of children of ex-servicemen, often with relatives, and their welfare was reviewed at regular intervals. Later this provision was extended to delinquent children, who were placed in care of the local authority with a view to boarding out (which indeed was obligatory save in special circumstances). The number of children boarded out grew steadily, but the quality of their care and supervision remained variable.

It was not until after the Second World War that the collective social conscience on behalf of deprived children was fully aroused. The experiences of war-time evacuation had drawn attention to the emotional needs of children separated from their parents, whilst the avoidable death of young Dennis O'Neill in a foster home led to increased public awareness of the dangers of casual supervision (Monckton Report 1945). Yet the Curtis Committee (1946), the first of several bodies appointed in the post-war era to look into arrangements for children cut off from normal home life and to make recommendations to the government, came down heavily in favour of boarding out as the second best alternative to adoption.[1] As a direct consequence (would that other government-sponsored committees were as influential!) the local authority children's departments were founded in 1948 and children's officers appointed. Their staff included boarding-out officers (later called child-care officers) whose duty it was to find foster homes for all children in care of the local authority except where such a measure was considered undesirable or impractical. This obligation continued until the implementation of the Children and Young Persons Act of 1969 (DHSS 1976).

The recruitment of satisfactory foster homes has never been easy, and the frequency of boarding out (especially as a long-term solution) has always varied from one authority to another. This is partly a matter of local conditions, in that close-knit rural communities are a more fertile source of potential foster parents than decaying inner city areas. But it is also affected by departmental policy, with not all children's officers – or their more versatile successors, the directors of social services[2] – equally enthusiastic about the merits of foster care in preference to residential care. In practice the proportion of children in care who are fostered was found on a recent estimate to range between 27–67 per cent, with a mean of about 47 per cent (Rowe 1983). In absolute numbers this amounts to more than 37,000 foster children in England and Wales, with fairly marked fluctuations over the past two or three decades. Such an estimate takes no account of private fostering, which is known to add at least another 11,000 cases apart from those not notified to the local authority (Holman 1980).

Fostering is not only a more generic term than adoption, it also for that very reason embraces a wider variety of objectives. At its simplest and most straightforward, it serves to bridge a gap during a mother's acute illness or confinement, or between an infant's birth and placement for adoption at 6 weeks (which is the earliest that the legal probationary period can begin). Here the time limit is fairly predictable. Medium-term fostering is a more open-ended arrangement, brought about by an unsatisfactory situation rather than by a temporary crisis. This situation – be it mental or chronic physical illness, marital failure, inadequate housing, or sometimes a combination of adversities – may or may not be expected to resolve in time, but the aim initially at least is restoration to the natural parents. The likely time scale may be hard to gauge, and indeed there is no clear demarcation line between medium and long-term fostering. The latter is undertaken when there is no realistic expectation of reclaim by the natural parents, who may nevertheless remain in the picture for a while or even indefinitely. The foster parents may have always intended to adopt the child, or this may emerge as an option even when not originally envisaged, or they may not wish for it (Rowe *et al* 1984). Long-term fostering differs from adoption in that parental rights are retained whether or not they are vested in a local authority, responsibility is shared with the authority, and weekly allowances are payable on a variable and far from uniform scale.

Even so the boundaries between long-term fostering and adoption are becoming increasingly blurred with the step-by-step implementation of the 1975 Children Act, which now gives foster parents the unconditional right to apply for adoption after five years and has also opened the way to allowances for adoptive parents. (The foster parents' application may not succeed but it is not dependent on local authority support, nor can the child be removed for a certain period except by court order).

Short-term fostering is not without its stresses, in that often enough it may arise from a degree of family disorganization sufficient to prevent relatives from stepping into the breach (Schaffer and Schaffer 1968). Yet for obvious reasons there is more to interest us in the social and psychological problems of the medium to long-term foster child, or what Rowe and Lambert (1973) have called 'indeterminate' fostering. Such will be the focus of this chapter.

RECRUITMENT OF FOSTER PARENTS

Whilst there may be differences of opinion among child-care workers as to the merits of adoption, there is rather more agreement that fostering without guarantee of permanency is a more hazardous undertaking. Who are the intrepid volunteers prepared to dedicate themselves wholeheartedly to the task, yet without becoming too possessive towards the child? How are they to be located within the local community, or even confidently identified when they do come forward? Much effort has gone into the task of recruiting foster parents, with increasing use of the media in recent years to publicize the needs of individual children judged suitable for fostering. However, although various investigators have commented on the crucial importance of motivation, scant progress has been made towards evolving reliable methods of assessment. What we do know is that borderline applicants have been repeatedly accepted through pressure of immediate needs, as emerged from several earlier studies both British and American (for example, Hutchinson 1943; Trasler 1960; Wolins 1963; Parker 1966; George 1970). One can hardly begin to study a couple in depth if the child has to be placed as a matter of urgency and there is no well-tried foster home available. Child care was ever a crisis service, with decisions having to be made at a speed that would be unthinkable for adoption workers.

As compared with adopters, prospective foster parents have always been in short supply. Socially they have tended to belong to different strata of the population, with a bias towards middle-aged couples of working-class origins. Whilst younger childless couples may be willing to accept fostering as an alternative to adoption, especially in the present shortage of normal infants, they have in the past been outnumbered by couples whose children have left home or are approaching that stage. Fostering is traditionally an extension of the maternal role for married women who are not particularly interested in work outside the home. This is not to deny that spinsters or widows can sometimes excel as foster mothers, but they are in a minority. Gray and Parr (1957), for example, in a study of 438 homes found that 90 per cent of foster mothers were married, 59 per cent were over 40 when recruited, and 77 per cent did not go out to work. The proportion of non-working mothers is likely to have declined over the past thirty years rather more than the other two categories.

Few reports have included detailed information on motives for fostering, but Jenkins (1965) provides a useful exception. In a qualitative study of ninety-seven British couples she found that many applications could be construed as attempts to compensate for past or present deprivation. On the basis of searching home-interviews, nine motivational categories were extracted, such as: companionship for own child or completion of family, compassion for children in need, reliving of happy relationships, compensation for poor relationships, and reparation for guilt feelings. The placement was rated as unsatisfactory when one or both foster parents, child-care officer, and interviewer agreed that it should never have been made. When the thirty homes so rated were examined in relation to the motivational categories, success was conspicuously (though not significantly) associated with compassion and reliving; it was negatively associated with compensation and reparation ($p < 0.01$, present author's calculations). In addition, couples reporting that both partners had experienced an unhappy childhood accounted for half of the unsatisfactory placements (also $p < 0.01$). Unlike Jenkins, most other authors have delved into the past history or current experience of the foster child without paying as much heed to the positive and negative characteristics of the foster parents.

In a sense the quality of foster care depends as heavily on the social workers who select and supervise the substitute parents as it does upon the children who find their way into the system. George (1970) has castigated old-style child-care officers for the innocence of their approach to human frailty, especially when it comes to appraising the strength of a marriage. A home visit can be far more revealing than an office interview, yet vital opportunities would appear to have been lost when prospective foster parents are described in the case notes as happily married on the grounds that the wife was found to be preparing the husband's meal, which 'showed concern'. (To be fair, this was not the only evidence recorded; George 1970: 140). George was unable to satisfy himself that the skills of trained workers were in any way superior to those of untrained workers, at least in respect of psychological assessment. So whilst the proportion of trained social workers has increased significantly since this study was done, it is not entirely clear how much benefit has accrued from this change. Possibly there is an element of 'role handicap' for the substantial number of female officers who lack marital and parental experience at the start of their career, and who find subsequently that the work is too demanding to combine with family life. From conversations with clients we have learnt that they are apt to be reassured by evidence that the worker herself has a family.

The DHSS Working Party's Guide to Fostering Practice (1976) is somewhat idealistic in places, yet it does acknowledge a recurrent problem with which teachers on social work courses must be all too familiar. Thus the social worker (here conventionally designated as female) is

brought face to face in a stressful way with her own childhood feelings and experiences which may make it difficult to maintain an objective approach. Her situation is often further complicated by the fact that she may have a very small number of foster homes on her case-load, and therefore little opportunity to develop her skills. A prime requisite is that she should receive good supervision and support in extending these skills from a senior member of staff experienced in fostering, who can understand her feelings and, in sharing her anxieties, can help her to keep them within acceptable bounds.

(DHSS 1976: 162)

This is surely no less true today, nor is it likely to change. It is among the less readily measurable factors contributing to the success and failure of fostering, which we shall consider next.

OUTCOME OF FOSTER PLACEMENTS

In her foreword to a unique follow-up study of adult adoptees in Britain (Raynor 1980), Jane Rowe has written: 'Success in adoption cannot be properly measured for there is no yardstick. In fostering we have usually considered the placement successful if it lasts.' This neatly apostrophizes the extreme crudity of one of the two best known British studies of fostering breakdowns. Parker (1966), in search of a predictive index, took five years' uninterrupted duration of a placement as his sole criterion of success. In extenuation it must be said that he writes most persuasively, and is obviously only too aware of the limitations of a study confined to documentary evidence compiled by one local authority (hence the reliance on a single objective measure). His work has been justly acclaimed, yet in our opinion it falls well short of an earlier study by Trasler (1955; 1960).[3] He again worked with just one authority, and included all children in its care who were removed from long-term foster homes in a three-year period 'whatever might be the immediate, overt reason for this change of plan', apart from those returning directly to their own parents. This produced a sample of fifty-seven children who had suffered a total of eighty-six removals, including fifteen who had failed twice and six who had failed three times or more. A second group of eighty-one placements were rated by two or more assessors as highly successful in terms of the following criteria:

(i) The foster family should meet the child's emotional, intellectual, and material needs as fully as possible;
(ii) there should be no indication that the child might later find this environment restrictive or lacking in any characteristic important to his development;

(iii) the relationship should be satisfying to both the foster parents and the child;
(iv) the child should show no serious behaviour problems.

(Trasler 1960: 8)

These criteria are certainly stringent, and whether they are unduly so is a matter of opinion. It is of course unrealistic to expect any child of school age, with a history of emotional damage and/or restricted life experience, to settle quickly into even the most tolerant and supportive foster home. There may be an initial 'honeymoon' period but this is soon followed by a phase of 'testing out', in which the child may be unconsciously driven to explore the limits of his acceptability to the new parent-figures. But Trasler was surely right to stress the importance of meeting the foster parents' needs as well as the child's. If what they really wanted all along was a quasi-adoptive relationship they may be doomed to disappointment or else it may take many years to achieve, and then often enough be subject to the whims of the natural parents. Unrealistic expectations of the child's behaviour and emotional responsiveness was pin-pointed as a major cause of breakdown in this study, which was based on extensive interviews with staff and (whenever possible) the foster parents as well as on close inspection of the case notes.

With his narrower approach Parker (1966) reached a number of similar conclusions from an analysis of 209 foster placements. Early placement was an obvious advantage, and the most successful arrangements were those which approximated most closely to traditional adoptions. Pre-school children of the marriage, and older children not too different in age from the foster child, were an equally obvious disadvantage, with success and failure almost equally distributed in such circumstances. Trasler's finding was even more striking here, with 87 per cent of failed placements where the foster parents' own child was of the same age and sex.[4] Sibling rivalry is healthy enough in itself, but a sense of hopelessly unequal competition must be severely damaging. In both studies (as in those of George 1970 and Napier 1972) it was found that placements were at their most vulnerable during the first year or two, with a diminishing rate of breakdown thereafter. Judicious support from the case worker might help to prevent some of these early failures, and it is therefore peculiarly

unfortunate that the minimum rate of visiting as laid down by
the boarding-out regulations can so easily become the norm.
Again in both studies it was the older foster parents who tended
to fare better even when entrusted with the older and consequently more disturbed children. Among the younger foster
parents it was those without children of their own who did best,
probably because they were more likely to be given the opportunity of a quasi-adoptive relationship.

George (1970) in his study of three children's departments
relied on postal questionnaire data supplied by 28 child-care
officers and 135 foster parents (mothers and fathers). All the
workers responded but only two-thirds of the parents. He was
principally concerned with the gulf between theory and practice,
as already indicated in the section on recruitment. However, he
was also interested in comparing his findings on outcome with
those of previous investigators. Only two of Parker's prediction
factors were found in this study to discriminate between success
and failure, namely age at placement and presence or absence
of behaviour problems. Through using more than one sample
George was able to lay more emphasis than most other resear-
chers on the significance of local factors, such as departmental
policy and geographical features. He can also claim credit for
allowing the foster father's voice to be heard, sometimes with an
intriguing difference of perspective. Indeed, it is only in recent
years that male parents of any kind have managed to break
through the barriers erected by blinkered social scientists!

The most recent British study of foster care (Rowe et al 1984) is
both comprehensive and nationally representative. However, it
has little to say about the causes of failure, since all the children
had been in the same foster home for at least four years and almost half (67/145) for more than ten years. It is refreshing to
learn that during the two years of field work only six youngsters
left their foster home, and in only two instances could this be
construed as a genuine breakdown. An adolescent girl was expected to rejoin her original parents whom she had not seen for
fifteen years, during which time the foster placement had somehow lingered on despite the misgivings of her social workers. A 9
year-old boy had been bereaved of his elderly foster mother, and
the grieving foster father had been forced to give up after a while
when his own health began to deteriorate. So there is obviously

no reason to despair over the stability of foster care once the first
year or two have been safely negotiated.

Perhaps enough has already been said to indicate that fostering
is an emotional minefield for all parties, including the professionals, and more will be added. Trasler considered that more
than half of the breakdowns he studied could be attributed to
emotional disturbance due to previous rejections. We are easily
persuaded by his argument, having long believed that the role of
foster parent called for monumental patience if not recognized
therapeutic skill. The evidence of long-term stresses confronting
adoptive families will be reviewed in the next three chapters, but
we can note meanwhile that this protected form of surrogate
parenthood is a good deal less demanding than foster care for all
its shared responsibility and social support. Yet at its very best
fostering may bring most of the same rewards, or even become
hard to distinguish from adoption. Indeed, the concept of *open*
adoption is an acknowledgement of the common ground between the two forms of substitute care.

It may be helpful at this point to recapitulate and summarize
the evidence so far reviewed as to the relationship between outcome and age at placement (Table 2.1). We have included data
from Napier (1972), who in trying to replicate Parker's prediction
table on a sample of seventy-nine children in Lancashire found
that age at placement was the only factor to survive. Trasler's

Table 2.1   *Age at placement: comparison of five studies*

Study	Age at placement					
	All placements studied			Successful placements		
	under 2 %	*2–4* %	*5+* %	*under 2* %	*2–4* %	*5+* %
Trasler (1960)			50			46
Parker (1966)	24	31	45	31	35	34
George (1970)	26	33	41	47	31	22
Napier (1972)	28	30	42	38	36	26
Rowe *et al* (1984)				52	32	16

Source: Adapted from Rowe *et al* (1984: 28)

figures are incomplete owing to his use of different age bands, whilst those of Rowe *et al* are confined to successful placements. There is fair consistency between the four comparative studies, except that Parker's figures do not reflect the value of early placement in successful cases to the extent that might have been anticipated from his prediction table. The evidence from the Rowe *et al* study is altogether more compelling, but as already indicated their sample was selected on a different basis.

So far we have concentrated on outcome over a limited time span. Only two studies, both in Scotland, have followed children growing up in foster care into early adulthood (Ferguson 1966; Triseliotis 1980). Ferguson's sample of 205 children in the care of Glasgow Children's Department included 139 (68 per cent) who had been brought up mainly by unrelated foster parents, usually as a result of parental death or desertion. All were born in wartime and grew up in a period when social services were strained; about half were illegitimate, and the great majority were taken into care before the age of 5. IQ, school performance, and employment record were all poorer than in the author's previous study of working-class Glasgow boys not in care, and there was an enhanced crime rate. A few did well even if the group's overall social adjustment fell short of accepted standards. On the whole relationships with foster parents were remarkably good, and contact was maintained in 75 per cent of families. Thus although a quarter of the group had lost touch within two years of passing out of care, it is

> perhaps even more significant that at the age of 20, two years after they were entirely free to shape their own lives and many had in fact moved far away, 30 per cent of the young people still continued to live with their foster parents and many, in other parts of the country and overseas, still regarded their foster home as 'home'.
>
> (Ferguson 1966: 139)

Triseliotis (1980) interviewed a smaller group of forty young adults born in 1956–7, who had spent an average of twelve years in a single foster home. Most had been taken into care during the pre-school years, and half had been fostered before the age of 4.

All came from disorganized families, and on average there had been four moves between the reception into care and final placement. A four-fold classification was evolved from narratives of the fostering experience by both parties, and the largest group of twenty-four ex-foster children (60 per cent) had enjoyed their substitute care and were coping well with life at the age of 20 or 21. Adoption, whilst often wanted on both sides, was not pursued on account of local authority anxieties over age, parental consent, or genetic factors. At the other extreme were ten with negative perceptions of their foster care who were coping rather poorly. There were no differences in age at placement or other background factors, and inferior outcome was explained by the author mostly in terms of parent-child interactions. In particular, he refers to an earlier study by Rutter *et al* (1964) suggesting that through his inborn temperament a child could contribute to his own difficulties in social learning. Clarke and Clarke (1976) have commented on the disturbed ex-institutional child who may elicit hostility from the foster mother which has the effect of accentuating his instability. Such a sequence may also occur after delayed adoption, but is perhaps less likely in the long run owing to the greater security of the adoptive relationship.

In general, these ex-foster children had left school at the earliest opportunity and were currently in unskilled or semi-skilled occupations. In this way they seemed destined to recapitulate the life-style of their original parents, rather than being all set to rise above it like some of the late adoptees also pursued to early adulthood by Triseliotis and Russell (1984). At the same time many showed signs of having absorbed some of the outlook on life communicated within their foster home. As the author observes:

> Given certain conditions, this process could have been more effective. Instead, both foster parents and social workers seemed to have low expectations and aspirations for the children, and the children had few aspirations for themselves. Setting low sights and expectations appears to be endemic to foster child placement, in contrast with adoption.
>
> (Triseliotis 1980: 158)

The possibility that adoptive parents may be at risk of erring in the opposite direction will be considered in the next chapter.

THE ROLE OF THE NATURAL PARENTS

The continuing involvement of the natural parents, while varying a good deal from case to case and not always encouraged by social workers, still constitutes one of the major differences between fostering and adoption. For the foster parents it can so easily turn what would otherwise have been a perfectly manageable enterprise into a prolonged obstacle course. In his eminently readable even if no longer up-to-date *An Introduction to the Child Care Service*, Stroud (1965) gives the example of a foster child with a large working-class father, who visited frequently and regularly but always with two equally large 'mates'. The three men, having said a few words to the child, would promptly settle down to spend Saturday afternoon watching television and munching the refreshments provided by the foster mother. Such provocation would be unthinkable in the closed world of adoption.

Even so the contrast between the two forms of surrogate parenthood may be less clear-cut than we are giving the reader to understand. For example Holman (1980), in a penetrating discussion of 'exclusive' and 'inclusive' concepts of fostering, portrays a recurring dilemma of social work. In a comparison of private and local authority foster parents in the Midlands (Holman 1973) he established that almost two-thirds of the latter regarded the children as their own and would like to have adopted them. Similarly, George (1970) found that the same proportion of his sample of foster parents regarded 'own parent' as the best description of their position, whilst Adamson (1973) in South Wales found that more than 50 per cent of her sample of foster mothers did not like to think of themselves as such. By devising a scale of 'possessiveness' she was able to elicit powerful evidence of misunderstandings on the part of her informants, at least half of whom said they had expected the child to remain with them until 18 if not forever. Some long-standing foster mothers could plausibly argue that the ultimate aim of fostering (that is, to restore the child to its own family) had never been properly explained to them, whereas others were 'hiding behind a psychological blindfold, shielding themselves from views and attitudes they could not face' (Adamson 1973: 197).

A realistic understanding of the foster parents' task calls for some appreciation of the circumstances that bring children into

care, which may in turn demand an acceptance of the inclusive
concept of fostering. There is usually an interaction between psy-
chosocial and economic factors even where the admission is
likely to be of a short-term nature, as with confinement or acute
but temporary illness. After perusing 145 records, Rowe *et al* (1984:
42) were left with an 'overwhelming impression of poverty and
deprivation'. Nevertheless other factors may play a part, as is
clearly apparent from Table 2.2. The percentage figures indicate a
good deal of overlap between categories, and other relevant
factors have been omitted. For instance, 14 per cent of mothers
and 26 per cent of fathers were known to have a criminal record
in adulthood, which is scarcely conducive to good parenting even
if it does not constitute an inevitable handicap. Again, twenty-
nine mothers and ten fathers had spent an extended period of
their own childhood in care, which can be regarded as a vulnerability factor (Wolkind 1977). But easily the most conspicuous
feature of the child's family background was parental conflict.
Marital and sexual relationships can be seriously impaired without any of the children having to come into care, but where other
adverse features intrude the risk is obviously enhanced. In this
particular study only a third of the children's parents were
known to be cohabiting at the time of admission, and a substantial minority of these households were internally at war. The
fluidity of intimate relationships in such families must mean that

Table 2.2   *Known handicaps to parenting*

	n	%
Single parent family	79	59
Parent(s) suffer from physical, mental, or emotional ill health[1]	48	36
Unsatisfactory accommodation	47	35
Financial problems	37	28
No wider family support	32	24
Family discord[2]	29	22
Child rejected by mother's or father's partner	14	11

Source: Rowe *et al* (1984: 44)

[1] Including drug taking and alcoholism.
[2] Including discord in parent's own family if still living at home.

rejection of a child by the parent's new partner is probably rather more common than the table indicates. Where this has happened the child cannot afford to experience further rejection in a foster home, and unless suitably mature foster parents are ready to take over there may be no sensible alternative to a longish period of observation in a reception home.

Once a foster placement has been made, parental visiting becomes a vital factor in any long-range planning and calls for adroit stage management. Rowe *et al* report that the rate of visiting in their own enquiry was lower than that of any other British study (Table 2.3). They were

> frequently dismayed and sometimes angered by the way in which social workers failed to provide the necessary support and encouragement to maintain visiting. Sometimes they actually seemed to set up 'no win' situations for natural parents, first discouraging visits 'to let the children settle' and later saying that after such a long gap renewed visiting would be upsetting. But this was by no means the whole story. We found that ambivalence towards visiting seemed to be a prevalent attitude in natural parents and foster children as well as in social workers and foster parents. Everyone seemed to draw back from the pain and potential conflict involved.
>
> (Rowe *et al* 1984: 99)

Table 2.3   *Parental visiting pattern*

	n	%
No visits since admission	51	35
No visits since placement in this foster home	11	8
No visits since the first year after this placement	21	14
No visits since the second year after this placement	8	6
Visiting has now ceased	23	16
Continued or recent visits	31	21
Total no. of children	145	100

Source: Rowe *et al* (1984: 99)

The picture is complex and facile generalizations are to be avoided, but some specific statements can be made with confidence. As in an earlier study of parentally-deprived children who had failed to achieve a substitute family (Rowe and Lambert 1973), the younger the child on admission and hence the longer in care, the more likely that parental contact would be severed – and often sooner rather than later (Table 2.4). This is a sad reflection of the chronic sense of ambiguity and stalemate that can so easily creep in when children are parted from their family of origin without a clear goal in view, such as adoption or rapid restoration. Ideally there will be relatives to step into the breach, and Rowe *et al* studied an additional group of fifty-five children who were fostered within the extended family.[5] Where there is no option of this kind, and in the absence of a measurable time-scale for restoration, then adoption may be seen as far and away the most desirable plan. Of course the parents may oppose it, and grounds for dispensing with parental consent may remain elusive even after the five years have passed which allow the foster parents to apply for an adoption order regardless of prevailing circumstances. Often enough they have no wish to adopt their long-stay foster child, or an earlier interest in doing so may have lapsed. Rowe *et al* concluded that, apart from fear of losing the child which was a recurrent theme, foster parents' attitudes to adoption were not readily amenable to statistical analysis. On the contrary,

Table 2.4   *Parental contact in relation to years in care*

Parental contact	No. of years in care									
	4–6		7–9		10–12		13–15		16–18	
	n	%	n	%	n	%	n	%	n	%
Yes	16	42	6	19	6	21	3	8	–	–
No	22	58	25	81	23	79	34	92	10	100
No. of children	38		31		29		37		10	

$x^2 = 16.39$, d.f. = 4, p < 0.01

Source: Rowe *et al* (1984: 101)

The decision to adopt a child, like a decision to marry, is personal and intimate...the key to the whole subject may well lie in the answer the adopters so often gave to our question about their reasons for adopting: 'This particular child was very special to us'.

(Rowe *et al* 1984: 205)

In practice, therefore, the social worker is commonly forced to make the best of a bad job. The foster child's perspective will be addressed more fully in the next section, and here we shall merely note that opinions are divided on what is best for the child in terms of parental contact. Goldstein, Freud, and Solnit (1973), who were aptly concerned with the 'least detrimental alternative', have argued that if long-term foster parents are fulfilling the role of psychological parent then *they* should be the final arbiters on the question of parental visiting. In contrast, Fanshel and Shinn (1978) have put forward the view (not strongly supported by their data) that it is better for the child 'to have to cope with the *real* parents who are obviously flawed in their parental behaviour, who bring a mixture of love and rejection, than to reckon with *fantasy* parents who play an undermining role on the deeper level of the child's sub-conscious' (489). This smacks of special pleading, especially as they had already conceded that 'there are adults who are apparently intact emotionally and in their ability to function in many areas of their lives but who seem entirely undeveloped as parental figures' (485). Rowe *et al* wisely refuse to take sides in this debate, being content to point out that they could find no evidence in their own study of any relationship between the pattern of parental contact and the child's social adjustment as measured by behavioural rating scales. On the basis of previous research they had predicted that the best-adjusted children would be those whose contact with their original parents had ended early in life, leaving them free to form new bonds, *or* whose parents had remained in close touch. In the event it was those who were no longer being visited, but were of school age when contact ceased, who fared best.

One is left with a strong conviction of missed opportunities all the way along the line. Not only was there a degree of passivity among the social workers in their dealings with the natural parents, but there could and should have been a more imaginative approach to the use of resources for maintaining contact with the child's family. Why was there only one department which encouraged grandparents to remain in touch after the parents had dropped out? Such an arrangement appeared wholly beneficial and caused minimal friction with the foster parents. Contact with siblings was also potentially important where they were in care but could not be (or at any rate had not been) placed in the same family. Correspondence was another vital means of keeping open the channels of communication with the original family, and more could have been done to exploit it. There was a mother who wrote to the foster mother as follows:

> Thank you very much for everything you have done and are doing for them both. I mean that from the bottom of my heart. . . I know you must have wondered why I don't visit and take them out. Well, simply I don't want all your good care to be affected by opening any healed wounds for them or for me.
>
> (Rowe *et al* 1984: 98)

Apart from understandable guilt feelings it is plainly not all that easy for parents to fit in with the system even where the foster parents are ready to co-operate. Journeys can be expensive and time-consuming, whilst a tendency among social workers to prefer meetings on neutral ground (doutless to protect the foster parents' privacy) is hardly conducive to the maintenance of warm family relationships. When face-to-face contact has to be discouraged at least for the time being, there is no reason why links should not be preserved through letters, gifts, and photographs (Bentovim 1980). If rehabilitation with the natural parents is the avowed aim of social work with many fostered children, then until it has come to be recognized as unattainable it must be pursued with the utmost vigour. And if in particular cases the aim is rather to create a viable substitute family that will see the child through to independence, this too must not be allowed to founder from lack of sustained effort. There is always scope for improvement in the matter of goal setting and goal-directed behaviour.[6]

There is nothing novel in these suggestions, as any experienced child-care worker will recognize. It is nearly ten years since the literature on foster care was reviewed by Prosser (1978), and little seems to have changed since then. But it is frankly disconcerting

to find such a familiar passage in the review by Pringle and
Dinnage (1967) published more than ten years previously:

> With regard to the child's own parents, it is required of foster
> parents that they put no obstacles in the way of continued
> contact between the child and his family, to put it at its lowest;
> while at best, they are expected to help with keeping alive the
> child's bond with his family to facilitate his eventual return.
> Since in many cases the foster parents will practise a much
> higher standard of child care and will also be more stable and
> mature than the child's parents, this is demanding a great deal
> in terms of tolerance, compassion, and unselfishness. In cases
> where the real parents are feckless, unreliable, or generally
> inadequate, the foster parents are faced with a task which
> would tax the skill and understanding of a highly trained and
> experienced case worker, let alone someone who is (and
> should be) emotionally involved, rather than skilled in 'de-
> tached professionalism'.
>
>   (Pringle and Dinnage 1967: 27)

Surely this says it all, but will it still need saying at the turn of the
century? We hope not, yet fear so.

GROWING UP AS A FOSTER CHILD

From what has been said already, it will come as no surprise to
learn that foster children as a group are liable to experience more
than their fair share of developmental problems, whether in
the form of anxiety symptoms or troublesome behaviour. Yet by
comparison with the now voluminous psychiatric literature on
adoption, mental-health workers have had less to say about
fostering.[7] It is not entirely clear why this should be so, yet
George (1970) is probably not alone in lamenting the inadequacy
of supporting services available to child-care workers. Among
these psychologists and psychiatrists deserve pride of place.

   Drawing yet again on the all-embracing study of Rowe and her
colleagues, Table 2.5 lists in order of frequency the behaviour
problems reported by more than 25 per cent of the foster parents
interviewed by the team. Lack of concentration is hard to define
and temper tantrums hard to interpret out of context, but the

Table 2.5   *Behaviour problems reported by foster parents*

	n	%
Lack of concentration	59	42
Temper tantrums	56	40
Stealing	50	36
Demanding attention	49	35
Sleeping difficulties	40	29
Speech difficulties	40	29
Lying	39	28
Enuresis	37	27
Eating difficulties	36	26

Source: Rowe *et al* (1984: 77)

occurrence of stealing and attention-seeking behaviour in more than a third of the children raises the possibility of rejection by the foster parents as well as by the natural parents earlier in life. Among the twenty-seven families where specialist help had been sought were five mentally handicapped children, another seven children requiring speech therapy, and one child who was seen by a psychiatrist with regard to wardship proceedings. This left only fourteen cases where a psychologist or psychiatrist had been consulted specifically about disturbed behaviour. Treatment had been often perfunctory and the benefits uncertain, but if the problems were relatively intractable then more could scarcely have been expected. To quote an understatement from the authors: 'In view of the severity and persistence of some children's problems this level of psychological and psychiatric support seems low.' (Rowe *et al* 1984: 77) One in four foster parents admitted that they had felt like giving up at some point, or possibly over an extended period. We share the authors' surprise at finding that the peak age for problems was 7–9 rather than the teenage years, but from their account this could be a statistical artefact. Even so they are again worth quoting when they speculate that 'the developmental tasks of this period are perhaps made particularly difficult by the ambiguities of status and conflict of loyalties inherent in being a foster child' (78). Concern over one's origins may be just as typical of the so-called latency period as it is of adolescence, and several authors have made the same point about adopted children (for instance, Bohman 1971; Lambert and Streather 1980; Raynor 1980).

An overall disturbance rate of 30 per cent in the 145 foster children, as judged from behavioural rating scales, was regarded by the authors as minimal; however, it is already more than four times higher than the figure of 7 per cent quoted by Rutter, Tizard, and Whitmore (1970) in respect of their Isle of Wight study of 10–11 year-olds who with few exceptions had never left home. Whilst for a variety of reasons it would be inappropriate to press the comparison too far, there can be little doubt as to the prevalence of deeply unhappy children among those in long-term foster care. Interestingly, neither age at initial separation nor age at final placement were major contributory factors in predicting the level of disturbance. Yet it was the children who had been disturbed at an early stage in their foster homes who were most likely still to be so described. As with delayed adoption, so with indeterminate fostering it could well be the experiences of the first year or two that count in the long run. Blessed are the foster families who can recover completely from an unfortunate start.

Just as the foster parents themselves are vulnerable to 'role ambiguity' and 'role strain', so the foster child whose original parents are still familiar or even vaguely recalled must somehow come to terms with the *bête noire* of split allegiance and insecurity of status. Of the specific dilemmas commonly arising in foster families we shall give but two examples. Should the child identify with the foster parents to the extent of taking their name, or is it better for the sake of the self-image to accept the obvious disadvantages of being known by a different name? No general answer can be given, but if the link with the original family is to be preserved it may cause confusion to change one's name. The adopted child is lucky to be spared this conflict, although as we shall see in chapter 5 the discovery of one's original name can have considerable symbolic import for the adult adoptee.

Secondly, how is the foster child who has spent some years in the parental home to reconcile what may well be a contrasting set of standards and values attaching to the foster home? Household routines, table manners, and bedtime rituals may differ markedly, to say nothing of the quality of family relationships. Weinstein (1960) was one of the first to address these issues in research, and although his data came from a rather small and possibly atypical sample (sixty-one children covering a wide age range) his study is still widely quoted. He concluded, reasonably enough, that a strong and stable identification was crucial for the child's sense of well-being; whether there should be a bias towards identifying with the natural parents (in the absence of any specific indications to the contrary) is more debatable. The much larger sample studied intensively by Fanshel and Shinn (1978), who assembled multiple data on 624 children in New York over a period of five years up to a maximum age of 18, ought to have provided a more reliable basis for generalization. Yet their findings on the management of divided loyalties are strangely inconclusive, and their emphasis on the value of maintaining contact with the natural parents appears to stem from prior conviction rather than from the evidence they had so laboriously amassed.

The need for ancestral knowledge among children reared by substitute parents will be discussed more fully in the context of adoption, but it applies equally to long-stay foster children. Trasler (1960), in a thoughtful discussion of the issue, has this to say:

> It is a serious mistake to assume that if a child has no recollection of his parents, they must consequently be of little importance to him. Our culture is permeated by a recognition of the importance of kin relationships: the development of a consciousness of personal identity is closely connected with the growth of the child's understanding of these special ties of kinship. Any child is keenly interested in these matters: even if he does not remember his parents, he is nevertheless deeply curious about them. Finding out or imagining things about them is reassuring to him; it helps to allay his sense of loss, and the nagging feeling that he is abnormal, different from other children, because he has no parents.
>
> (Trasler 1960: 233)

The social worker has the delicate task of helping foster parents to maintain open communication even where they would probably much rather forget that the child ever had other parents.

NEW TRENDS IN FOSTER CARE

Just as adoption is no longer what it used to be, so there has been a steady expansion of the frontiers in foster care. Not all the deficiencies exposed by a national study of 'children who wait' (Rowe and Lambert 1973) have been remedied, yet there has been a mounting campaign to bridge the gap between imagination and reality. Only a few brief examples will be given. The recruitment of West Indian foster parents for deprived children belonging partly or wholly to their own ethnic group has been described by Sawbridge (1980). This campaign, known as 'Soul Kids', took place in London in the mid–1970s, and worked better than many social workers would have predicted. Further examples of such initiatives have been reported (for example, Schroeder, Lightfoot, and Rees 1985).

At about the same time the Kent special family placement project was launched under the direction of a senior research fellow at the University (Hazel 1980; 1981). The project was designed as a five-year experiment to cater for adolescents aged 14–17 with severe problems, which fell roughly into three categories: delinquent boys, girls deemed 'beyond control', and casualties of the system – that is, boys and girls with a long period in care 'moving through many placements and becoming increasingly rootless and alienated' (Hazel 1980: 104). While this might seem like a recipe for disaster, the project got off to a promising start thanks to a 'methods package' with four essential components: recognition of foster care as professional work with an appropriate fee, regular group meetings to prepare families and monitor each placement (with the family of origin involved whenever possible), specific treatment plans with a written contract over a flexible time-span, and discreet publicity through the media. During the first three years of the project forty-one boys and thirty-four girls were placed, and an independent evaluation of the first twenty-five placements was reported by Yelloly (1979). Success was defined liberally as non-failure, with at least one transfer permitted within the system. After-care has presented problems, and at the time of writing it was uncertain how many of these young people would be capable of living independently in the community. Yet Hazel argues that foster care, quite apart from its educative value, is significantly cheaper than residential care.

A broader account of specialist fostering is offered by Shaw and Hipgrave (1983), and some persuasive contributions to a DHSS-sponsored workshop have been edited by Wedge and Thoburn

(1986). Among other examples of recent trends which would be worth discussing if space allowed are: respite care for the physically and mentally handicapped, assessment of abused children in temporary foster homes, and 'bridging' arrangements for children whose foster placements have come to grief.

Despite this rustling of the winds of change, foster parents still have to be seen in essence as care-takers. Let Rowe (1983), in a brief commentary on what is coming to be known as permanent fostering, have the last word: 'The emphasis on permanence sharpens perceptions about what can and should be done to offer security within the framework of fostering as well as through adoption.' (20) And it is to adoption that we shall now turn.

3 Adoption (1): inherent stresses

Among the helping professions there is now considerable currency for the notion that adopted children are developmentally at risk. Such was not the view of a distinguished psychiatrist writing nearly forty years ago (Bowlby 1951), who stated that they were not unduly frequent visitors to child guidance clinics. Nor was any support for the notion provided by Addis, Salzberger, and Rabl (1954), who conducted a survey for the National Association for Mental Health. Among a series of 1,152 children seen at a child guidance clinic only seventeen (1.5 per cent) were legally adopted. If this figure was acceptable (and the authors themselves regarded it as surprisingly low) it gave grounds for optimism, as the proportion of adoptees in the general population was unlikely to be much lower; yet the method of enquiry, which seems to have relied on the help of a psychiatric social worker in identifying cases, leaves room for doubt whether a clean sweep was achieved.

In contrast, Schechter (1960) aroused alarm and despondency by claiming on the basis of his private practice in Southern California that adopted children were over-represented by as much as a hundredfold. Of a total of 120 children seen between 1948–53 the adopted group accounted for 13 per cent, whereas statistics compiled from twenty-nine states yielded a national average of 0.13 per cent. What Schechter failed to appreciate was that his base rate was drawn from a period of only twelve months, yet some of his patients were adolescent. He later modified his position somewhat (Schechter et al 1964), and the fallacy in his reasoning was vigorously attacked by Kirk, Jonassohn, and Fish (1966). However, extravagant claims die hard, and it was perhaps unfortunate that Pringle (1961) had meanwhile compounded this bad propaganda for adoption by quoting a prevalence rate of 8 per cent among nearly 2,600 children in residential schools for the maladjusted. There is no reason to challenge this figure, but children deemed maladjusted and separated from their parents on that account are an even more atypical group than those seen in private consultation.

During the decade that followed Schechter's first paper several further studies of adoption in a clinical setting appeared from America (for example, Goodman, Silberstein, and Mandell 1963; Sweeny, Gasbarro, and Gluck 1963; Menlove 1965; Simon and Senturia 1966; Offord, Aponte, and Cross 1969). There is no need to dwell on these as they have been comprehensively reviewed by Pringle (1967) and Hersov (1985). In the same period only two British studies of this kind were published (Humphrey and Ounsted 1963; 1964; Jackson 1968). It is fashionable to decry evidence from biased samples, and there can be no doubt that children referred for a psychiatric opinion (even if it be no more than that) are unrepresentative in various ways. Still, the apparent surfeit of psychiatric consultations by adoptive parents is so consistent from one study to another that it probably cannot be dismissed as an artefact arising from faulty statistics or variations in local prevalence. Nor is Kadushin (1966) altogether convincing when he argues that the social characteristics of the modal adoptive family, with its middle-class values and curtailment by a late start, may be more important than any psychological stresses inherent in the adoptive relationship. The only child of elderly parents features commonly in psychiatric series of adoptive families, yet there is no evidence that the only child as such is more vulnerable (indeed he has been almost ignored by psychiatrists). Again, if middle-class or upwardly mobile working-class parents are more sensitive to their children's failings and therefore readier to seek professional advice, we might expect that paediatricians too would see more than their fair share of adopted children; but Schechter *et al* (1964) looked in vain for such a trend. A further possibility is that adoptive parents find it harder to identify with their children because they cannot see their own characteristics mirrored in them, but this hypothesis is equally unsupported.

The purpose of this chapter is to re-evaluate the Humphrey and Ounsted study in the light of subsequent research. Begun in 1959, it was concerned with all the adoptive families (n = 78) who had been referred for psychiatric help in the Oxford region between 1951–62. The eighty children[1] comprised twice as many boys as girls (fifty-three as opposed to twenty-seven), in

keeping with the usual pattern of psychiatric referrals in childhood. Age at placement ranged from 0–6 and age at first interview from 3–19. Three-quarters of the parents were infertile
prior to adoption although eight couples had produced a child
afterwards. Most of the clinical data (including psychological
tests) were collected routinely but a structured interview was
devised for the purpose of the study and used with two-thirds of
the adoptive mothers, the fathers being seen too wherever possible. The timing of this special interview varied, some taking place
shortly after the initial consultation and others in a follow-up
months or years later. Those exluded had either ceased to co-
operate (case closed) or moved to another area.

Here we shall examine three main themes: incidence of referrals, presenting symptoms, and the concept of adoption stress.
The possible relevance of genetic factors will also be considered,
especially in the light of evidence from children who were
adopted in early life rather than remaining with an alcoholic
or schizophrenic parent.

INCIDENCE OF REFERRALS

Our figure of 2.9 per cent was derived from a consecutive series
of forty-five adoptees attending the Park Hospital for Children
in Oxford from 1958–62. This neuropsychiatric centre served a
wide area of the South Midlands (nine counties contributed to
the present sample) and specialized in the investigation and
treatment of epilepsy. Throughout the course of this study it dealt
also with a variety of emotional problems and conduct disorders
without known organic basis, including court cases on remand.
An average of 25–30 new cases were referred every month but
most of these were seen as out-patients only. The fact that twelve
of these forty-five adopted children required hospital admission[2]
for periods ranging from a few weeks to over a year gives some
indication of the severity of disturbance, but there were only five
cases of confirmed neurological disorder. No upper age-limit was
laid down but those who had left school were more likely to be
seen elsewhere.

The sample was increased to eighty by including thirty-three
children seen at the Oxfordshire and Oxford City child guidance
clinics and two adolescents who were referred to the parent

hospital.[3] It is regrettable that our incidence rate could not be calculated from the total population, but we did not attempt this for two reasons. First, the system of record keeping at the child guidance clinics did not allow rapid ascertainment of the total number of children seen over a given period; and secondly, we were less confident of being able to identify all the adopted children seen from 1951 onwards (this being the earliest referral we could trace). Reluctantly therefore we confined our attention to the hospital group in the firm belief that this smaller series would at least yield a reliable figure. In retrospect even this confidence must be seen as misplaced, since one or two other cases came to light after the study was completed. These omissions were due to the failure of colleagues to notify all cases seen at the weekly remand-home clinic, where the psychiatrist might not even spend long enough with the patient to learn of his adoption. Since a considerable part of the new intake was via this clinic (for example, 30 per cent in the years 1960−61) it would have been better for our purposes if the delinquent population could have been screened more thoroughly. Alternatively, there might have been some justification for excluding the remand-home group on the grounds that delinquency introduces a special bias from its recognized link with early parental deprivation.

At all events we must acknowledge that our reported incidence was a conservative estimate, the true figure being above rather than below 3 per cent. We calculated that this was more than twice the expected incidence (Humphrey and Ounsted 1963: 600). Our slight underestimate is of no great consequence in itself but does perhaps raise doubts about the accuracy of other reported figures. In a sense all published work has to be taken on trust, yet material gathered with reference to service rather than research needs and analysed retrospectively is peculiarly fallible. The unreliability of an earlier British survey (Addis, Salzberger, and Rabl 1954) has already been noted, and it is possible that some of the American incidence rates are equally suspect. It is ironical that the highest reported figure is one of the more trustworthy, being based on a limited number of children seen by a psychoanalyst (Schechter 1960), yet it is also the most distorted by sampling bias. With this exception the figures quoted in the literature should probably be regarded as minimal.[4]

Some of the variation in the American incidence rates (from

2.4 per cent to 13.3 per cent) may reflect differences in income levels as well as in the prevalence of adoptive families in the local community (Hersov 1985). Adoption today may be less imbued with the prejudices of middle-class social workers appraising a middle-class clientele, but it remains true that the less affluent couples tend to prefer the shared responsibility of fostering. In their review of nearly 600 children seen at the Staten Island Mental Health Centre in New York State, which caters for families of lower income, Goodman, Silberstein, and Mandell found only fourteen cases of extra-familial adoption. They comment that

> This over-representation of extra-familially adopted children in our clinic case-load (2.4 per cent) as compared with their ratio in the community (1.7 per cent) is of a magnitude which, though statistically significant, is not believed sufficient to warrant social consequence. Our findings suggest that child-care agencies might postpone their anxieties pending further investigations.
>
> (Goodman, Silberstein, and Mandell 1963: 456)

It is safe to assume that Schechter's private patients were at the opposite end of the social spectrum.

Another possible source of discrepancies is the scope of the clinical interview, which must vary from one setting to another. In our experience the fact of adoption was usually easy to elicit from the parents if not from the child, but if a couple chose to conceal it professional workers would have no means of finding out unless their suspicions were aroused. In one case it did not come to light until the couple was being recruited into a control group, and the wife's air of embarrassment when asked about the interval between marriage and childbirth led to a more penetrating enquiry. There may have been other cases that slipped through the net altogether, and by definition these would be impossible to enumerate. In practice, however, it seems unlikely that many couples would hold out against questions about pregnancy and labour. One might suppose in any case that adoptive parents would be ready enough to confide in a doctor even if they might avoid mentioning the fact to a teacher (Humphrey 1973a).

The situation is quite different with adult adoptees as patients. The patient who is his own witness might well refrain from referring to his adoption where he knew of it, or he might have been brought up in partial or complete ignorance of the fact. A further point is that legal adoption was comparatively rare before the Second World War, so that older adults are less likely to have been adopted. It is possible also that adoptive status is perceived as less obviously relevant to adult psychiatric illness. Whatever the explanation of this focus on the adopted child, neither the psychiatric nor any other literature has much to say about the adopted adult. Simon and Senturia (1966) reported higher rates of clinic attendance for children and adolescents but not for adult patients, while Bratfos, Eitinger, and Tau (1968) found no raised incidence of mental disorder or crime in 250 Norwegians who had grown up in adoptive homes. As Hersov (1985) remarks, it may be that family tensions leading to psychiatric consultation in childhood and adolescence are relieved when the adoptee leaves home. On the other hand Bohman and von Knorring (1979), in an epidemiological study of over 2,000 adults adopted in early life, found that a history of psychiatric illness in adulthood was indeed more common in the adoptees than in control subjects pair-matched for age and sex (19 per cent versus 13 per cent, p < 0.001). In view of a bias towards personality disorder − including alcohol and drug abuse − in the diagnostic records of the adopted group, these authors were inclined towards a genetic explanation of the difference. As will be discussed later in the chapter, there is now growing evidence of a genetic basis for alcoholism and other antisocial behaviour of a kind that is relatively common in the biological parents of children released for adoption but rare in adoptive parents.

A defect of all these clinical studies is that they involve a comparison of incidence with prevalence, which is theoretically unsound when nothing is known about the distribution of adoptive families in the clinic's catchment area. In Britain we are hampered by the limitations of our national as well as local statistics, and the proportion of adoptive families in the com- y at large is still not precisely known (though usually ited at 1−2 per cent). There is also the problem of how to for the exclusion of certain categories, such as children ed by their stepfathers from our own study or all extra-familial adoptions from most other studies. The incidence of such adoptions is recorded but fluctuates over time. Objections of this kind may appear to border on the pedantic, and certainly do not detract from the consensus of evidence that psychiatrists have become unduly familiar with adoptive families. Yet ultimately the most satisfactory method of exploring the mental health aspects of adoption is by epidemiological enquiry, as in the Swedish study just quoted (Bohman and von Knorring 1979). This is in line with current trends in psychiatric research, where the emphasis has switched from the patient in the consulting room to the individual in the community who may or may not be complaining of symptoms. Seglow, Pringle, and Wedge (1972) have already underlined the value of this approach to adoption by refuting any expectation that the adopted children in the 1958 cohort would have been referred to child guidance clinics more often than children remaining in their biological families. The significance of their study is limited by the fact that adolescence was still some years ahead, and a report on the same cohort at age 11 found that, even when enjoying all the social advantages of a small middle-class family, the adoptees were apt to be seen by their teachers as less well-adjusted (Lambert and Streather 1980). Nevertheless, the higher clinic attendance rate of 7 year-old illegitimate children reared by their own mothers was well worth demonstrating.

PRESENTING SYMPTOMS

We found no difference in the frequency of various symptoms between children received before the age of 6 months and a carefully matched control group of non-adopted children attending the same clinics. What did emerge most strikingly was a higher incidence of antisocial conduct in children received *after* that age, which is when the average child is beginning to form specific social attachments (Schaffer and Emerson 1964). This finding was confirmed by Offord, Aponte, and Cross (1969) although not by Menlove (1965), who had set out to look for it.

The frequency of placement after the age of 6 months (thirty-four out of eighty children, or 43 per cent) appeared suspiciously high even without a firm basis of comparison, which we lacked at the time. Since then two independent enquiries have agreed on a more representative figure of about 15 per cent, derived in one case from a sample of 3,400 adoption applications made in

1966 (Grey and Blunden 1971) and in the other from the 1958 cohort already mentioned (Seglow, personal communication). Thus children whose placement was delayed to this modest extent were apparently almost three times as numerous in our psychiatric series as in the general population. Their pre-adoptive histories were not well documented, but in nineteen cases there was unmistakable evidence of inadequate parental care. Nine children adopted after the age of 2 had suffered an uneasy introduction to life in the hands of unstable mothers − two of whom were later certified as mentally defective − and/or a reluctant grandmother or a series of indifferent foster mothers (one of whom had her licence revoked for neglect). It is therefore doubly unfortunate that the couples who took older children were mostly childless and had been so for a longer average duration (p < 0.05) than those who managed to secure infants.

At one time it was not hard to believe that the mother who had her child's welfare at heart would decide on adoption at an early stage, usually during the first few months of pregnancy, whilst the mother who elected to keep her child under unfavourable circumstances was thereby demonstrating her emotional instability (Yelloly 1965). In a changing social climate this is less likely to be true, but between 1940−59 when all but one of the children in our series were born there would certainly have been pressure on the mothers to reach an early decision on their future. It follows that in most cases of delay there were likely to be adverse factors in mother or child, and sometimes in both. So, tempting as it was to explain the triad of stealing, cruelty, and destructiveness − which was conspicuous in some of our adolescent boys though not confined to them − in terms of early parental deprivation and its effects upon character development, this is probably not the whole story.

Two additional possibilities have to be borne in mind. The first is that, at the time of these adoptive placements, a child's prospects of finding a good home would have diminished sharply after early infancy. This was certainly the experience of most adoption agencies until the shortage of available infants from 1970 onwards made adopters more willing to consider older children. Although we made no attempt to measure the parental qualities of our adopting couples, it was our impression that some of the children who had been parentally deprived before adoption were also singularly unfortunate in their chosen family. This dual handicap could have been almost insurmountable, for it is now firmly established that the success of post-infancy adoption is particularly dependent on the warmth and sensitivity of those who finally assume the parental role.

The second possibility, which is more speculative, is that the natural parents – and perhaps especially the mothers – of these children were themselves suffering from personality disorders to a greater extent than the mothers who had given up their children without delay. Since a careful study of psychiatric disorder in identical twins (Tienari 1963) has shown a concordance rate of 67 per cent for sociopathic personality, genetic transmission is a factor that cannot be ruled out. More recent studies pointing in the same direction will be reviewed below.

Several authors have alluded to the adopted child's propensity for aggressive and sexual 'acting out' (Schechter *et al* 1964; Menlove 1965; Simon and Senturia 1966; Jackson 1968; and others). The following passage from Simon and Senturia is of special interest in this connection:

> In cases we have seen there has always been one partner, usually the wife, much more anxious to adopt than the other. The entrance of the adopted child into the family may upset a carefully established equilibrium around need gratification. The child can be both a competitor and a weapon in the interpersonal conflicts of the parents. The adopted child can, in addition, serve as a vehicle for the acting out of forbidden parental impulses and wishes.
>
> For example, in a typical case, the father, a very passive man, was actively concerned about and subtly encouraged all types of aggressive and destructive behaviour in his adopted son. The mother, a controlling and aggressive woman but very restricted in the area of sexuality, was concerned almost exclusively about the patient's sexual acting out.
>
> (Simon and Senturia 1966: 863)

A tendency on the part of adopted adults to express their disturbance through sexual acting out and also alcoholism was noted by Schechter and his colleagues. Such behaviour may have something in common with the antisocial conduct reported in our own series, and again appears to be associated with delayed placement and possibly also with adolescent turmoil (though data on age at placement and age at referral in some of the the American studies are meagre). Attempts at explaining this form of disturbance in terms of adoptive family dynamics may seem plausible enough, but information about the adopters and their marital and family relationships is often minimal.

On balance, the advantages of early transfer from natural to surrogate parent are thus strongly upheld. The challenge for to-day's adoption workers is to recognize couples with the patience to endure a slower process of bond formation and the resources to counteract the child's initial difficulties in social learning. Such couples are surely to be found, but perhaps not primarily among those who are still feeling acutely deprived by their childlessness. For those who are equipped for the task the chances of a reward-ing family life are by no means bleak, as there is now ample evidence that the effects of traumatic experience in the pre-school years will fade unless subsequently reinforced (Clarke 1968; Clarke and Clarke 1976). If this were not so the recruit-ment and supervision of foster homes for children of school age would be even more problematical.

ADOPTION STRESS

In our second paper (Humphrey and Ounsted 1964) the clinical material was analysed for indications of how far the adoptive situation might itself have contributed to the need for help, regardless of whether there had been a delay in placement. In a few cases we knew it had played no part whatsoever. For example, an adolescent girl was referred in connection with a compensation claim for the after-effects of a severe head injury, prior to which she had given no cause for concern. At the other extreme were several cases where the parents' (and hence also the child's) feelings about the adoption had an obvious bearing on the presenting problem. Thus a chronically over-active boy had been referred originally at the age of 3 with a diagnosis of hyperkinetic syndrome (Ounsted 1955), but in this case no or-ganic basis for the condition was discovered. Some years later the adoptive father (a general practitioner) happened to mention that his wife had never found it easy to relate to children, and it was in the hope of overcoming this deficiency (and perhaps thereby achieving conception) that she had decided to adopt when medical investigations revealed no clear-cut reason for her childlessness. There appeared to be an element of unconscious parental hostility towards this likeable rogue, who was later severely burnt in an inexplicable accident. Where a child of the marriage might have relieved the wife's feelings of inadequacy, the adopted child merely symbolized her failure as a woman. However, in the majority of cases the contribution of the adoptive aspects was more nebulous.

After a careful search through the case histories and interview data for factors of possible relevance to the presenting complaints that were either absent or comparatively rare in biological families, we listed nine such factors in addition to the pre-adoptive deprivation already discussed (Table 3.1). Since this was an exploratory study we were content with simple enumeration of these factors in order of frequency, believing them to merit discussion even if further experience were to modify our view of their importance or bring new ones to light.

The literature of the last twenty years would certainly call for a re-evaluation of most of these factors. For example, no major follow-up study of more representative adoptive families has shown any relationship between outcome and parental age (factor 1) or subsequent childbirth (factor 7), whilst prolonged childlessness before adoption (factor 4) is likely to be relevant only where it is associated with depressive or other neurotic reactions (factor 6). Fear of unknown heredity (factor 3) is harder to evaluate because it is more subjective. Our finding that almost one couple in three harboured anxieties of this kind was probably an underestimate, since elicitation depends on how the question is put. It was seldom mentioned spontaneously, and could in most cases be construed as a reaction to the child's deviant behaviour. It was most conspicuous among the parents of aggressive boys ($p < 0.01$), some of the mothers complaining of physical assault. Although such behaviour might well occur in response to parental attitudes, as in the case of the adolescent girl who becomes promiscuous by way of acting out her adopters' spoken or unspoken fears, the genetic anxiety itself is unlikely to be a sufficient explanation of the disturbance. However, one would certainly expect it to be expressed more commonly by the parents of disturbed adoptees, just as the latter may be more prone to want

Table 3.1 *Factors related to adoption in 70 disturbed families*

		No. of families	%
1	Mother adopting at age 30+, no child previously	37	53
2	Disclosure of adoption avoided, postponed or mishandled	29	41
3	Fear of unknown heredity	20	29
4	Ten or more years of childless marriage before adoption	19	27
5	Child parentally deprived before adoption	19	27
6	Mother haunted by sense of biological failure	13	19
7	Child of marriage born after adoption	12	17
8	Third parent (natural mother or father) known to child	6	9
9	Child adopted to replace recent loss by death or stillbirth	5	7
10	Child adopted in hope of relieving mother's infertility	3	4

Source: Humphrey and Ounsted (1964: 550)

to seek out their natural parents when they come of age or later in life (Triseliotis 1973).

Since the last three factors listed are rare in practice as well as in our clinical experience, the remainder of this section will be devoted to disclosure of the child's origins (factor 2). This we did not discuss at all fully as our data were rather meagre. But we were not unduly impressed by the warning issued by the Standing Conference of Adoption Societies (from which the present British Agencies for Adoption and Fostering originated) in its pamphlet 'Adopting a child', to the effect that children 'have become delinquent – have even run away from home – through learning too late and in the wrong way that they have been adopted' (11).[5] Dramatic episodes of this kind were foreign to our clinical experience, and only one referral was prompted by the need for advice on how to broach the subject to an adolescent girl. But we were sceptical about the recurring statement from parents who raised the matter, that the child had shown no curiosity about his origins at any time. We suspected that in truth the parents were unresponsive to the child's curiosity, and this suspicion was later reinforced by the findings of McWhinnie (1967).

Writers on adoption have been so consistently preoccupied with this theme that it must have some importance for the adults involved if not for the children. Slowly the realization has dawned that it is not sufficient to issue a prescription to adopters that they must at all costs tell the child of his adoption before he starts school, nor on the other hand is it feasible to offer more than broad guidelines on how this should be done. There is agreement on only two general propositions: that the fact of adoption cannot be concealed indefinitely even if this were desirable, and that many adoptive parents find the process of communication harder than they had anticipated. The second statement must apply equally to natural parents in the matter of sex education.

Among the many interesting discussions in the research literature that of Jaffee and Fanshel (1970) may be singled out. In their quest for a detailed portrait of adoptive family life as experienced by 100 families over more than twenty years these authors had intended to include interviews with all the adoptees, who by then had reached early adulthood, but in the event only thirty-three interviews of this kind were achieved. Their examination of the stresses of adoptive family life was based entirely on the parental interviews, which enabled them to classify the families into three groups according to the number of problems reported. The thirty-three with the smallest and largest number of problems respectively formed groups I and III, with group II intermediate. All but four couples had told the children of their adoption, but the difference in adjustment between children who had always known and those who discovered later was negligible. The circumstances of the telling and the parental attitudes surrounding it seemed to be more crucial than the timing, both past and current problems being associated with clumsy and precipitate disclosure. Repeated discussion of adoptive status over the years was also a negative factor, although not enough was known of the emotional climate in which these conversations took place. Only a minority of the couples had shared the whole story as fully as they could, and withholding of information was commonest in group III. As the authors concluded:

> The way parents dealt with revelation was by and large a reflection of a more basic underlying orientation to child rearing in general. Families which tended to take a sheltering approach to the general upbringing of their children – e.g., supervising closely, not encouraging the development of autonomy and independence, etc. – were also likely to de-emphasize the adoption component in their children's lives. They tended to postpone revelation, to give minimal information about the child's biological background, to decrease the visibility of the adoptive status, and, in effect, to simulate a biological parent-child relationship. On the other hand, parents with a less protective orientation towards the rearing of children were likely also to be more 'open' about adoption, to reveal more information about natural parents, and to acknowledge freely the non-biological nature of their relationship with the adoptee. Revelation, in other words, tended not to take place as a separate and isolated parental activity but rather as an integral part of the overall raising of children.
>
> (Jaffee and Fanshel 1970: 311–12)

It is a reasonable assumption that those who feel most comfortable about both the child's background and their own role as adoptive parents are likely to cope best with the communication problem, neither glossing over the essential facts nor belabouring them. We saw many couples who appeared distinctly uneasy in the parental role; and whilst in a few cases this could be viewed as a normal reaction to the child's inherent abnormality, such situations were atypical. Yet so far as we could ascertain only one couple had genuine grounds for anxiety over the child's background, knowing that his father had been in Broadmoor. Clinical experience leaves no doubt that, in family life as elsewhere, fantasies can be more noxious than the most unpalatable of facts.

A concept that was fundamental to Jaffee and Fanshel's approach, although they were unable to verify it, is that of 'entitlement'. This refers to the hypothesis that some of the stress in adoptive family relationships stems from the parents' inability to look upon the children as truly theirs, leading them to engage in 'as if' behaviour. This could have the long-term effect of undermining the close sense of unity and mutual belonging that characterizes the nuclear family at its best. It is scarcely surprising that a subtle handicap of this kind should elude the research worker's grasp, but it has been noted in clinical work. For example, Walsh and Lewis (1969) in a study of twelve adoptive mothers attending a child guidance clinic found a major common source of difficulty in the apparent feelings of guilt about taking children who did not belong to them, and this guilt was said to arise from unresolved anger and rivalry towards their own mothers.

Psychodynamic theories of this nature are superficially attractive, yet they should not be given too much weight. The fact that adoption can pose problems of its own must not be taken to mean that it will inevitably bring more anxiety than satisfaction to adoptive family members. Moreover, major follow-up reports on more representative samples (for example, Jaffee and Fanshel 1970; Raynor 1980) have been heartening in their message. The available evidence does not suggest that in the long run adopted individuals are any less likely to make a success of their lives.

Studies of adopted children who are in trouble or distress, whilst interesting in their own right, must be interpreted with due caution (Shaw 1984). Where pre-adoptive deprivation in the child is compounded by pre-existing emotional problems in the adoptive parents (as was all too apparent in some of the Oxford families) the outcome may indeed be compromised. But it is now abundantly clear that devoted care by loving adopters can largely reverse the ill effects of parental neglect (Kadushin 1970) or institutional life (Tizard 1977) in the pre-school years. And whilst neither of these last two investigators followed their adoptees into adult life, Triseliotis and Russell (1984) have produced optimistic findings on a group of young adults who had been adopted between the age of 2–8 in Scotland and were evidently faring rather better than a control group who had spent most of their early years in residential care. Most of these forty-four adoptees (including twenty-eight men) were employed, and a few had already married by their mid-twenties. In choosing such a control group the authors had obviously recognized that it might be unfair to compare late adoptees with those who had spent all their formative years in the family of origin, since this is seldom a realistic alternative for children who are adopted at any age. Even so, there is no longer any reason to suppose that delayed placement for adoption, with all its attendant disadvantages, need set the stage for a disastrous childhood or adulthood. It all depends on the quality of parental care in the adoptive home.

The main lesson from clinical studies of an earlier era is that grotesquely unsuitable placements have been made in the past. It would be idle to pretend that they are no longer made today even if adoption workers are more sophisticated than thirty years ago. The difficulty facing today's agencies is the acute shortage of straightforwardly adoptable infants. The older child, the non-white child, and the infant with known or suspected defects (be they mental, physical, or genetic) has a better chance of finding an adoptive home than in the past. But who are the adopting couples who can cope with such a variety of challenges? Previous experience of rearing a damaged or disadvantaged child is likely to be a major asset (Kadushin 1970), whereas the couple who are feeling emotionally deprived by their childlessness may be at risk of deluding themselves that any child is better than no child. Such couples should not be required to become therapists to an adopted child, and it may be that adoption is not in their own best interests. (Nor is fostering with a view to adoption a satisfactory alternative in view of the obvious hazards for both parties in the event of failure.) The National Association for the Childless was founded in 1976 to provide information, advice, and support for those who at an earlier period would have found it easier to solve their problem by adopting an unblemished infant, but are now forced to rethink their attitudes. For above all, adoption is no longer to be construed as a service for childless couples.

Despite this change of emphasis whereby adoptive homes are increasingly being sought for children with a chequered history,[6] traditional adoptions are still taking place albeit on a small scale (at the time of writing less than 1,000 annually). Even a copy-book adoption may run into serious problems, and as in any other family the parents may find themselves wondering where they have gone wrong. A crucial difference for adoptive parents is that they may have a more pervasive sense of the unknown which will colour their attitude to the child; and doctors or social workers may be tempted to collude with them in this matter. Hence the chapter will end by examining the notion that, even where the child is transferred to the adopters soon after birth and with an absolutely clean history (including a normal pregnancy and delivery), there is still an element of risk from unknown genetic factors.

WHAT ABOUT THE GENES?

The use of adoption as an alternative to twin studies in the quest for evidence on the relative importance of nature and nurture in human development has burgeoned over the past twenty years. Psychiatrists in particular have been interested in the possible genetic basis of alcoholism, schizophrenia, and psychopathy, whilst criminal and other antisocial behaviour has attracted the attention of social scientists. This approach depends heavily on the existence of reliable information about the birth parents, which explains why so much of this work has been done in Denmark and Sweden where adoption and twin registers are of better quality than elsewhere. It also calls for assiduous follow-up after an interval that allows ample time for the emergence of the illness or behaviour in question. For this purpose a twenty-year follow-up is barely sufficient, whereas an interval of thirty to forty years is more acceptable.

To begin with schizophrenia, which has an incidence of barely 1 per cent, yet prior to effective drugs was responsible for some 25 per cent of psychiatric bed occupancy (Storey 1986), a pioneering research was conducted in Oregon (Heston 1966; Heston and Denney 1968). The focus of the enquiry was a group of forty-seven subjects born to schizophrenic mothers in state hospitals and separated from them in the first few days of life without further contact. They were placed either in orphanages or foster homes (usually with paternal relatives), and there was no evidence that type of placement had made any difference to the long-term outcome. They were matched with adoptees of normal parentage, and both groups were interviewed by Heston in their mid-thirties. The follow-up was not blind but the case material was reviewed blindly by other judges, and police and hospital records were consulted. Schizophrenia was diagnosed in five index subjects (11 per cent) but no controls. There were also thirteen cases of neurotic personality disorder and nine cases of

antisocial personality, both significantly higher rates than the
seven neurotic and two antisocial personalities found among the
fifty controls (28 per cent versus 14 per cent and 19 per cent
versus 4 per cent respectively). In all, serious psychopathology
was discernible in more than half of the offspring of schizophrenic mothers, and their risk of developing frank schizophrenia
was apparently no less than that of individuals reared by a
schizophrenic parent.[7] This last finding was confirmed by Karlsson (1970) who, by pooling data from several studies including
his own, found that 14 out of 137 adoptees born to a schizophrenic parent had themselves developed schizophrenia.

The well-known work of Rosenthal *et al* (1968; 1971) using
national adoption and psychiatric registers in Denmark produced
comparable findings. Here the biological parents were diagnosed
as falling into the 'schizophrenia spectrum' of disorders, with
twice as many mothers as fathers affected. Almost a third of the
seventy-six index subjects as against fewer than a fifth of the
sixty-seven controls were similarly classified. Both groups of
adoptees had been placed with non-relatives at a median age of 6
months, and they were interviewed blind at a mean age of 33.
From the different methods of ascertainment it is reasonable to
infer that the parents were less severely ill than Heston's group of
mothers; the fact that almost three times as many of the adoptees
as in his study (32 per cent versus 11 per cent) were classed as
psychotic is probably a reflection of less stringent diagnostic
criteria.

A parallel study of thirty-three schizophrenic adoptees and
matched healthy controls, again traced through Danish registers,
compared the incidence of schizophrenia spectrum disorders both
in the biological and the adoptive relatives, that is, in parents,
siblings, and half-siblings (Kety *et al* 1968; 1971). Again, the difference between 21 per cent of the index biological relatives and
11 per cent of the controls is highly significant, whereas among
the adoptive relatives these disorders appeared to be no more
common than in the general population.

Finally, a study by Wender *et al* (1974) compared twenty-eight
adoptees of normal parentage, but reared by schizophrenic adopters (who must have somehow slipped through the net unless
they had become ill after adopting), and a control group of
seventy-nine adoptees with no history of schizophrenia in either
set of parents. The incidence of schizophrenia spectrum disorders

was only marginally lower in the controls (10 per cent versus 11 per cent). In reviewing this unusual study Crowe (1975: 359) concludes that 'schizophrenia in a parent figure does not appear to facilitate the development of that disorder in a child in the absence of a genetic predisposition'.

Turning now to alcoholism, we find that parallel studies involving samples of much the same size have yielded consistent findings that point in the same direction. The child of an alcoholic parent who is reared in a foster home after early separation is more likely to succumb to alcoholism as an adult (Goodwin *et al* 1973; 1974; Bohman 1978), whereas exposure to an alcoholic foster parent has no such effect (Schuckit, Goodwin, and Winokur 1972). But whereas there is only a small excess of male schizophrenics (after allowing for later age of onset in females), alcoholism remains substantially more common in men despite indications of a growing incidence among women (Camberwell Council on Alcoholism 1980). Moreover, although the incidence of alcoholism is harder to estimate owing to problems of definition, it is undoubtedly more prevalent than schizophrenia. This has implications for the study of adoptive families, in that a history of schizophrenia in a biological parent is likely to be more accessible than a history of alcoholism. Twenty years ago the offspring of a schizophrenic parent might well have been considered unadoptable, and it would have been harder in any case to find suitable adopters. And if in today's adoption famine it has become easier to place children with this kind of history, at least the prospective adopters can be warned of possible long-term hazards. In contrast the male parent of a child up for adoption is often a shadowy figure, so that a genetic loading for alcoholism may remain a latent risk.

Another factor in comparing alcoholism and schizophrenia is the question of associated conduct disorders in childhood. Whilst it is rare for either disorder to become manifest before late adolescence or early adulthood, there is no strong evidence to suggest that children destined to become schizophrenic are harder to rear than their healthy siblings. Thus although a proportion of diagnosed schizophrenics are seen in retrospect as odd personalities, it would seem that they are not unduly prone to antisocial character development when adopted as infants. In contrast, childhood problems of this nature are fairly common in the histories of alcoholics, including those separated from alcoholic parents in early life and raised in foster homes (Schuckit et al 1970; Goodwin et al 1975; Cadoret and Gath 1978; Cadoret, Cain, and Grove 1980). In case alcoholism might be seen as a direct outcome of poor social learning rather than as genetically transmitted, Cadoret, Cain, and Grove (1980) looked at the biological backgrounds of adoptees with a dual diagnosis of alcoholism and antisocial personality. On the basis of rather small numbers in sub-groups with a background of alcoholism, other psychiatric diagnoses, or no diagnosis, they concluded that alcoholism in the biological relatives was a specific predictor of alcoholism in the adoptee regardless of whether it was associated with antisocial personality. However, ideally a prospective enquiry would be needed to disentangle the influence of these two factors.

Finally, we need to look at more recent evidence than the aforementioned study of monozygotic twins concordant for sociopathic personality (Tienari 1963). Again we can thank the Danish system of registration for two useful adoption studies of psychopathy and criminality. Schulsinger (1972), from a search through hospital records of fifty-seven adoptees classified as psychopaths and matched controls with other diagnoses, found that deviations of this sort (including criminality, drug abuse, and hysterical character as well as psychopathy) were significantly more common in the biological relatives of the index group. Biological relatives of the control group were affected with approximately the same frequency as either group of adoptive relatives. The second study involved the screening of 1,145 male adoptees aged 30–44 in Copenhagen and the same number of matched non-adopted controls, together with their biological and adoptive parents, for a record of criminal offences (Hutchings and Mednick 1975). It was found that 16 per cent of the adoptees but only 9 per cent of the controls (the same proportion as in the local population) had a criminal record; corresponding figures for adoptive and control fathers were 13 per cent and 11 per cent, which raises the question of whether prospective adopters were screened as carefully in Denmark between the wars as they are in Britain today.[8] Notably, however, almost a third of the adoptees' biological fathers (31 per cent) were past or present criminals. With the focus narrowed to criminal adoptees, the proportion of criminal adoptive fathers rose to 22 per cent and biological fathers to 49 per cent. Thus, as Crowe (1975) points out, criminality in an adoptee was positively correlated with criminality in either the biological or the adoptive father. The effect of rearing by a deviant parent was apparently greater when there was a genetic predisposition, and interestingly a psychiatric diagnosis in the biological mother emerged as an independent contributory factor.

It was predictable that age at placement and quality of pre-adoptive experience would also have a measurable effect on the crime rate. The criminal adoptees in Hutchings and Mednick's series were adopted no later than the rest; on the other hand Crowe (1974) found that whilst only a small number of adoptees born to female offenders in correctional institutions (with evidence of assortative mating in at least a third of the cases) were rated as antisocial personalities in early adulthood or later, such an outcome was more probable with a history of more than twelve months in temporary care. The same interaction between genetic predisposition and early experience (at least for male offenders) was noted in the latest report by Mednick, Gabrielli, and Hutchings (1984) on more than 14,000 people adopted in Denmark between 1927–47. In this study 'crime' covered anything from traffic offences to murder, and the biological linkage appeared independent of the type of crime – even embezzlement seemed to have been lurking in the genes! A striking exception was violence, which was not appreciably more common in adoptees with violent ancestors (5 per cent as against just over 4 per cent).[9]

The collection of relevant data continues apace but without throwing much light on the mechanisms involved. Before we can confidently postulate an inherited propensity towards crime we need to clarify our ideas on the nature of what is being transmitted. The at first sight paradoxical absence of a genetic link for violence may in fact help to steer us in the right direction. Mednick himself has suggested that we might look towards 'autonomic nervous system responsiveness' for an answer. The level of autonomic activity (as reflected in how fast the heart beats and how much we sweat, for example) is known to govern our experience of anxiety. Those whose pulse rate responds only mildly to stress, or who become accustomed to it more rapidly than others, may be more prone to offend against society if only because they are cool customers with a better chance of escaping justice. But violence is typically both unpremeditated and directed against a member of a family, whereas non-violent crimes are more likely to be both impersonal and foreseen. It is the sangfroid of the hardened criminal rather than the impulsiveness of *crime passionnel* that is more likely to be an inherited trait (Humphrey 1984).

This discussion of the family history of adoptees has opened up new vistas, and the interaction between genetic and environmental influences is an alarmingly complex issue. For practical purposes adoption calls for an environmentalist stance, and adopters cannot allow themselves to be mesmerized by the unknown genes. We would need more compelling evidence than hitherto available (for example, Cunningham *et al* 1975) to believe that adoptees are to an appreciable extent genetically at risk, in terms of their mental health, as compared with individuals who remain with their family of origin.

Whether their academic and vocational achievements are likely to fall short of parental expectation, in view of possible disparities between the two sets of parents in favour of the adopters, is equally debatable. In the Oxford study the nineteen children placed early in middle-class homes had a mean IQ just short of 120, which implies that quite a few were of university potential. This points to the importance of environmental factors, but interpretation is complicated by the policy of selective matching espoused by most adoption agencies at that time. For example, in all but three of the fifteen cases where the natural father's occupation was known, it tallied with the adoptive father's. Seglow, Pringle, and Wedge (1972: 145) in their national survey found that a small sub-group of adoptees in middle-class homes were apparently vulnerable in terms of their scores on the *Bristol Social Adjustment Guide* (Stott 1966), as completed by their teachers. All but three of these sixteen children were boys. The reason for this link between possible maladjustment and type of home must remain conjectural in the absence of a testable hypothesis. It is possible, though perhaps not all that likely in middle childhood, that the parents (especially the fathers) were disappointed by their school progress. Intelligence was not tested individually, as in the Oxford study, but we would doubt whether inherent lack of ability played any part in the teachers' estimates of social adjustment. However, the pressures acting upon children adopted by well-educated couples would most certainly repay further study.

The reader who wishes to pursue the question of genetic and environmental effects on measured intelligence in adopted children should begin by consulting a detailed review by Munsinger (1975), who takes a predominantly genetic stance. In rather more polemical fashion Kamin (1974; 1981) leans heavily in the opposite direction. The work of Horn (1983) in Texas and Scarr and Weinberg (1978; 1983) in Minnesota allows room for both kinds of influence. Unlike most previous workers these investigators were able to test the adoptive parents, whilst Horn also presented data on the natural mothers. Both studies gave reasonably clear evidence of the operation of genetic factors, and Scarr and Weinberg found these to be more conspicuous in older children (mean age 18.5 years). Their conclusions are worth quoting:

> Younger children, regardless of their genetic relatedness, resemble each other intellectually because they share a similar rearing environment. Older adolescents, on the other hand, resemble one another only if they share genes. Our interpretation is that older children escape the influences of the family and are freer to select their own environments. Parental influences are diluted by the more varied mix of adolescent experiences.[10]

(Scarr and Weinberg 1983: 265)

These findings largely bear out the classic studies of Leahy (1935), also in Minnesota, and Skodak and Skeels (1949) in Iowa. Leahy compared 194 early adoptees aged 5–14 with individually matched non-adopted controls. When mean IQ was correlated with adoptive father's occupation in five sub-groups she found more than three times as much variability in the control group: from 102 (semi-skilled) to 119 (professional), as against 108 and 113 respectively in the adopted group. Interpreting this difference as a reflection of genetic diversity, she reached the following conclusion: 'Apparently environment cannot compensate for the lack of blood relationship in creating mental resemblance between parent and child. Heredity persists' (Leahy 1935: 284). Skodak and Skeels, following up 100 children adopted in early infancy, found that the correlation between child's and natural mother's IQ on the same test repeated several times increased until at a mean age of 13–14 it reached approximately the same level as is typical of parent-child resemblance in ordinary families (about 0.4). Even so the adoptees, with a mean IQ of 106, were several points above the population mean and twenty points above the mean of their natural mothers.[11]

In support of their much more recent IQ data Scarr and Weinberg cite the results of aptitude and achievement tests (Table 3.2). They argue that

> The effects of being reared in the same family, neighbourhood, and school are negligible unless one is genetically related to one's brother or sister. The correlations of the biological siblings were modest but statistically different from zero, whereas the aptitude and achievement scores of the adopted siblings were virtually unrelated.
>
> (Scarr and Weinberg 1983: 264)

Considering that performance in the classroom over time has been regarded, on the basis of twin studies, as more susceptible to family and other environmental influences than immediate performance on an IQ test (Jensen 1969), such findings are indeed remarkable. However, it might be prudent to await replication before taking them too seriously.

Most research workers, be they clinicians, social scientists, or behavioural geneticists, have been content to look at adoptive families from the outside. What has been missing from the story

Table 3.2 *Sibling correlations of aptitude and achievement test scores of adopted and biologically related adolescents*

	Biological no. of pairs	r	Adopted no. of pairs	r
Aptitude				
Verbal	141	0.29	68	0.13
Numerical	61	0.32	49	0.07
Achievement				
Reading	106	0.27	73	0.11
Maths	104	0.35	58	−0.11

Source: Scarr and Weinberg (1983: 264)

so far (as indeed from much of the literature on adoption) is any awareness of what growing up adopted means to the adoptee. This gap in our knowledge is what the next two chapters are designed to fill.

4 Adoption (2): the need for identity

If some foster children are handicapped by uncertainties over their sense of identity, as noted earlier, this will apply to a larger proportion of adopted children. Loss of contact with the original parents is a standard feature of adoption, and once the legal order transferring all parental rights to the adopters has been granted, it is as if an iron curtain has descended. The historical reasons for this philosophy of a totally fresh start are clear enough when we recall the stigma attaching to illegitimacy and single parenthood during the late Victorian era and beyond. However, it is only over the past two or three decades that concern has been expressed over the psychological consequences of this fresh start for the children as they grow up. In this chapter we shall consider what it means to be permanently cut off from one's roots. Is the sense of rootlessness of which adoptees have sometimes complained too heavy a price to pay for the protection from interference by the biological relatives? We have already noted some of the problems of 'dual parentage' that can impinge on children in foster care, and the resistance displayed by social workers as well as foster parents when faced with the challenge of integrating the two sets of relationships. But are those adopted as infants, with neither memories of an earlier life nor even much concept of an alternative biography, really so much better off with the approach of adulthood?

GENEALOGICAL BEWILDERMENT

It was Sants (1964) who went so far as to suggest that ancestral knowledge was a prerequisite of mental health, whatever that may mean. His message may have struck a chord, but it was drawn from a distillation of clinical experience and literary insights. His collaborator at the same child guidance clinic, Wellisch (1952), is believed to have introduced the notion of genealogical bewilderment, and we ourselves have recently reviewed the evidence in support of it from research studies conducted over the past fifteen years or so (Humphrey and Humphrey 1986). Here we shall try to take our ideas a stage further in assessing the frequency and importance of this now familiar syndrome. We shall argue that it should be accorded no more than a modest influence on either professional practice or popular thinking as to what it means to grow up adopted. Whilst not wishing to discount the value of clinical speculation, we would be happier to put our trust in findings from research (including our own small-scale enquiry to be reported in the next chapter) when they all seem to be pointing in the same direction. There can be no doubt whatever that some adopted individuals are acutely disturbed by ignorance of their origins; the question is whether such ignorance is the primary cause of their disturbance, or whether their unknown parentage has become the focus for a more pervasive sense of dissatisfaction with themselves and their lives.

Again, we would gladly acknowledge that genetic curiosity is a perfectly normal response on the part of children who have had little or no contact with their family of origin. The question here is, at what stage does healthy curiosity turn into a morbid preoccupation? Presumably there is some kind of a continuum between passive acceptance of one's fate as an adoptee and over-whelming determination to seek out one's biological relatives; and whilst no scale of measurement has been or indeed is ever likely to be devised, it might not be too difficult to place any individual at some approximate point along this continuum at any given time. And as always, extremes are easier to recognize. According to Sorosky, Baran, and Pannor (1974), the 'adoptee activist movement' was pioneered by Jean Paton, an adopted social worker who located her original mother when she herself was 47 and her mother 69. After publishing her first book (Paton 1954) she was in great demand as a lecturer, and at one time headed an organization called 'Orphan Voyage' with its main office in Colorado. She has recorded the poetic sentiment that 'In the soul of every orphan is an eternal flame of hope for reunion and reconciliation with those he has lost through private or public disaster.' (Sorosky, Baran, and Pannor 1974: 196)[1]

An equally energetic campaigner on behalf of adoptees' rights was Anna Fisher, who was adopted by a Jewish couple as an infant in New York before the Second World War. At the age of 7 she discovered her adoption papers, but was made by her outraged adoptive mother to feel that this was a shameful secret. She became obsessed with her lack of family resemblance in looks or abilities, and after the failure of a youthful first marriage she began what proved to be a long-drawn-out search for her original parents. She came up against bureaucratic and other obstacles, but finally managed to trace her mother when she herself had turned 40. Her reception was cool if not hostile, perhaps partly because she had pretended to be a long lost cousin in order to gain an entrée. Fortunately her father's family were more welcoming, and she achieved an ecstatic reunion with him in California. She discovered that the couple had been married very briefly in their early youth, and it was on the maternal grandparents' insistence that she was surrendered for adoption. Flushed with the triumph of her delayed success, she went on to found ALMA (Adoptees' Liberty Movement Association) as a means of helping others in the same position. Her book (Fisher 1973) is a highly emotive account of her unhappy childhood and self-torturing early adulthood, but her passage through to a more tranquil middle age was sustained by her second husband as well as by the ultimately rewarding outcome of her search.

Our third and last example of an indefatigable searcher comes from nearer home. David Leitch, an investigative journalist of some renown, has published two instalments of his autobiography. *God Stand up for Bastards* (1973) opens with a *cri de coeur*: 'Mother, where are you?' At 8 days of age he had been offered for adoption through a small advertisement placed by his mother in the personal column of the *Daily Express*. Prospective foster parents were invited to a private viewing at the Russell Hotel which, as the author remarks, 'dominated the east end of Bloomsbury with its lunatic facade − all in all, a happy choice' (Leitch 1973: 9). In effect, he was to be auctioned to the highest bidder; and in case this might strike some readers as an inauspicious start to life, we would merely comment that in 1937 there were worse ways of arranging an adoption.[2] A year after its publication, his natural mother, Truda, borrowed the book from her library and promptly fainted when she saw the photograph of the baby she had given away. But the gamble paid off, and in due course − after a gap of more than thirty-six years − contact was renewed.

In his sequel, *Family Secrets* (1984), he wrote of his gradually unfolding relationship with his long lost mother, who was able to
explain her reluctance to delve too deeply into their common
past. Through her he was able to locate one of his younger sisters,
and at the time of writing he was still hopeful of tracing the other
one. Leitch appears to have been happy enough with his surrogate family, even if he grew up without siblings. What distin-
guishes him from the vast majority of adoptees is his unflagging
curiosity, which was doubtless what propelled him into journal-
ism. At all events we would hesitate to accept him as a reliable
guide to the psychological needs of adopted people.

Nor can we altogether share the conviction of another
journalist, Polly Toynbee, that her small series of adoptees in
search of their mothers can be viewed as representative of all
adoptees. Her book (Toynbee 1985) is evidently the product of
three years' research and writing, yet according to her publishers
it is

> not a 'sociological' work, in the narrow sense of that term,
> although she comes to some hard-hitting conclusions. Rather it
> is a series of thrilling stories which portray people at their most
> determined and their most vulnerable, engaged on a search of
> supreme importance to them and revealing truths about blood
> ties which bind us all.

She herself in the Acknowledgements expresses some confidence
that these stories are 'reasonably typical of adopted people in
search of their origins', and for all we know some of them may
be. Yet we cannot help wondering about the thrice-married
Georgina Enston, for instance, who discovered her adoption at
the age of 8 by rummaging through her adoptive mother's
underclothes drawer. Sadly she had no hope of ever meeting her
natural mother, Ruth Ellis, who was convicted of shooting her
lover and became the last woman in Britain to hang for murder
in 1955. With such an unhappy history how could she be typical?
It certainly sounds as if her adjustment to life as an adult was
somewhat precarious, although her middle-aged adoptive parents had done their best to make up for an uncertain start (for
the first two or three years she was mostly in the care of her
grandmother, until removed by her father). Whilst not wishing to
disparage such an intriguing contribution to the literature, we
feel bound to cast doubt on its scientific value.

These pioneering and well-publicized ventures by adopted individuals who succeeded in finding their own original parents are unlikely to have made a significant impact on adoption policy and practice. In the USA there is still inter-state variation in the provisions for assisting in such a search, but it is not made easy for the candidate. In Minnesota, for example, an application is forwarded by the Department of Public Welfare to the most appropriate local child-placing agency, which then embarks on a series of manoeuvres to locate the birth parent(s). Only if these are successful and written consent is given by the parent(s) will access to the birth records be permitted (Weidell 1980). The approach to potential birth parents is anything but discreet, as it typically involves telephone calls to people with the same surname. Where a blank is drawn presumably no harm is done, but when the call is taken by an innocent child or spouse there is no knowing what the repercussions might be. By comparison the British experience has been quite circumspect, if we can rely on the testimony of adoptees interviewed in Scotland by Triseliotis (1973; 1984). But Scottish adoptees have been entitled to inspect their birth certificate on coming of age ever since 1930, a privilege at one time shared only with natives of Finland. In the ten years or more since the 1975 Children Act has been in force, a more open and liberal attitude towards searching has spread throughout Britain, until it has become almost the 'done thing'. In order to set current trends in perspective, it may help at this point to present a brief résumé of developments over the past sixty years.

EVOLUTION OF ADOPTIVE PRACTICES

The first Adoption Act was introduced in 1926, and during each of the next four years an average of 3,500 orders were granted by the courts. After this modest start there was a steady rise until the 1950s, when the annual rate remained fairly constant at 13,000–14,000. It then rose again until 1968, when almost 25,000 orders were granted. Since this peak year it has shown a striking though not wholly unpredictable decline, bearing in mind a falling birth rate, easier abortion, and more widespread social acceptance of single parenthood. But it must be made clear that a fluctuating proportion of children over the years have been adopted within the family. In a small minority of cases this has meant adoption by grandparents or by an uncle and aunt, but far more often these intra-familial cases have resulted from the natural mother's marriage or remarriage to a man who is not the child's father but wishes or at least is willing to formalize the quasi-paternal relationship. Such step-parent adoptions have ranged in frequency between 30 per cent and 70 per cent of the annual total, in round figures. Interestingly, Masson, Norbury, and Chatterton (1983) state that resort to this kind of legal artifice, which is not how the public thinks of adoption, has 'dwindled dramatically' since implementation of the relevant sections of the 1975 Children Act.[3] However, in 1984 step-parent adoptions still contributed a little over 50 per cent to the total figure of less than 9,000. Whatever the theoretical arguments in favour of abolishing step-parent adoptions as such, it would seem that judicial practice is taking a while to catch up.

What are the likely consequences for children adopted within the family who are only partially cut off from their roots? On the face of it this would appear to be a much simpler situation, but it is not necessarily so. Clearly the acquisition of a step-parent can pose problems of its own, the nature of which will depend on the age and stage of occurrence. Some of these will be discussed in Chapter 6, but meanwhile we will refer to a perceptive study by Goodacre (1966). This focused on all adoptions (nearly 300) over a four-year period in the administrative area of a single children's department. Interview requests were sent to 108 adopting couples, of whom 90 (83 per cent) accepted. But there was a marked difference (p almost 0.001 on the present writer's calculation) between the refusal rate of step-parent adopters (10/27 or 37 per cent) and the remainder (8/81 or less than 10 per cent). And the author comments that

> Of all the adoptive couples seen, these were the ones who had perhaps had to make the most subtle and complex adjustment of any. They had realized that theirs had not become an 'ordinary' family simply by virtue of the making of the order: adoption had, indeed, solved some problems but it had created others.
>
> (Goodacre 1966: 141)

Paramount among these other problems, it would appear, was the young stepfather's reluctance to tell the child that he was not the true father, thus putting pressure on the true mother to remain silent. Honesty may come harder when the child has no memory of the stepfather's arrival in the family; and in the absence of any evidence that over the past twenty years single mothers have become more inclined to delay marriage when opportunity offers, the temptation to conceal the truth under these circumstances may be no less powerful today. However, the chances are that an uneasy silence cannot be maintained forever. In our series of couples seeking donor insemination (Chapter 7) a husband related how the man he had always thought of as his father had, in a rare moment of anger, told him that he was really his stepfather. As they had spent most of the previous sixteen years living under the pretence that they were father and son, the sudden disclosure could have risked damaging their relationship beyond repair. The fact that, to all outward appearances, it had not done so, was hardly the stepfather's fault!

Nor are adoptions by relatives guaranteed to make it any easier to confide in the growing child. Goodacre quotes the case of a conscience-stricken woman with a supportive husband who found herself committed to adopting her sister's new-born daughter only five days after the birth of her own, with older children already in the family. They had lost no time in telling Fanny that she once had another mother, yet were understandably perplexed as to how they would ever be able to convey the whole truth to her in an acceptable form. They had no intention of letting her know that her mother did not want her, but what were they to say if pressed for an explanation when they themselves had always found the sister's attitude utterly baffling? Intra-familial adoptions of this nature have the merit of conferring security and legal rights that could be gained in no other way, although there is no reason why the child should not be known by the family surname even without going to court. However, the author is surely entitled to query whether the difficulties created within the extended family might be a high price to pay:

> For the evidence showed that the effect of granting orders was to confuse relationships – grandparents becoming parents, natural mothers becoming sisters and so forth...possibly, through amendment to the present guardianship laws, a

means of conferring the same security on proxy-parents might be provided, while releasing them and the child from some of the constraints and anxieties implied by adoption.

(Goodacre 1966: 174)

What prophetic insight!

This brief digression may serve to demonstrate that genealogical confusion, if not actual bewilderment, can arise just as easily when adopted children retain some or even all of their family connections. But it is probably fair to suggest that, until the 1975 Act, legislation was framed primarily for the benefit of children adopted by strangers. In 1954 the Hurst Committee had already laid great stress on the need for complete honesty between adoptive parents and their children, having heard from witnesses that the children had a right to satisfy their natural curiosity. Nevertheless the Committee refrained from making any stronger recommendations in this direction which would have anticipated the Houghton Committee (1972), who finally overcame their reluctance to compromise the natural mother by reneging on promises of absolute confidentiality made when she surrendered her child for adoption. For this Committee, unlike the earlier one, had commissioned various pieces of research to guide its deliberations. That was how Triseliotis (1973) came to produce the evidence that, within a remarkably short time, brought England and Wales into line with Scotland by giving adopted persons right of access to their birth certificates on reaching the age of majority (which in Scotland meant adding a year). The lasting influence of his enquiry has belied the modesty of its scope.

The seventy adoptees interviewed by Triseliotis had visited or written to Register House in Edinburgh over a period of two years for information about their origins. There were approximately equal numbers of men and women among the ninety-eight from whom his sample was drawn, but a better response rate from the women resulted in forty-one interviews. Most were in their twenties or thirties, and some were living outside Scotland at the time. Often their curiosity had built up over a long period, finally reaching a head in response to some key event such as marriage, the birth of a child, or the death of an adoptive parent. They were only a small minority of those entitled to make enquiries, in that on average only forty-two people per annum (or 1.5 per 1,000 adoptees over the age of 17) had contacted the Registrar General for this purpose over the previous decade. The knowledge to be derived from a birth certificate is of course minimal: name of parent(s), child's original name, date and place of birth, parental occupation(s), and their usual address at the time. So those who intended to use the information as a starting point for a search must have been inspired by enthusiastic optimism rather than by rational expectations. In reality almost 40 per cent of these adoptees were merely seeking the truth about their origins, and had no wish to take active steps towards confronting their blood relatives. Only eleven (16 per cent) got as far as a meeting, be it with a parent, a sibling, a grandparent, or an aunt. The experience had sometimes proved disenchanting, and further contact might be severed at the behest of either party.

Predictably enough there was evidence of personality problems and/or disturbed family relationships among those with a compulsion to search. Most of these amateur sleuths conveyed an air of alienation and impaired self-image which they themselves were apt to attribute to emotional deprivation within the adoptive home. A good many of these had received psychiatric treatment in the hope of promoting their adaptation to life. Moreover they 'expressed feelings of shame and embarrassment about their adoptive status and the implied illegitimacy. The greater their sense of isolation and insecurity, the greater the possibility they would be searching for their original parents' (Triseliotis 1973: 91). Where the home background was more favourable, the individual was more likely to be content with the information on offer. Similar findings were reported by Raynor (1980) from interviews with 105 young adults traced through their adoptive parents, mainly in London and the home counties. Although only 22 per cent of her sample (as against 62 per cent of the Scottish one) declared an interest in meeting their original parents, they were younger (aged 22–27) and had not been selected with this question in mind. However, the association between wanting to meet and a less satisfactory adoptive experience was equally clear-cut. Evidence of this kind is alone sufficient to challenge the assumption that detailed knowledge of one's origins is essential for healthy development, as postulated by Sants (1964). It begins to look as if ignorance of one's forebears is perfectly compatible with security about one's self. Much will depend on the quality of adoptive family life.

And further evidence continues to accumulate. When Section 26 of the 1975 Children Act was implemented in November 1976, there was a spate of almost 2,000 applications from adoptees wanting access to their birth records during the last five weeks of the year. This level of interest was not maintained, with fewer than 3,500 enquiries for the whole of 1977 and then on average only a little more than 2,000 annually during the next six years. At this stage it was estimated that only about 2 per cent of all adoptees had taken advantage of the counselling facility (Children Act, Second Report to Parliament, HMSO 1984). And despite a recent upsurge in the number of enquiries, with an average of 4,200 over the past three years (Registrar General, personal communication), we still anticipate that only a minority of adoptees will attempt to trace their origins through official channels.

Interviews with the first 500 enquirers at the General Register Office in London revealed that 28 per cent had already made up their mind to search for their parents or other relatives, the rest being either uninterested (39 per cent) or undecided (33 per cent). Not many of the resolute searchers betrayed signs of emotional disturbance, although a determination to pursue their quarry went with adverse factors in the adoptive history (such as early death of an adopter, marital discord, or an unexpected birth to the adopting couple). In all, only eighteen applicants (3.6 per cent) still gave cause for concern after skilled counselling (Day and Leeding 1980).

The impact of counselling upon the potential searcher has become a live issue. The Houghton Committee (1972) did not specify counselling in their recommendations, and it was introduced mainly in response to parliamentary pressure. It was seen as a necessary safeguard, not only by MPs but by senior social workers and other professionals, in a situation that was ripe for mischief. A knowledgeable counsellor could make sure that the adoptee was sufficiently aware of the hazards of confrontation (especially where the parent or other relative had not been warned), and might in appropriate cases offer to act as an intermediary. Consequently it was laid down that those adopted before November 1975 would be required to undergo prior counselling from an accredited social worker, whereas children adopted more recently will be under no such obligation because their blood relatives will have been familiar with the new law at the time of placement. Obviously, however, the opportunity for discussion with a disinterested party will remain available to one and all.

A study of forty-five applicants and their counsellors by Haimes and Timms (1983; 1985) has brought out some of the hidden implications of this mildly controversial requirement. Counsellors' approach to the task, and their level of background knowledge, was found to vary a good deal. Where several meetings took place (which was entirely at the counsellor's discretion), the adoptee's attitudes to a possible meeting might be open to modification. Thus the effect of repeated discussions, at what was often a time of heightened emotion in the individual's life, was sometimes to convert a quest for information into an active campaign for a meeting. The authors took an entirely different view from Triseliotis in arguing that the need to search went with an urge to correct one's marginal status rather than with an unhappy adoptive experience. Some of their informants had come to regard themselves as having two life stories, as if their adoptive lives could be construed in part as 'living under a bogus identity' (Haimes and Timms 1983: 72). This is an interesting notion, and it cannot be denied that an introspective but essentially normal adoptee might be tempted to dwell on the might-have-been, especially at times of crisis. Divergent viewpoints can sometimes arise from differences in research method, as where dissimilar samples are studied by different techniques and from a different angle. But in disputing the relevance of individual psychopathology and disturbed family relationships, Haimes and Timms (1983) would be on firmer ground if they had not excluded adoptees with overt mental instability from their sample.

These authors have invoked the concept of *social identity* as a means towards a better understanding of adoptees' psychological problems. The underlying premise here is that the adopted person has an intense need to know where he or she stands in relation to society. This may well turn out to be a useful correction to the committed psychological approach of other authors, including ourselves. Yet it does not dispose of the argument that whether to embark on the hazardous process of searching for blood relatives is *au fond* an emotional decision, even if it is also heavily influenced by the social climate. This was brought home to us when our own adopted daughter, immortalized by Heim (1983: 22) in the guise of Audrey Medlar, informed us of her decision to make enquiries with a view to meeting her original mother. Not long after marrying at the age of 18 she wrote to Dr Heim that she had never felt any desire for such a meeting, 'as I am aware of the upset it could bring her, my parents, and possibly myself'. But such cool objectivity, though allied to a sensitive nature, proved hard to sustain. At 24 she gave birth to her own daughter, and her reactions to this experience were reinforced by pressure from her mother-in-law to discover more about her own side of the family. At the time of writing she is still at an early stage of the search, in which we wholeheartedly support her. We doubt whether anyone who knows her well would regard her as psychologically disturbed, and so we find ourselves having to reconcile this unanticipated event with our previous acceptance of what the literature had to say about the psychopathology of the search (McWhinnie 1967; Triseliotis 1973; Raynor 1980; Triseliotis and Russell 1984; Stein and Hoopes 1985).

In view of our own findings from a group of mature adoptees recruited through a self-help organization (Chapter 5), which yield the same message, we can hardly abandon our previous stance without a qualm. Perhaps the simplest way out of the dilemma is to quote the final sentence of Triseliotis and Russell's chapter on genealogical and personal information: 'The adoptees' motives for access to their records, leading perhaps to the tracing of a natural parent, are not static. Besides personal factors, social attitudes and changes influence such decisions.' (1984: 107) The behavioural repercussions of the new legislation have taken a while to become apparent, but they are slowly gathering force.

What a pity that the search-mindedness of adoptees in the 1958 cohort has so far gone unreported. Now into their thirtieth year, they were only 8 or 9 at the time of the original interview with the adoptive parents (Seglow, Pringle, and Wedge 1972), and still pre-adolescent when followed up by Lambert and Streather (1980). They are a national sample, and it would be fascinating to learn how they have coped with the genealogical factor. All but 6 per cent had been told of their adoption by the age of 9; and although background information was described as meagre in 55 per cent of cases, Seglow, Pringle, and Wedge report that only one adopting couple in six would have welcomed further details. In contrast, Triseliotis (1973) was under no illusions of having captured a representative sample; and whilst the adoptions studied by Raynor (1980) were probably fairly typical of those arranged by voluntary societies between 1948–51, times have changed since then. The research worker, like any other writer, is at the mercy of the *Zeitgeist*. The choice lies between articulating what seems to be true today, or maintaining a dignified silence until tomorrow. And in the present economic climate more than ever before, those who delay publishing for fear of error or distortion are less likely to have their contracts renewed!

THE ADOPTEE'S SELF-CONCEPT

It has become almost part of the received wisdom that adolescence can be a particularly trying time for the adopted individual. The capacity for abstract thinking is supposed to reach a peak during these years, allowing even the serenest of articulate youths to formulate and become preoccupied with previously unthinkable questions such as 'Who am I?' For this is also a period when social, sexual, and occupational roles may be tried for size, even if only in the imagination. Those who have reached this stage of life with little or no knowledge of their ancestry may indeed be at some disadvantage, if in seeking a stable self-concept most of us are likely to benefit from whatever we have learnt about our family history. Yet we are aware of no hard evidence on this matter, and have already argued that the psychology of heredity is a curiously neglected topic (Humphrey and Humphrey 1986). We shall therefore end this chapter by attempting to clarify what the search for *identity* means from a developmental perspective.

In the Oxford study (Humphrey and Ounsted 1963) it was found that adopted children, when compared with unselected controls, were more likely to be referred for psychiatric consultation after the eleventh birthday ($p < 0.02$). This would fit in with the notion of increased genealogical anxiety at the onset of puberty, but on the available data it must remain no more than a notion. It is not clear from published work whether other ins vestigators have replicated this finding, nor did our own series include more than one or two families in which this had been identified as a major problem. On the whole it seemed more likely that the bias towards adolescent crises in these families was a long-term outcome of pre-adoptive parental deprivation, in that 30 per cent of the girls and almost 50 per cent of the boys had been placed for adoption well after the optimal age (and typically with no history of adequate substitute care). Had their adoptive parents been more warmly supportive, as well as more insightful than was usually apparent, the flight into juvenile delinquency or other forms of antisocial conduct might have been averted in some cases.

A more recent study by Stein and Hoopes (1985) has approached the question of adolescent identity in a community setting. A sample of fifty teenage adoptees was recruited from a possible total of ninety; they were all white, mainly middle class, and had been placed for adoption before the age of 2. They differed from a carefully-matched control group only in the lower incidence of marital disruption in their families. Those with a history of severe psychopathology or known retardation were excluded from the sample. Neither interviews nor tests designed to measure aspects of identity were effective in discriminating between adoptees and controls; and the authors rightly take clinicians to task for creating the stereotype that adoptive status is in itself a source of psychological problems. The fact that none of these teenagers could have retained memories of other parents would appear to strengthen the authors' case, but ideally we should await similar evidence from those adopted after infancy before regarding the matter as settled. And it has to be added that a sample loss of almost 45 per cent is cause for concern.

Perhaps, however, the time has come for a more analytical approach to the question of identity formation before further studies are launched. Coleman (1980) has a helpful chapter on the development of the *self-concept,* which he takes to have essentially the same meaning as *identity* in this context. It refers to every aspect of the individual's view of his or her self, thus embracing *self-image* (description of the self) as well as *self-esteem* (evaluation of the self). Coleman's own work has incorporated the vital distinction between present and future self, first adumbrated by Douvan and Adelson (1966). He and his colleagues (Coleman, Herzberg, and Morris 1977) have devised a sentence-completion test for the express purpose of tapping this dimension; and whilst their preliminary work is of limited relevance to adoption, being focused on the rather bleak sentiments of working-class boys in an urban area, it might open the way to a better understanding of the adolescent adoptee.

Another important aspect of the self-concept is *body image*, which could have a special meaning for individuals cut off from their ancestral roots. In having to come to terms with a pre-pubertal growth spurt followed by the characteristic physical changes of adolescence, the adoptee cannot hope to learn as much as his peer group from gazing into the mirror of genetic resemblance. How much of a handicap is this likely to be? Some of the earlier work by social psychologists to which Coleman refers (for example, Jourard and Secord 1955; Gunderson 1956) has a bearing on this issue because of the readily demonstrable link between self-esteem and satisfaction with one's physique. But, quite apart from any specific anxieties experienced by adopted teenagers as they become aware of themselves as members of a minority group, the bodily preoccupations of growing youths have been relatively neglected by psychologists. Rosenberg (1979) is somewhat unusual in noting the importance of physical characteristics as part of the self-concept; and it may well be that adolescence is the time when adoptees are most vulnerable to a sense of dissimilarity between themselves and the only parents they have ever known. As we shall see in the next chapter, adopted adults in search of their biological relatives are often concerned to establish family likenesses in terms of appearance as well as temperament.

Nor is it only after puberty that such concerns may become apparent, as Kirk (1964) among others has noted. A child psychiatrist, too, may be exposed to revelations of this kind. A 10-year-old's fainting spells were found to occur when he attempted to visualize his natural parents:

> With great difficulty, he told me that he would sit in class, and begin to paint a mind picture of his real daddy and his real mummy. And he could manage the whole picture – nearly. He would start with the feet and the legs, and the body, and the shoulders – and he waited, and I waited, and then I said, 'And the faces?', and he said, 'The faces won't come'.
>
> (Stone 1969: 27)

A similar experience of our own is brought to mind by this story. When he was about 8 our adopted son woke one night with an attack of wheeziness (he was never actually diagnosed as asthmatic). When he could at last draw breath again, he said in great distress, 'I can't remember what my first mummy looked like.' Curiously enough he has shown little interest in the story of his adoption at any time (unlike his older sister who has always been eager to discuss the subject), and at 23 has yet to indicate any desire to embark on a search.

One can hardly conclude this discussion without reference to the work of Erikson (1963; 1968; 1980). If Haimes and Timms (1985) were right to lay stress on *social identity*, Erikson's concern was with *ego identity*. The development of this 'core' sense of self is a lifelong process, originating normally in early family relationships and subsequently tested and redefined in a wider milieu as the various stages of life are negotiated. A reflective being will soon get caught up in his or her life story, and historical events relating to the family may assume a significance of their own. Where the past is a closed book, recollections of life experience will suggest where it may be desirable to fill in the gaps if at all possible. Those who can take their genetic background for granted are unlikely to attach much importance to it as they progress through adolescence into adulthood. It is often only as they mature and have families of their own that inherited characteristics really begin to matter. A sense of unfolding family history is aroused when they see their children growing to look like themselves or their parents, and developing talents or traits which they feel gratified (or dismayed) to have passed on. Finally, as grandparents, they may use the leisure of retirement to compile an extensive family tree. An adopted person would be hard put indeed to follow this developmental sequence, but does this necessarily betoken an impaired sense of identity?

It should come as no surprise that theoreticians like Erikson (who as far as we know has little to say about adoption) hold firmly to the concept of *identity crisis* as an essential hurdle of adolescence. So far there have been few attempts to put this theory to the test of empirical research, which has an inconvenient habit of failing to deliver the goods. When evidence of adolescent turmoil is sought from field studies (for example, Rutter *et al* 1976) it is scarcely overwhelming. The awkward transition between dependent childhood and the robust self-sufficiency of mature adulthood is demanding at the best of times, especially when major decisions loom up (what line of employment or course of study to follow, or whether to get married and settle down, for example). But somehow most of us cope, at whatever level. There is nothing to suggest greater frequency of stress-related disorders in the teenage years, whether among those reared by surrogate parents from infancy or their biologically anchored contemporaries.

We are coming to believe that this more recent emphasis on *social identity* may clear the way to a more balanced view of growing up adopted. Elsewhere (Humphrey and Humphrey 1986) we have suggested that feedback from 'significant others' in the long run has more influence on an individual's self-concept than any amount of genealogical information. This deceptively simple view of human development owes much to the philosophical writings of Mead (1934), and was later elaborated in a psychiatric context by Sullivan (1953). As we expressed it in our earlier contribution:

> In the final analysis it is surely life experience that contributes most to self-awareness; and until we can add to our store of facts we may be in danger of over-estimating the handicap of ancestral ignorance to children cut off from their roots. . . . Further enquiry into the curiosity displayed by children in all kinds of substitute family would be welcome as an antidote to clinical speculation. We need also to consider how far the yearning to get to grips with a mysterious past is dictated by the conspiratorial nature of the adoption process rather than by individual psychopathology.
>
> (Humphrey and Humphrey 1986: 139)

If *open* adoption should ever become more widespread this could lead to a more satisfactory appraisal of the theme of this chapter. For it would then become possible to compare those growing up in a state of ignorance or mystification with those who had always known about their past. Even as it is we ought perhaps to look more closely at the genealogical concerns of those who spend most of their formative years in long-term foster care, without having been altogether cut off from their roots. Otherwise we can always fall back on the world of fiction. About three years ago we wrote to the editors of the *Times Literary Supplement* and *London Review of Books*[4] asking for readers' help in tracing examples of fictional characters who were mystified about their origins. The response was gratifying, and we were directed to Charlotte Brontë, Charles Dickens, George Eliot, and Thomas Hardy as well as other lesser-known authors. Amidst the other pressures of preparing for this book our enthusiasm for this line of enquiry was regrettably allowed to wane, but it is a topic that would surely benefit from further research.

Another rich source of insight is autobiography, and we have already referred to David Leitch. By chance the year in which Leitch published his *Family Secrets* (1984) was also notable for the publication in Britain of Anthony West's hard-hitting account of his troubled upbringing, thinly disguised as a novel. His mother was Rebecca West, and it was an open secret that his father was H.G. Wells; however, from the way he writes he could clearly have done without this genetic complication. It was in the same year that Angelica Garnett, daughter of Vanessa Bell, published a memoir in which she wrote of her poignant discovery in her late teens that her father was not Clive Bell (as she had always assumed), but the painter Duncan Grant. The message would seem to be that you do not need to be parted from your mother in order to grow up confused. Since legal adoption belongs to the twentieth century one must expect the great works of literature to be more concerned with illegitimacy, but there is considerable overlap. As examples of modern fiction dealing explicitly with the psychological problems of adoption we shall end by drawing attention to John Stroud (*On the Loose* 1961), in his *alter ego* as a creative writer, and P.D. James (*Innocent Blood* 1980). Readers wanting a less academic introduction to the notion of genealogical bewilderment could do worse than begin here.

5 Adoption (3): the pursuit of origins

It has been suggested that adopted people may have more difficulty than others in developing a satisfactory social identity. In order to test this theory we employed a small postal survey of adult adoptees who felt the need to research their origins and who had joined the National Organization for Counselling Adoptees and their Parents (NORCAP). This is a self-help group which was established in 1982 and has a current membership of just over 2,000, of whom approximately 60 per cent are women and 40 per cent are men aged 18 and over. It provides support, counselling, and practical advice to those contemplating the search for natural relatives. It also has suitably trained people who will act as intermediaries before direct contact is made with the natural family.

We felt that a sample of equal numbers of men and women over the age of 30 would be the most likely to yield the type of information we sought, in that the uncertainties of adolescence would be behind them and most were likely to be established in some kind of career pattern and stable relationship. We expected that the majority would have children and that this would be an important factor in their decision to seek more information about their genetic backgrounds. We were interested to discover if there were differences between men and women in our sample in the way they construed themselves, and in their motives for the research they were now undertaking. Other studies since the implementation of the 1975 Children Act have shown that more women than men sought information about their natural families and that they did so at an earlier age (Day and Leeding 1980; Triseliotis 1984; Triseliotis and Russell 1984; Haimes and Timms 1985). A pilot version of the questionnaire was first sent to twenty NORCAP members who had been selected as likely to respond promptly and constructively to such an approach.

In both the pilot and the main study the respondents were unknown to us and were free to remain anonymous if they so wished. Seventeen of the twenty pilot questionnaires were completed and returned. The revised questionnaire (Appendix I) was then circulated to fifty men and fifty women over the age of 30 selected at random from the NORCAP register. We later discovered that two or three of our pilot respondents had been included in the main study, but this had little effect on the results. A reminder was sent to non-respondents after eight weeks, and this resulted in a further thirteen replies (three male and ten female). In total we received seventy-six completed questionnaires, forty-two female and thirty-four male, together with additional information in a number of instances, and nearly a third of our respondents in the pilot and main studies offered further help either by telephone or letter. We took up most of these offers, and three personal and eighteen telephone interviews were conducted.

RESULTS

(1): Age of respondents

Table 5.1 shows the age distribution of our respondents. Although there were more women than men in the 30–39 and 50–59 age groups, the largest group of both sexes fell in the 40–49 age band, where there were twenty men and nineteen

Table 5.1   *Age distribution of respondents*

Age	Male n = 34	Female n = 42
30–9	12	18
40–9	20	19
50–9	1	4
60+	1	0
Not stated	0	1
Range	32–65	31–56
Mean	41.8 yrs	41.1 yrs
s.d.	6.19	5.80

women. The one male respondent over 60 was still interested in tracing his origins even if the likelihood of finding a natural parent alive must have been small. Three people failed to state their occupation. Of the remainder, twenty were in social classes I and II, forty-five in social class III, and eight in social class IV (Registrar General's classification). Where information was available on their adoptive parents' occupation, sixteen were in classes I and II, eighteen in class III, and thirteen in class IV.

(2): Age at placement and family structure

As can be seen in Table 5.2, the majority of adoptees had been placed with their adoptive parents by the time they were 6 months old. Of the two men who were not adopted until they were more than 10 years old, one advertised for a family at the age of 11, the other was finally adopted at age 16 (after living informally with the family for two years), so that he could pursue his education, which would not have been possible had he remained in the children's home where he had spent most of his childhood. Although he was fairly non-committal about legally becoming a member of the large family he had joined, he was able to look back on his experience of family life as thoroughly enjoyable and to acknowledge the extent to which his adoptive parents had helped him (Appendix II: 4).

Our first impression was that many of our respondents had been adopted by elderly parents with Victorian values, whose strictness and grandparental appearance had caused their children embarrassment and a sense of isolation from their peers.

Table 5.2   Adoptees' age at placement

Age	Male n = 34	Female n = 42
Up to 6 months	20	32
7−11 months	6	3
1−5 years	4	7
6−10 years	2	0
Over 10 years	2	0

Whilst this was true in a minority of cases, Table 5.3 shows that most of the adoptive parents were in their thirties when their children were placed with them, although there were ten couples where both partners had been aged over 40 when the child arrived. We pursued this point further in our interviews with respondents, and learned that in many instances the adopters had been married for some considerable time before they became parents. Often the wives had experienced repeated miscarriages before finally turning to adoption as a solution to their childlessness. It was probably as much the fact that couples had had ample time to establish a cosy routine of mutual self-sufficiency as their actual age which made them appear old-fashioned to their children. Several male adoptees complained that their adoptive mothers had been both strict and possessive, looking to their sons to provide them with a purpose in life, while more than one daughter was aware that she had become the apple of her father's eye, driving a wedge between her parents and making it difficult for her mother to accept her wholeheartedly.

Situations like this were unlikely to happen where there were other children in the family, and Table 5.4 shows that for fourteen men and sixteen women this was the case. Of those who had siblings, four of the seven women with siblings who were born to their adoptive parents maintained they had not had a happy experience of adoption, compared to only one man in this situation. One of these women was placed when her adoptive mother must already have become pregnant, again after several

Table 5.3   *Adoptive parents' age at placement*

Age	Father	Mother
20−9	6	11
30−9	40	43
40−9	20	13
50−9	1	1
Insufficient information	9	8
Range	24−55	22−57
Mean	37.4	35.3
s.d.	6.28	6.46

Table 5.4 *Sib-ships in adoptive families*

Number of siblings	Male n = 34	Female n = 42
None	16	22
1 adopted sibling	3	6
2 adopted siblings	0	1
1 born sibling	4	5
2 born siblings	3	1
3+ born siblings	1	1
Mixed born and adopted	3	2
Not stated	4	4

miscarriages, and her younger sister was born prematurely so that the age gap between them was only eight months. However, just under half the total sample of men and just over half the women were brought up as only children.

The notion that an adopted child is often an only child with elderly parents may seem out-dated today, but the adoptees in our survey were all born before 1955, and until the 1950s adoption workers, operating within the framework of moral welfare with its emphasis on the need to rescue the child from the stigma of illegitimacy, tended to favour the older couple with strong Christian principles, ignoring the threat of a generation gap when the child reached adolescence. Private adoptions, too, were not uncommon and there were several in our sample. We also learned of one man who had never been legally adopted and whose position only came to light when he needed a birth certificate before joining the Armed Forces. There were, in fact, fewer people than we expected who had been only children with parents over 40 at the time of their placement; only three men and seven women had mothers of this age, and in these instances the fathers had also been correspondingly older. Of these, two of the three men reported being unhappy in their adoptive home, as did three of the seven women. Several of our respondents who were only children told us of their loneliness. Some had over-protective mothers who discouraged them from mixing with other children, some lived in very isolated places so that even if friends were theoretically welcome there were practical difficulties over their visiting, whilst others would doubtless have had siblings if their mothers' health had permitted. One man told us how he had invented a sister when he was in his teens in order to keep up with his friends, and regaled them with stories about her. However, when he no longer needed this fictional sister and wanted to 'kill her off' he found it very difficult, and even after he started work former friends would ask after her, to his considerable embarrassment.

(3): Quality of childhood

When asked if they had been happy in their adoptive home (Table 5.5), thirty out of the thirty-four men but only twenty-seven of the forty-two women reported a happy childhood ($p < 0.05$). This was not related to the presence or absence of siblings, however, as only three out of seventeen men and six out of twenty-two women without siblings reported unhappiness. The fact that a larger proportion of women considered their experience of adoption unsatisfactory is in keeping with the national trend, in which more women than men at every age feel the need to research their origins. It is also reflected in the greater number of women in this series who had already met a natural parent or relative, and we shall return to this point later.

With hindsight, several of our respondents, particularly the women, acknowledged that they had had a better start in life in their adoptive homes than they would have had if they had remained with their natural mothers. This was not merely a material advantage, as it seemed unlikely that their emotional needs would have been any better met by biological than by adoptive parents. They felt cherished and secure in their adoptive families, even if there were occasions when their parents seemed unable to understand them. One man spoke of 'my adoptive

Table 5.5   *Happy in adoptive home*

	Male $n = 34$	Female $n = 42$
Yes	30	27
No	4	15

$x^2 = 4.54$, p < 0.05

parents, who will never be replaced', and a woman wrote to us: 'I have always felt very much wanted and loved. Mum and Dad always encouraged us in everything, school, interests, etc., and found a way to provide us with opportunities which they could ill afford.'

(4): Knowledge of adoption

Other surveys have shown that the way in which adopted children learn of their status is more important than the time at which they find out (Humphrey and Ounsted 1963; McWhinnie 1967; Triseliotis 1973). Nevertheless, there are obvious advantages in being told a certain amount before they start school. Table 5.6 shows that nearly a third of the men and one fifth of the women were told of their adoption after the age of 10. Two men and five women did not discover until they were adult. The source of their information is given in Table 5.7. Several men reported being embarrassed at the efforts made by their adoptive mother to tell them of their adoption at around the age of 10 or 11, and thereafter found it impossible to ask more questions. The adoptive mother may have felt that her obligations had been discharged once the topic had been brought up and then closed; the adoptee felt very differently.

Our sample is too small to draw more than tentative conclusions, but it appears that those men who discovered their adoptive status between 9–13 years had particularly unfortunate experiences. It is easy to speculate that adoptive parents who were uneasy about telling had left it late and then bungled it. Three men to whom this happened said that communication with their

Table 5.6   *Age at which first told of adoption*

Age	Male *n = 34*	Female *n = 42*
Always knew	11	14
Before age 5	2	7
Aged 5–10	10	13
Aged 11–19	9	3
Aged 20+	2	5

Table 5.7   *Source of information on adoption*

	Male n = 34	Female n = 42
Adoptive mother	13	19
Adoptive father	4	5
Both adoptive parents	6	10
Other relative	2	2
Outside source	3	4
Found papers	1	1
Not stated	5	1

parents had always been difficult and learning of their adoption made it worse. One man suggested that his mother's inability to explain the facts to him and her restrictive possessiveness had led to confusion about the establishment of close personal relationships in his adult life, particularly with women. All three felt that lack of communication with parents (particularly their mothers) while they were growing up had made it difficult to commit themselves to lasting heterosexual relationships, and though two of them were now married the third had still not resolved this problem in his thirties. Of the two who had married, one was a recent occurrence, while the other had rushed into marriage at 21, only to find he had made a mistake which took fifteen years to put right; however, he felt that his second marriage stood a much better chance of succeeding.

Perhaps the most unsatisfactory way of all to learn of one's adoption occurred to the man who was taken to court at age 11, so that an order could be made, without any explanation from his adoptive parents as to what it all meant. He had been in care until the age of 2, and presumably his adoptive parents had then fostered him until the mother's consent to an adoption order had been obtained. Even after their rocky marriage had broken up when he was 15, they continued to say nothing by way of explanation, and only his grandmother (whom he described as a Victorian schoolmarm) told him he should consider himself lucky to be adopted.

One woman, who was finally told by an uncle after her father's death when she was 31, had in fact picked up a comment by a neighbour when aged about 4. Her parents' reaction had been to move promptly to another district before any more awkward questions could be asked. Before the war many adoption workers advised their clients to say nothing to the child, and many parents would have been relieved to take the easy way out. However, even when parents were recommended to be open, the information they were given about the natural mother and the circumstances in which she had decided to part with her child was usually minimal, and rarely committed to paper. Small wonder, then, that over the years even those adoptive parents who were willing to discuss the situation frankly with their children had pitifully few facts to disclose, and time may well have distorted those they had. One informant was so relieved to discover, eventually, that her natural mother had wanted to keep her if it had been possible, that she sent us a copy of the letter she had received from the adoption society telling her of this. Often the information passed on by the adoptive parents turned out later to have been wildly inaccurate, and those involved in complicated searches for their natural families have attributed their difficulties to poor record-keeping and possibly deliberate propagation of misleading information by agencies. We already knew that one of the better-known voluntary societies used to advise its clients to tell the child that its natural parents had died, possibly in a car crash.

Half the women but only just over a third of the men knew of their adoption by the time they were 5 years old, and although this difference might easily be due to chance, it seems possible that adoptive mothers, who were largely responsible for introducing the subject, found this less difficult when talking to daughters than to sons. It would be interesting to know whether the same is also true in natural families when the facts of life are discussed. In our own personal experience, telling about adoption in the early years was inevitably linked to explanations as to where babies came from. We are reminded that the majority of our respondents were adopted by people who themselves grew up in the first half of this century, when reticence about sexual matters was the norm and illegitimacy was a shameful secret, so it is hardly surprising if they said little to their children.

(5): Marital and parental experience

In selecting a group over the age of 30 as our sample, we anticipated that most would be married, and this proved to be the case (Table 5.8). Only three women had never married, and six of the men also remained single. Two of the men were in their forties but the rest were younger. One of the women, now in her early forties, had spent twenty years with the same man but did not feel able to commit herself to marriage; while the two younger women who were single had both had particularly unhappy experiences of adoptive family life, and each had been sexually abused by an adoptive parent. Of the twenty-eight marriages reported by the men only three (or barely one in nine) had ended in divorce; whereas the same applied to eight of the thirty-nine marriages reported by the women, which is more than one in five. Again with such small numbers this difference could well be due to chance, but it is worth adding that men whose marriages had failed were more inclined to risk a new relationship than were the women.

Table 5.9 gives the number of children born to respondents. Where ages were stated (by twenty-three men and twenty women), the majority of children were in their teens or older for both groups. Nine of the men and just six of the women had children under 12 years old, presumably because the latter had tended to marry earlier. In addition, one woman told us that she had had an illegitimate baby whom she had given up for adoption when she was in her teens, and that subsequently she had been married and divorced without bearing further children. We asked those respondents whom we interviewed whether they saw having children of their own as important in view of their adoptive status. Six of the ten men felt it meant or would mean a

Table 5.8 *Marital status of adoptees*

	Male *n = 34*	*Female* *n = 42*
Single	6	3
Married	25	31
Divorced	3	7
Separated	0	1

Table 5.9   *Number of children born to adoptees*

	Male n = 28	Female n = 39
None	3	5
One	4	2
Two +	20	24
Not stated[1]	1	8

[1] This question was inadvertently omitted from the main questionnaire, necessitating a follow-up letter to establish this information where it had not been mentioned spontaneously.

lot to them to have children with a biological link, but three of them said that adopting a child would be preferable to remaining childless. Of the women, all but one of those who were married had produced children of their own, and only one of those with children said it was not particularly important for her. There appeared to be a link for both sexes between their own experience of adoption and the importance of biological children to them, with those who recalled their childhood as unhappy rating the importance of the blood-tie most highly. Those respondents with children all felt they would like to be able to pass on information about their genetic background when the children were old enough to value this. However, in many cases, particularly among the men, there appeared to be major difficulties in obtaining information about their natural families, and one man said that his children had never been told of his adoption as there seemed little point when he had no facts about his background to pass on.

(6): Prior knowledge of parentage

In fact, nearly two-thirds of the sample were told nothing by their adoptive parents about their natural mothers (Table 5.10). Only nine of the thirty-four men and eighteen of the forty-two women knew anything about their background before they decided to investigate. Only those sent reminders and those who failed to indicate their own parental status on the questionnaire were specifically asked if they knew their natural father's name, and a

Table 5.10   *Information on natural parents*

	Male		Female	
	Yes	No	Yes	No
All respondents (n = 76)				
Natural mother	9	25	18	24
Selected respondents (n = 36)				
Natural father	6	13	9	8

minority of these (six men and nine women) could state that they did. More than half of our respondents reported that they knew their own original name. Those who knew were asked how important this had been for them, and thirteen of the twenty-one women replied that it had been very important to them compared with six of the twenty men, which underlines the women's greater concern about their identity. Both men and women were asked if they had been told why they were offered for adoption (Table 5.11) and the women were more likely to have been given an explanation by their adoptive parents (p < 0.01). Often this was more conjecture than hard fact, and more than one adoptee discovered later that the story told by their adopters was a long way from the truth, though not necessarily a deliberate deception.

(7): History of search

Children brought up by their biological parents with access to a full family history nevertheless enjoy fantasies about additional

Table 5.11   *Reasons given for adoption*

	Male *n = 34*	Female *n = 42*
Told why offered		
for adoption	10	26
Not told	23	15
Not stated	1	1
$x^2 = 8.02$, p < 0.01		

relatives – the older brother a girl would have liked, a younger sister for a boy, or parents of royal blood perhaps – so it is hardly surprising that adopted children wonder about their unknown background. For twenty-two of our respondents the decision to find out all they could was taken in childhood (Table 5.12), whereas theorists on the development of identity would expect the most curiosity to be shown in the teenage years. Twice as many women as men remembered wanting to find out about their origins before the age of 12, but once out of their teens the men showed somewhat more curiosity than the women in this group. For those who did not find out they were adopted until they were adult (three men and five women), the need for information was immediate and consuming.

When asked what had prompted them to seek information about their backgrounds, many reasons were put forward (Table 5.13). Three times as many men as women were able to admit to frank curiosity as their prime motive, and more men than women gave the need to verify their identity as the most important factor; women for their part were more inclined to spell this out in terms of physical resemblance, which seemed considerably less important for men. None of the men were prepared to admit that an unhappy experience of adoption had influenced their decision, whereas for women this was an important factor. Those who had felt the most unloved in their adoptive homes and particularly those who had never had good relationships with their adoptive mothers, were the most inclined to feel that their natural mothers would supply the warmth and acceptance they had missed as children. They had usually decided to search for their natural mothers by the time they had reached their teens,

Table 5.12   *Timing of decision to research origins*

	Male *n = 34*	*Female* *n = 41*
Before age 12	7	15
In teens	3	8
Since teens but more than 5 years ago	12	10
Within last 5 years	12	8

Table 5.13   *Reasons for decision to research origins*

	Male	Female
Curiosity	12	4
Who am I / Who do I take after?	9	6
Unhappy experience of adoption	0	7
Total lack of information from adoptive parents/others	3	3
Need to pass on background information to own children	0	4
Need for medical information	0	3
Need to find siblings	1	2
As a result of therapy	2	2

and as one of them said, 'I always thought things would be different with my real mother.' Several of our female respondents appeared to have carried somewhat unrealistic assumptions with them into adulthood and had not taken into account the passage of time and life events which would conspire to make a new mother–daughter relationship difficult if not impossible. Women mentioned the need for family and medical information to pass on to their children more often than men in their questionnaire responses, though several of the men we interviewed talked of this too. One man was actively involved in researching his adoptive family history, but was frustrated by dead ends when he attempted to find out anything about his own, and one of the women mentioned her adoptive father's interest in compiling a family tree and her own strong feeling that it was nothing to do with her.

We had anticipated that the birth of their own children would act as a trigger on adoptees to take up the search for their origins. In fact, though many of our respondents, male and female, agreed that they were more interested in their own backgrounds once they had families, a number hesitated to pursue the matter whilst their adoptive parents remained alive for fear of hurting their feelings. This is in line with previous research (for example, Triseliotis 1973), and would help to explain why so many of our respondents had only recently embarked on their search although already into their forties. However, where the lines of communication remained open and both parents and children felt comfortable about the adoption, respondents mentioned their adoptive parents' support for their decision to search. Two men and two women who were undergoing therapy for personal problems had been encouraged to research their origins within this context, and we shall return to this point later in the chapter.

Since our sample was drawn entirely from adoptees who had become members of NORCAP to facilitate their research, we were interested to learn how far they had taken it (Table 5.14). The most striking fact was that 60 per cent of the women compared with only 26 per cent of the men had actually made contact with their natural mothers or members of their families ($p < 0.01$). Although equal numbers of men and women were actively engaged in trying to trace their natural families at the time of the survey, when all those who had not yet effected a meeting were asked their intentions nearly twice as many men as women were unsure or saw such an event as something to be considered in the future.

Several of the respondents we interviewed told us of the speed with which they were able to trace their natural mothers, once

Table 5.14 *Progress made in the search*

	Male *n = 34*	*Female* *n = 42*
Counselling only	3	1
Inspection of birth certificate	8	2
Search for natural mother/ relatives	14	14
Meeting with natural mother and/or relatives	9	25
If not the latter, intentions to take it further:		
Now	5	5
In future	8	5
Not sure	7	3

Meeting: No meeting, $x^2 = 8.30$, $p < 0.01$

they devoted time to it. This fact underlines the need for counselling before attempts at contact are made, and the value of using an intermediary to make the first approach. All our respondents had been placed for adoption at a time when the natural mother was protected by the law, and the changes implemented under Section 26 of the 1975 Children Act have exposed women who are now middle-aged or elderly to the risk of their hitherto successfully-buried past catching up with them. The social climate may have changed greatly since the time when they gave away their illegitimate babies, but many will have kept that secret to themselves. To be confronted by an adult stranger with undisputed evidence of kinship poses problems of disclosure which some natural mothers have been unable to face. The consequent rejection which the adoptee must accept is very hard to bear (Fisher 1973). Several respondents spoke of their concern about approaching a natural mother who might no longer be in good health. One woman told us how she had made contact by letter and telephone with her natural mother, but a few days before the date arranged for their first meeting her mother died as a result of heart trouble from which she had suffered for the previous four years. Our respondent had to ask herself whether her reappearance in her mother's life had contributed to her early demise. In several instances the adoptee's search had ended with a death certificate. Some said that although they were sad to have missed the opportunity to know their parents, they felt relief that there would be no chance of a confrontation.

Any feelings of disappointment they might have, however, were mitigated if they succeeded in meeting a sibling. All those who found they had either full or half-siblings commented on how much this had meant to them. It will be remembered that half our sample had grown up as only children in their adoptive families, and many had stressed their loneliness. Even those who had not missed a playmate felt that an adult sibling, particularly a sister, would enrich their lives; one woman only joined NORCAP in case the half-sister she knew existed might be looking for her, and another, who very much hoped to find a sister, learned with sadness that the half-sister she sought had died from cancer a few years earlier. Making a relationship with a new-found adult sibling was easy compared to establishing a bond with the mother who had parted with her child when young, whatever the circumstances. Several of those who found they had older half-siblings were surprised to discover that these remembered nothing about a baby who may have remained for several months in the family before disappearing out of their lives. However, thirty out of our total sample of seventy-six adoptees (almost 40 per cent) had been born during World War II, when families had often been separated or forced to make frequent moves.

In contrast to those who had little difficulty in tracing their natural mothers, we were made aware of the plight of those whose adoption had been preceded by a spell in residential care. The four men who told us they spent their early childhood in children's homes had all experienced considerable difficulty in obtaining information about their natural mothers. There seems to have been a deliberate policy on the part of welfare services at one stage to discourage contact between a mother and her illegitimate child. Practices appear to have been modified by most agencies in the light of modern child-care concepts, and one of our respondents was able to see his file, which did much to explain the circumstances of his placement in care. The others were not so lucky, and at the time of the survey were still totally frustrated by lack of information. In the case of one man, not only had the records from the children's home where he lived till the age of 8 disappeared, but his adoptive mother had systematically destroyed all evidence of his existence before her own death sixteen years ago (see Appendix II.5).

Many of our respondents had thoroughly enjoyed the detective work they had undertaken in the search for their origins, and their first meeting with a relative, whether natural mother, half-sibling, or more distant kin, had been approached with excitement even if also with a degree of apprehension. For several of the women, the strong physical resemblance to their mothers had come as a shock, albeit a welcome one, and this had been followed by much comparison of tastes and temperament. One woman said of her first meeting with her natural mother that it was 'unreal, like looking into a mirror'. Several of our female respondents had stressed how the difference in temperament between themselves and their adoptive parents had led to misunderstanding when they were growing up or had served to emphasize their adoptive status, and they were relieved to find a context in which their personality was not out of step. The men who had made contact with their natural mothers tended to be more detached about their initial meeting, though no less apprehensive. The need for physical resemblance was considerably less for them possibly because there was little prospect of meeting their same-sexed parent; their chief interest was in their family history and the circumstances which necessitated their being placed for adoption.

Once regular contact had been established and the gaps in family history filled, a number of our respondents reported a distinct feeling of anticlimax. Most of those who had made contact with a natural mother discovered that the role they came to play in the new relationship was more that of friend than son or daughter. Those with a comfortable experience of adoption felt no need to acquire extra parents as such, while those who had retained expectations of replacing an unsatisfactory adoptive mother with an idealized, perfect natural mother were doomed to disappointment. Often the natural mother was reluctant to explain the presence of her new-found adult offspring to relatives or friends, and considerable discretion was called for on both sides to maintain a relationship which did not cause the mother embarrassment.

No mention has yet been made of the natural father and this is because he appears to have been a shadowy figure, of considerably less importance than the natural mother to the majority of adoptees. When asked they expressed curiosity about him, but conceded that they were much less likely to be able to trace him. The natural father's name is rarely to be found on the birth certificate of an illegitimate child, though adoption agencies did sometimes succeed in persuading the mother to give a name for their records. How often this was accurate we have no means of knowing, but several respondents who were now in touch with their natural mothers reported their considerable reluctance to divulge anything about the father. Only one informant maintained that it would be more important to find her natural father than her mother, though two others had switched their search to the father when the natural mother refused contact.

(8): Adoption stress

A short inventory was devised to test our hypotheses about the factors which would most influence adoptees to research their origins as a means of validating their sense of identity (Table 5.15). It comprised eight items. One point was scored for each negative response with a maximum possible score of ten. The sub-sections in Item 8 ranged from three points for 'Often' to none for 'Never'. Table 5.16 gives the total scores recorded. Women scored more highly than men on every item: omitting the five respondents who missed out more than one item, the mean score for men was 3.73 and for women 5.10 (t = 2.25, p < 0.05). Twenty-one respondents failed to complete every item of the inventory but their responses to individual items have been included in Table 5.15.

Over half our respondents said they were sure of their place in the world (Item 1) regardless of sex, and few people had experienced negative reactions from their friends when adoption was revealed (Item 2). More than half the men in our sample were happy about their status as adoptees but the women were equally divided on this question (Item 3). One woman had only discovered for certain that she was adopted at the age of 36, but said she had always had a 'chip on her shoulder' because she was aware of being out of place physically and academically in her family and of being treated very differently from her siblings.

Relatively fewer men than women felt that their adoptive parents had cramped their style as they grew up (Item 4), and several women specifically mentioned their adoptive parents' need for them to conform to their preconceived pattern. One respondent told us of her lifelong disappointment at not being allowed to pursue the career of her choice, and of the alarm with which her adoptive parents had viewed any expression of independence, fearful that 'blood will out' and that she would follow in her natural mother's footsteps and disgrace them. The most extreme example of the adoptive parental need to influence the future of their child was given by the woman whose adoptive parents decided from the outset that she was destined for university and a high-flying career, and whose early childhood was devoid of playmates or dolls as her parents systematically laid the foundations for her future academic achievement (see Appendix II.2).

Only one in eight of our sample were able to assert that they had no doubts about their identity (Item 5), and it is interesting that the only two women who felt positive enough to say so both

Table 5.15 *Responses to adoption stress inventory*

		Male		Female		x^2	p
		True	False	True	False		
1	I am sure of my place in the world	21	12	24	17	0.20	—
2	Friends who know I'm adopted have usually accepted the fact without comment	28	3	36	6	0.35	—
3	I've never felt comfortable about my adoptive status	14	19	19	20	0.34	—
4	My adoptive parents have always respected my individuality	18	11	21	20	0.81	—
5	I have often wondered who I really am	26	7	40	2	3.31	<0.10
6	I've never felt that I was living under a bogus identity	25	9	15	24	9.02	<0.01
7	Learning more about my background has helped (or would probably help) me to come to terms with myself	27	5	37	4	0.16	—
8	I find myself wishing I had remained with my original family:						
	Often	1 ⎫		7 ⎫			
	Sometimes	3 ⎭		9 ⎭		5.19	<0.05
	Rarely	5 ⎫		8 ⎫			
	Never	18 ⎭		15 ⎭			

Table 5.16   *Scores on adoption stress inventory*

Score	Male n = 34	Female n = 42
0–4	14	13
5–10	8	20
Incomplete	12	9

had careers in the helping professions and came from secure and happy adoptive homes. One of the men who answered similarly had discovered his adoption only within the last year when aged 40, and was happily married with a family of his own, which mitigated the shock of discovery. At the other end of the scale, the man for whom no records appeared to exist said that he sometimes felt that he didn't exist either as he had only his adoption certificate to prove his identity.

The greatest discrepancy between male and female responses occurred for Item 6: 'I've never felt that I was living under a bogus identity' (Haimes and Timms 1985). More than half the women in the sample declared that this was untrue compared to only nine of the thirty-four men (p < 0.01). Several of our respondents underlined their feeling of dual identity by giving both their present name and the one they were given at birth, and these included the oldest man in the sample who had been born in 1921 and joined his substitute family several years before adoption was recognized in law.

If the scores for both sexes on Items 5 and 6 are combined a number of interesting correlations become apparent. These two items pin-point most clearly the doubts about identity expressed by the adoptees in the sample, and there appears to be more uncertainty among those under 40, where sixteen out of thirty showed a positive stress score (p < 0.05). Three-quarters of this group are women; and in the over-40 group, although only 29 per cent scored significantly on both items, eight of these thirteen people were also women. If we look at those who rated their experience of adoption as unhappy, four times as many who had high stress scores were unhappy (p < 0.01) and twelve of these fifteen people were women. Being an only child in the adoptive family did not increase the likelihood of identity stress, although those with an adopted sibling appeared to have been mildly protected against it, compared to those with born siblings. It appears that those in the sample who had felt the need to find out about their background as children were likely to have significantly higher stress scores (p < 0.01), and thirteen of the nineteen respondents in this group were women. It is perhaps not surprising that those who were searching for their natural relatives but had not yet made contact showed higher stress levels than those who had achieved a meeting, and here the men out-numbered the women by fourteen to eleven. A significantly higher proportion of women in the total sample had established contact with their natural families (p < 0.01) and they mostly expressed the view that this had been helpful in sorting out their own identity problems.

Both sexes agreed that 'learning more about my background has helped (or would probably help) me to come to terms with myself' (Item 7). Several of the women who had made contact said that they now felt 'more comfortable' about themselves, and one wrote, 'I do have a lot more confidence in myself now that I have met people who are very like me in personality as well as looks.' The male respondents did not comment on this aspect of a successful outcome to their search, possibly because they harboured fewer doubts about their identity in the first place, but they still felt it important to research their origins to set the record straight about themselves.

When asked to rate the statement: 'I find myself wishing I had remained with my original family' (Item 8) the majority of those who answered this item replied that they 'rarely' or 'never' did so. Of those who 'sometimes' or 'often' did, sixteen (75 per cent) were women (p < 0.05). Thirteen of these women had reported being unhappy in their adoptive homes compared to only one of the four men who scored highly on this item. But this respondent had an interesting story. He told us that his adoptive parents had always seemed totally preoccupied with their business interests and had little time for their family of four, of whom three had been adopted. He discovered, however, that his natural parents had married a year after his birth and had gone on to have three further children. He was warmly welcomed by his natural family and fully expected that they would make up for what he felt he had missed.

(9): Help with personal problems

Finally, we asked respondents if they had received professional help for behavioural or emotional problems as children or adults (Table 5.17). Numbers were small but almost equal between the sexes, with twice as many seeking help for problems since becoming adult. Several of those who were taken to child guidance clinics by their parents were sceptical of any beneficial effects. One of the women whose experience of adoption had not been happy recalled her mother frequently taking her to such clinics for deviant behaviour such as running away from home. When professional attention was switched from child to mother, however, the visits ceased abruptly. One male respondent qualified his statement that he had been happy, on the whole, with his adoptive family by saying, 'With hindsight we were well looked after, but at the time I must have been unhappy, ran away a number of times, got into trouble with the law, etc.' He said that he was taken to child guidance on occasion throughout most of his school life: 'I must have been a pest!'

Those who had sought help for personal problems as adults had sometimes been treated by more than one method and for the most part saw such interventions as helpful. The two men who

Table 5.17   *Help received for behavioural or emotional problems*

	Male	Female
Child guidance clinic	4	5
Help for adult problems	10	9
This included:		
Out-patient treatment	5	5
In-patient treatment	0	3
Psychoanalysis	2	1
Psychotherapy	0	2
Hypnotherapy	0	2
Acupuncture	0	1
Other counselling	2	0

had entered psychoanalysis were still in treatment at the time of the survey and expected to remain so for some time to come. One of the women had tried psychoanalysis in the past but had not remained in treatment. Three women had received in-patient care, and depression was mentioned by several as the reason why they sought professional help. Only one of the men in this group reported an unhappy childhood, compared to seven of the women. Two-thirds of this group had learnt of their adoption after the age of 5 and several reported considerable distress at the way in which they found out. One woman was told when she became engaged at the age of 23 and felt that the unwelcome news precipitated her psychiatric problems. One man told us that he was taken to court at the age of 11 so that an adoption order could be made without any prior or subsequent explanation. His adoptive parents' marriage broke up soon after, and he took to a life of petty crime for a while as a means of getting even with them and with the society which had dealt so harshly with him.

Although by no means all those who had sought professional help also scored highly on the items in the adoption stress inventory which most closely correlated with identity confusion, there were a significant minority who did so. In this small group there were twice as many women as men (eight to four). Four of these women reported seeking professional help for depression, though two of them had other major problems as well which resulted from their sad experience of adoption (see Appendix II.1 and 2). When the overall scores for the adoption stress inventory are compared for those who sought help as adults, there was again a sex difference in that seven of the nine women scored more than five points on the inventory, compared to four of the ten men.

DISCUSSION

As Haimes and Timms (1985: 50) have pointed out, adoptees who feel the need to trace their origins are not necessarily ' "psychological vagrants" rushing around looking for a new set of relationships', and our survey of NORCAP members should be considered within the wider context of the need for social identity which adoptees in general feel. Rosenberg (1979) states that social identity is often the most concrete part of an individual's self-concept, and the adoptee who is unable to give a full account of himself in terms of his life history is at a disadvantage. The achievement of social identity is a continuing process throughout the life cycle, and the time at which it becomes important to complete their own life story will vary from one individual to another. In recent years the practice of constructing life story-books for children to take with them when placed in adoptive families has been used to remedy the lack of information accompanying an adopted child into his or her new life (Ryan and Walker 1985), and many an adult adoptee might wish that such a practice had been fashionable at the time of their own adoption.

The way in which identity develops is influenced by society's view of sex roles, and these are expected to become more clearly defined in adolescence. Thus, boys at this stage are encouraged to begin making decisions about future career and lifestyle which will lay the foundations for an adult personal identity (Marcia 1980). Girls, however, find their sex-role stereotypes are less goal-oriented and have more to do with personal relationships (Coleman 1980). Traditionally, girls have always looked towards marriage and motherhood as life goals, and worked at their interpersonal relationship skills towards this end, which is doubtless a factor in their earlier social maturity. In Erikson's schema of identity development, women were apt to reach the stage he calls 'intimacy' (which might be defined as proficiency at interpersonal relationships) at an earlier age than men (Erikson 1980); and biologically women are known to mature at an earlier age on average and to this extent are ready to take on family responsibilities sooner. Gaps in their personal life stories might well cause problems for adoptees as they attempt to develop a social identity; and since the social component of personal identity appears to play a larger part for women than it does for men, this would help to explain the greater number of women searching for their origins and the earlier age at which they do so.

In taking as our sample randomly selected members of a self-help organization, which exists to support adoptees and their relatives through their search for information about their origins, we were tapping the experiences of a self-selected minority of adoptees for whom the need for such information had become urgent. Since the implementation of Section 26 of the 1975 Children Act in November 1976 an increasing number of adoptees have made use of its provisions, including more than 80 per cent of enquirers who have been formally counselled; however, there is no recorded evidence of the proportion who have gone beyond obtaining their original birth certificate. Our survey has made us aware of the relative ease with which many adoptees can now trace their original families if they decide to do so. Of course, where sufficient information was available to adopters, it has always been theoretically possible for adoptees to conduct their own private search if they knew how to go about it, but the change in the law has made this legally respectable if not socially expected behaviour. Even those who have been unable to obtain information from adoptive parents or agencies have some hope of progress provided their adoption was legally ratified. However, as some of our older respondents pointed out, a proportion of adoptions were never legalized and a lot of luck may be needed before a search in such circumstances can be successfully concluded.

The age distribution of our respondents, with the largest group in their forties, to some extent reflects the recency of the Act which entitles them to research their origins, but it is also a reflection of their concern to avoid causing their adoptive parents distress by asking uncomfortable or unwelcome questions. They were aware that it might appear disloyal to the parents who had provided, for the most part, security and love throughout their childhood, if they made contact with those earlier parents who had renounced all claim to them. For this reason a large proportion had decided to wait until after the death of at least one adoptive parent before beginning their search. This fact alone bears out the contention of other writers that adoptees who seek information about their origins are usually thoughtful, sensitive people who do not wish to make trouble. Three of our female respondents specifically mentioned the support they had received from their adoptive parents over the decision to search, and their continuing interest in the outcome.

Most of our sample obviously felt affection for their adoptive parents, and 75 per cent said they had been happy in their adoptive homes. However, the greater proportion of those who reported an unhappy experience were women and this appeared to have affected how they perceived themselves in adult life.

Several stated that their adopted status had interfered with their ability to make meaningful and lasting relationships with the opposite sex, and some of the more detailed information we obtained bore this out. Waterman (1982) among others has suggested that the relationship with the same-sex parent has more effect on identity status in adult life than with the parent of the opposite sex, and there was evidence that this was so in our sample. In particular, several of the women who had sought professional help for emotional problems in adulthood complained of a poor relationship with their adoptive mothers. They also recorded high scores on the adoption stress inventory. From the evidence at our disposal it would be plausible to argue that they had reached adulthood with the lasting handicap of an unsatisfactory role model. It was as if they were still paying the penalty for an era in which adoption societies were committed to an emphasis on moral rectitude at the expense of maternal warmth.

When a child is born relatives and friends are eager to find physical resemblances to parents or siblings, and as he or she develops, temperament and aptitude are also compared by well-meaning outsiders as well as family members. The child who is adopted starts with a disadvantage from this standpoint; friends and relatives (if they approve of the adoption) may be quick to identify superficial likenesses between adoptive parents and child, but as the child grows up any such likeness will usually diminish or disappear. Early imitation of voice and mannerisms within the adoptive home will be unlikely to mask developing differences in temperament or abilities as the adoptee becomes an adult. People raised by their biological parents take family resemblance very much for granted, and nowhere in the literature on identity formation have we found a single reference to the part played by this physical belonging within a family in the development of mature adult identity. Yet it appears to have social connotations which cannot be ignored. To the adoptee whose origins are shrouded in mystery the lack of resemblance in looks and temperament to any known member of the family is an additional hurdle to overcome in the search for a rounded identity.

The male adoptees in our sample grew up at a time when men formed an overwhelming majority of the work force. Most of our female informants will, on the other hand, have learnt to construe themselves in terms of their social rather than occupational identity, and their role as wives and particularly as mothers appears to have brought home to them their lack of knowledge of genetic roots. Physical likeness is a very important factor for them, and those who have been able to verify this through meeting members of their original family have emphasized how much this has helped them to feel more secure in their own identity.

The need for a family medical history has also played a part in some of these adoptees' decisions to research their origins. With the emphasis on preventive medicine increasing, many an adult adoptee has found him- or herself in the embarrassing position of being unable to answer questions about family predisposition to this or that medical condition. Several of our respondents mentioned that they suffered from conditions that might be genetically linked, and a woman with Crohn's disease told us that she was often asked about her family health record of which she had no knowledge. NORCAP has suggested that a national computerized register be established for the exchange of medical and other suitable non-identifying information between natural and adoptive families. Many adoptees would be satisfied if such information was available without going to the lengths of tracing a natural parent in order to gain access to the family archives.

SUMMARY AND CONCLUSIONS

The seventy-six adult adoptees who completed the question-naire sent to them through NORCAP, seem to have given frank answers to the questions posed. More women than men replied (forty-two to thirty-four), mainly owing to the greater reluctance of men to respond to the reminder. The ten men and eleven women who were interviewed (mainly by telephone) gave additional substance to the picture we formed from the sample. All our respondents were over 30 years old, but there were more women at the younger end of the age range. There were six single men, and although all but three of the women had been married, there were more broken marriages among the women. Most of our married respondents had children and only one or two had deliberately avoided parenthood.

The majority of our sample had been placed in their adoptive home by the time they were 6 months old, but more than half did not learn of their adoption until after they had started school. Three-quarters of our respondents reported being happy in their adoptive family, but of the remainder four times as many women as men reported unhappy experiences. Fewer men than women had been given reasons for their adoption by their adoptive parents, but they were still more likely to be adult by the time they decided to find out for themselves why they had been given away. Twice as many women as men had decided in childhood that they would try to find their natural mother. Curiosity was the main reason given by the men for researching their origins, but both sexes felt an equally strong need to confirm their adult identity by filling in the background knowledge of their natural family which had been denied them. More women were influenced by their unhappy experiences of adoption, and they more often mentioned the need for medical information for the sake of their children. Nearly three times as many women as men had taken their search as far as meeting their natural mother or other relatives.

On the eight-item adoption stress inventory women scored more highly than men, and the items which particularly targeted anxiety about personal identity emphasized this trend. A quarter of the sample had sought professional help in adulthood for emotional problems, and in this group seven women but only one man reported an unhappy childhood.

The survey confirms the findings of other workers (Triseliotis 1973; 1984; Sorosky, Baran, and Pannor 1974; Day and Leeding 1980; Picton 1982; Haimes and Timms 1985) that adoptees have a healthy curiosity about their origins and a need for a full personal history in order to complete their sense of self. Women out-numbered men in their persistence with the task of tracing their origins and they attached a greater degree of emotional importance to their findings. A minority of our sample reported unhappy experiences of adoption and they were the most likely to score highly on the identity stress items and to have sought professional help for emotional problems.

It was already known that women outnumbered men in the search for biological relatives, and our findings suggest that this is because their sense of identity is more dependent on interpersonal relationships. Because of their greater investment in family life they are more likely to feel the need for genealogical information, not only for their own sake but more especially for the sake of their children.

6 Step-parenthood

The last four chapters will have made clear that fostering and adoption have never lacked appeal as topics of enquiry. Even if there are still plenty of questions remaining unanswered, there is now a wealth of literature on which to draw. In contrast, step-parenthood seems to have made surprisingly little impact on the clinician, the social worker, or the social scientist. It is almost as if there has been a conspiracy of silence, at least until recent years. A fortuitous illustration of this strange neglect has been provided by Standing and McKelvie (1986), in making the point that fashions in research have a bearing on 'publishability'. Psychological abstracts for the period 1981–3 listed about 330 entries on childhood autism (a rare condition) as compared with only thirty-five on step-families, which are commoner than most of us realize.

Why should this be so? The replacement of a missing parent or the merging of two families after death or divorce can have a variety of consequences for the adults and children involved – always intriguing, often demanding, sometimes dramatic, but never dull. So far it has been left mainly to investigative journalists (Simon 1964; Thomson 1966; Maddox 1975; 1980) and others with personal or professional experience of step-parenthood (Roosevelt and Lofas 1976; Rosenbaum and Rosenbaum 1977; Spann and Spann 1977) to fly the flag on behalf of a disregarded but fairly substantial minority. Maddox, whose pioneering work was inspired by the challenge of taking over the care of her husband's two young children after the suicide of his common law wife, has been particularly influential. She interviewed almost 100 step-parents with great sensitivity, yet was ill-equipped to attempt a quantitative analysis of her data. Visher and Visher (1979) took a more clinical approach to the problems faced by step-families, which came naturally to them as a psychiatrist married to a clinical psychologist. They too were in a position to draw on personal experience, although unlike

Maddox they reveal nothing whatever of their domestic life.
What Maddox and the Vishers had in common was a failure to
anticipate the complexity of their own family experience as step-
parents – and we may doubt whether they have ever stopped
learning! Adults can of course decide for themselves whether to
remain in touch with surrogate parents, regardless of whether
the latter have come into their lives through remarriage, adoption, or foster care; dependent children have much less choice.

In this chapter we shall examine the proposition that, painful
as the consequences of divorce may be for the parents, they can
be even more shattering for the children. And whilst it is true that
marital breakdown is relatively more common in the pre-parental phase, with a peak incidence of divorce after three years of
marriage (Haskey 1982), the proportion of divorces involving
children under the age of 16 has remained fairly constant since
1970 at about 60 per cent in England and Wales, and latterly also
in Scotland (Mitchell 1985). In absolute figures for England and
Wales, more than 150,000 children in this broad age-group
suffered the effects of parental divorce in 1982 (OPCS 1983). On
this basis it may be calculated that roughly one child in five is
now likely to meet this crisis before reaching the age of 16, and
one in eight before the age of 10 (Rimmer 1981; Haskey 1983a).
This estimate refers to Britain and takes no account of soaring
divorce rates in the USA, especially California.

Unfortunately, there are no accurate statistics on the numbers
of children currently living with a remarried or cohabiting parent.
We do know that there is no shortage of candidates, male or
female, for Dr Johnson's 'triumph of hope over experience',
which actually referred to a widower whose unhappy first marriage did not deter him from a second venture. In reality both the
pressures and opportunities to remarry are stronger among the
divorced, who are typically in their twenties or early thirties at
the time of separation. Widows and widowers are as a rule considerably older; and although some may have been protected from
marital failure by their partner's early demise, others will cling
obstinately to memories of a happy if not idealized relationship.
There is also the fact that while a widower can – after a decent
interval – choose a much younger spouse, the socially acceptable
options for a widow are somewhat narrower. Men and women
who have been through a divorce can more readily meet and
remarry at the same stage of the life cycle. Small wonder then

that in the twentieth century divorce has replaced bereavement as the major source of step-parenthood. It is now many years since premature death was the commonest reason for a marriage to end, and it is hard to believe that before the nineteenth century as many as 20 per cent of children were orphaned. We owe this apparently reliable estimate to Laslett (1977), who inferred that many of these children acquired a step-parent at some stage and often more than once. From a similar perspective Stone (1977) has estimated that during the seventeenth and eighteenth centuries about a quarter of all families contained a step-parent. Historically it is worth noting that the prefix 'step' is derived from the Old English *steop*, meaning bereaved or orphaned.

PREVALENCE OF STEP-FAMILIES IN THE COMMUNITY

For present purposes we can conveniently overlook the distinction between marriage and cohabitation, which is not always important and certainly does not filter through to the Registrar General. In a recent British enquiry Kiernan (1983: Table 10) found that in 1979, more than 5 per cent of all children under the age of 16 (that is, approximately a third of those not living with both parents) were living with a step-parent figure. There were more than five times as many mothers as fathers among the natural parents, and more than nine times as many mothers with sole care of their children. Thus although it is mothers who bear the brunt of parenting, as we have known for a long time, in reconstituted families stepfathers are much more often in the firing line. This is because women are a great deal more likely to retain custody of their children after divorce. Where a man initiates or acquiesces in the decision to end a marriage, he will not usually expect or want to keep any of the children, although there is obviously room for compromise where preferences for remaining with one or other parent vary within the family. Even when deserted by his wife and left with the children, he may still lose no time in making other arrangements for their day-to-day care. In recent studies the proportion of custodial fathers in Britain has ranged from 7 per cent to 13 per cent (Mitchell 1985). So although it is some years since Levine (1976) wrote of a growing trend towards paternal custody in the USA, there are no strong indications that it has taken hold either there or here.

Yet the remarriage rate for divorced men and women appears

to be much the same, regardless of whether there are children. This may run counter to preconceived ideas, but a record linkage study showed that some 50 per cent of both mothers and fathers had remarried within five years of divorcing in 1973 (Leete and Anthony 1979). It used to be assumed that the careworn mother of a young brood would find it harder to attract a new partner, whereas her carefree ex-husband would benefit from his freedom to play the field. Either this assumption is false, or the picture has been changing over the past decade or two. To us the second explanation would seem more plausible, but whether the change has arisen primarily out of the development of the women's movement (sexually and otherwise) or from other factors is a matter for speculation.

In the USA step-families are relatively more numerous, in keeping with the higher divorce rate. By means of data from the Population Reference Bureau, Visher and Visher (1979) were able to estimate that no less than 13 per cent of children under the age of 18 were living with a remarried parent and a step-parent in 1977. Maddox was more cautious, being content to note that this was an elusive question:

> Many householders do not want to report on a census that their wife has a child by another husband or lover and simply list stepchildren as their own children. Asking embarrassing questions puts the accuracy of all the other answers on a census form in jeopardy and census designers try to avoid it.
>
> (Maddox 1980: xvi)

THE PATH TO STEP-PARENTHOOD: DEATH VERSUS DIVORCE

Evidence from American studies of the past decade indicated that the average duration of custodial parenthood between marriages was again something like five years (Bane 1976; Bumpass and Rindfuss 1978). There can be no doubt that many children of divorced parents suffer a period of acute turmoil before there is any chance of settling into a reconstituted family. The parents too may be going through a turbulent phase as they try out new relationships of varying intensity and stability. The timing of remarriage or long-term cohabitation is likely to be crucial. Too soon, and the children will not have had time to mourn the departed parent (for even regular access is not the same thing as daily contact); too long an interregnum, and they may have adapted only too well to the absence of a father figure or even a mother figure. Clearly it is not entirely realistic to expect divorced men and women to regulate their emotional lives and new marital careers in such a way as to suit their growing children, even supposing that they were privy to the children's innermost feelings (and often they are not). But some consideration of the possible impact of a new partner on children still living at home[1] is an essential preparatory step that is sometimes overlooked. Children, perhaps especially during adolescence, are apt to be resentful when their acquiescence is taken for granted. In the euphoria of a promising new relationship, possibly following a number of false starts, the custodial parent may be tempted to move faster than the children can accept. As always, much will depend on the personal qualities of the new partner, who is all too easily seen as an intruder. Children can be uncompromisingly dismissive when the newcomer is neither tactful nor essentially likeable; moreover, he or she may be perceived as a competitor or threat to the non-custodial parent.

The different consequences of divorce and bereavement as causal factors in remarriage and step-parenthood have been debated in the literature without any firm conclusions. This is hardly surprising when one considers the enormous range of circumstances leading to death or divorce, and the varying intervals between the key event and the acquisition of a step-parent. It would be hard to design a convincing research project, particularly in view of the comparative rarity today of conjugal bereavement within the first ten years of marriage. Again there are no national statistics on which to draw, but an indication can be obtained from a small-scale study of step-families in Sheffield recruited mainly through the local Registrar and therefore not thought to be biased in any specific way (Burgoyne and Clark 1984). This series of forty remarried couples included only four men and three women who had lost a previous partner through death; and as there was one instance of a widower married to a widow, the frequency of prior bereavement was only 15 per cent. Although we cannot safely extrapolate from this local enquiry to the general population of step-families, we can surely reinforce our earlier statement that the great majority of such families are an outcome of marital failure.

It would be naive to imagine that the death of a parent, when it does occur, creates less of a handicap for step-family members than the departure of one who expects to be visited or is free to reappear on the scene from time to time. The vexed question of access will be discussed later, and meanwhile it has to be conceded that the legal wranglings and emotional conflicts over visiting are one of the more unfortunate aspects of divorce. The dead parent cannot intrude in this way, yet can exert a baleful influence none the less. Idealization is a recurrent hazard, and the fact that the surviving parent's earlier marriage may have been more than satisfactory in all important respects can contribute to a sense of disenchantment with the reconstituted family even when things are going tolerably well. Maddox (1980) has summarized the earlier literature on this issue. She too disputes the common assumption that the step-parent who replaces the dead parent has an easier time, pointing out that several studies have yielded contrary findings.[2] Apart from idealization and the age factor (if widows and widowers are typically older than divorced persons then their children are more likely to be adolescent), there will on average be more children in bereaved families if we can assume that couples with failing marriages will generally call a halt to reproduction. New step-parents can take small comfort from the principle of 'safety in numbers'; and if bereaved individuals can expect to take longer to find a new partner, the children will have had longer to become accustomed to life with a single parent. There is also no alternative home when the going gets rough for the stepchild whose other parent is dead. Maddox also suggests that divorce may lead to a sense of renewed hope and greater motivation to succeed as a surrogate parent. But she rightly regarded any statements that could be made on the available evidence as extremely tentative. Parental personalities and current circumstances will usually count for more than historical antecedents.

THE CONSEQUENCES OF DIVORCE FOR THE CHILDREN

The child's concept of death and the nature of children's mourning have been studied for a long time. In contrast it is only recently that the children of divorce have received attention in their own right. Major studies[3] have been carried out by Waller-

stein and Kelly (1980) in California, by Ferri (1984) in respect of
the 1958 British cohort, and by Mitchell (1985) in Scotland. The
American team started with 60 divorcing couples and 131 children, and were able to maintain contact with all but two families
for at least five years. Their report is disappointing in some respects, running to some 150,000 words but with minimal quantitative analysis (there are four tables with demographic data
hidden in an appendix). Yet their portrait of juvenile suffering
carries conviction. Initially the children ranged in age from 2–18,
and it was found that mother-child relationships were of paramount importance in the early years. After the age of 9 the
quality of the relationship with the same-sexed parent was
apparently a more crucial factor, and this finding carries social
implications in so far as older children related less easily to step-
parents.

At first almost 20 per cent of the children had aligned themselves with one or other parent, but five years later not one child
was aligned with the father and only three with the mother.
Anger against the parents for their part in the failure of the
marriage was sustained with remarkable intensity in some cases,
especially among adolescent boys against their fathers, leading
over the years to an inexorable decline in parent-child relationships. A decline in parenting capacity on the part of the custodial
mother had a particular impact on boys, whereas girls seemed
better able to 'switch off' the domestic turmoil when they got to
school (compare Rutter 1982). However, even within twelve
months of the separation acute responses had subsided if not
disappeared, with the children showing evidence of more rapid
recovery than the parents. The tendency of residual disturbance
in the children at this stage to become chronic was partly a
reflection of pre-existing family stress, but it was also likely to be
reinforced by the troublesome aftermath of divorce.

Almost half of the children were faced with further upheaval
when either or both of their parents remarried. Obviously this
was apt to be worse when it was the custodial parent (almost
invariably the mother) who remarried, especially where there
was a merger of two families. Nevertheless relationships between
step-siblings showed more positive than negative features, and
the main burden would fall on the parents – and disproportion-
ately on the mother or stepmother – in having to care for a large

brood. Much would depend on the capacity of the new parental couple to recognize that their own restored or often enhanced marital happiness was not in itself bound to improve the quality of the children's lives, and indeed they might well feel excluded by the close relationship between the two adults.

Regardless of the outcome in terms of step-parenthood, only 20 per cent of parents at the five-year follow-up looked back on their divorce as ill advised, whereas more than 50 per cent of the children evidently thought of themselves as worse off. It was children separated from a rejecting, belittling, or psychiatrically-ill parent who achieved the greatest gains. Wallerstein and Kelly cite the case of an intermittently depressed mother who was devoted to her family and functioned well between bouts of illness, and whose first husband nobly cushioned the children against its more devastating effects before reluctantly agreeing to a divorce. Unfortunately her rapidly acquired second husband was a poet, who not only lacked earning power but found the role of guardian angel much less to his liking (Wallerstein and Kelly 1980: 229)

Ferri (1976; 1984) took advantage of the 1958 cohort by following her survey of single-parent families with a study of step-children at a later stage of development. Whereas the Californian families were predominantly middle class, in no serious difficulties initially (at least so far as the children were concerned) and may even have benefited from the intervention as time went on, the British national sample was both unselected and spared the close scrutiny of the American team. Moreover as the families were studied at a single point in time, when the children were aged 16, they could not be expected to yield comparable data. A mainly quantitative analysis was applied to 455 families with a stepfather and 136 with a stepmother. Stepchildren were compared with children in unbroken families (n = 9767) and with those reared by natural mother alone (830) or natural father alone (152). Overall comparisons favoured the intact group on almost every measure, but with social class controlled, families with stepfathers in non-manual occupations suffered only in terms of housing tenure and mobility.

A sizeable minority of stepchildren were thought to have experienced multiple disadvantages after the breakdown of their parents' marriage, and the author lays considerable stress on financial hardship (compare Robinson 1980).[4] But interpersonal factors also played a part, in that only about two-thirds of the children reported a positive relationship with their stepfather, as compared with a good 80 per cent of children in unbroken families reporting favourably on their natural father. In the case of stepmother families the picture was complicated by sex differences, with more than twice as many girls as boys (37 per cent versus 16 per cent) expressing reservations towards their stepmother, but only 4–5 per cent of children of either sex discrediting their natural mother. These findings are in line with Bernard (1971). With regard to areas of conflict with parents, the author's findings support Burgoyne and Clark (1982: 293): 'The classic problems of adolescence are often compounded by step-relationships in which legitimate authority, mutual trust, and recognized family routines have not been fully worked out.' Sibling relationships emerged as relatively harmonious, with the hypothesis that solidarity between the younger members of the tribe had been promoted by parent-child friction. We suggest that this would make a particularly rewarding field of further enquiry.

Like Wallerstein and Kelly, Ferri was in a good position to appreciate that remarriage is no panacea for the many problems confronting one-parent families, especially when viewed from the child's perspective. Mitchell (1985) was influenced by this consideration in setting out to explore the psychological impact of divorce by interviewing seventy-one custodial parents (including only eleven fathers) and some of their adolescent children (twenty-five of each sex, aged 16–18), five to six years after the event. The marital status of the custodial parents, which covers most of the possible permutations, is shown in Table 6.1.

An impressive feature of her study is its insight into discrepancies between the parent's and the child's view of the situation. Time and again she would be assured by the parent that the children had taken the divorce in their stride, only to learn subsequently from the index child that this was manifestly untrue. A recurring theme was the parents' failure to make any attempt to explain what had gone wrong with the marriage. This could be due to a number of factors. In some cases they may have felt that the explanation was sufficiently obvious, for example, where drunken violence had been the father's habitual style. In others they were possibly at a loss themselves to understand the basis of

Table 6.1   *Marital status of custodial parents at interview*

Reunited with spouse	3
Still divorced	33
Remarried	15
Redivorced	3
Separated after remarriage	2
Widowed after remarriage	1
Cohabiting	9
Separated after cohabiting	5
Total	71

Source: Mitchell (1985: 146)

their incompatibility as marriage partners. Except where the violence (actual or threatened) was really terrifying, the children had not uncommonly accepted it as a fact of married life rather than as a reason for separating. And even where the nature of the marital difficulties was baffling to the adults (as without skilled help it so often can be), some discussion would have been welcomed by the children. It is quite remarkable too how children will cling to forlorn hopes of a reconciliation, even after one or both parents have remarried. Sometimes parents are so enmeshed in their own conflicts that they can turn a blind eye to their children's visible anguish.

Yet some of the more perceptive parents could hardly bring themselves to discuss such a painful topic, which therefore went by default. The author draws useful parallels with adoptive families, children in care, and the families of prisoners (Morris 1965). Here too there is sometimes a gross failure of communication despite good intentions on the parents' part. Often it is a matter of whether the adults appreciate that they need to make the first move, for it is no use expecting the children to make it easy for them. If fraught family relationships can be likened to a chess tournament, then it is nearly always the parents who hold the white pieces.

Interestingly, there were no consistent sex differences apart from the finding that teenage girls were more conspicuously upset by the divorce, and probably as a consequence found more difficulty in accepting a step-parent. It might have been expected that the trauma of family disruption and reconstitution would have interfered markedly with school progress, yet where initial problems were recalled, they had apparently resolved within a year or two. The lack of independent evidence from the children's teachers (unlike in the Californian study) may have helped to gloss over any long-term concern about academic attainment, whilst the author's non-clinical perspective may account for some of the divergence between her study and that of Wallerstein and Kelly (1980).[5]

At the same time it is not only the trained clinician who can persuade adolescents to speak their minds on sensitive topics. Mitchell's youthful informants could be cruelly honest. A girl whose stepfather had recently left the family dismissed him as follows: 'I didn't like my stepdad. He used to buy us presents and when he got angry with us he'd take the presents back again. He was bad to us.' (Mitchell 1985: 162) Similarly, a boy referred to the woman who was living with his non-custodial father: 'Dad found more time for her than what he did for me. I'd rather wash dishes than have her there.' (163) New partners of other non-custodial parents were described as 'a right pain' or 'a wee sly man, a ferret' (166). Granted that the role of step-parent is always apt to be problematical, it must help to promote smooth family relationships if the intruder is devoid of too many obnoxious characteristics! The author's final comment on the ups and downs of the transitional period is also worth quoting: 'Parents can change partners, but children cannot change parents: they can gain additional parents.' (169)

ACQUIRING A STEP-PARENT

This bring us to the question of how the fragile early stages of the new relationship are negotiated. Simon (1964), writing from her own experience of growing up as a stepchild and becoming a stepmother in her turn, utters a sensible warning:

> There is no reason to expect love-at-first-sight from the child, and every reason to know that at any age past infancy, memories will prevent it. If the step-parent-to-be needs the reassurance of immediate acceptance he will be frustrated; he might better be prepared to be insulted, rejected, and criticized, and

summon the strength to respond, not as adult to adult, but
as adult to child, continuing a slow, gentle courtship, which
may some day become mutual affection. If he considers the
child, than he will neither be over-zealous and aggressive nor
unaware of the child's existence but somewhere in between;
warm, accepting, and easygoing, he courts his future spouse's
children with a delicate touch.

(Simon 1964: 126)

The literature on the formation of step-families is anything but
scientific, yet sometimes helpful in its graphic descriptions of how
new encounters can be mismanaged. Where the parents' decision
to separate may have brought relief to them, to the children it
may have come as a catastrophe. A prospective step-parent must
find ways of establishing rapport with the loved one's children,
despite an often unconcealed lack of enthusiasm on their part if
not active disdain. He or she must allow the children to make
overtures when they are ready and not before. Resistance may
also be encountered from members of the extended family on
either side. A deserted husband or wife may be technically the
injured party, yet sympathies may lie predominantly with the
other party if the decision to leave the marital home was prompted by seemingly intolerable behaviour. Attitudes of the divorced
couple's own parents and siblings may have a powerful impact on
the reconstituted family, but are not always easy to anticipate.
While things are at their worst the new partner may be seen as an
interloper, and made to feel habitually in the wrong as the struggle for acceptance is met with a rising tide of hostility.

Such a situation has no obvious parallel in the other forms
of surrogate family with which we are concerned. Thus foster
parents and prospective adopters will have the advantage of a
stable marriage (whatever its hidden flaws) and can operate from
a position of strength at least in this respect. The child who has
spent some of his formative years in care, and/or has been
rejected by substitute parents in the past, will certainly need
wooing by his new parents-to-be; and they would be foolish to
count on a swift courtship. But with any luck it will be a case of
two reasonably mature adults supporting one another through
the quicksands of the engagement period until the *terra firma* of
adoption or permanent fostering has been reached. Now in

principle there is no reason why a parent and future step-parent should not behave in much the same way, and we would hope that in ideal circumstances they can and will. Yet whereas the majority of approved foster parents have shown competence in handling their intimate relationships, and it is to be hoped that fewer adoptive applicants today are driven by a sense of marital failure arising from their childless state, the same cannot usually be said of those planning to remarry. Step-parents without previous marital experience are in a minority; and although some commentators (including Maddox, who had not herself been previously married) have endowed second marriages with greater stability, the statistics of divorce do not support such an optimistic view (Haskey 1983b). Indeed, there is a distinct possibility that in a fair proportion of marriages which come to grief, one or other if not both partners may be short of what Terman and Wallin (1949) have called 'marital aptitude'. And the same lack of talent for sustained intimacy may make it harder for such persons to establish a strong bond with their prospective stepchildren. This is admittedly an unconfirmed hypothesis which we have not seen discussed by other authors, but we think it deserves to be taken seriously.

Another feature that differentiates between step-parents and foster parents is the likelihood of invidious comparisons, and this will obviously apply to spouses as well as parents. The value of getting off to a fresh start in a new home requires no emphasis. It is asking for trouble to seek to replace a lost or missing parent in the same physical setting or domestic aura. The second Mrs de Winter in Daphne du Maurier's novel of 1938 inherited a sinister housekeeper as well as the ghost of Rebecca, so perhaps it was just as well that there were no stepchildren lurking within the stately home. Tempting as it may be to take the line of least resistance by inviting the new partner to move in, a visit to the local estate agent is probably the wiser course. Were it not for the dire financial consequences of divorce such wisdom might be more widespread.

SEXUALITY AND THE STEP-PARENT

There are more live-in stepfathers than stepmothers, and some will acquire teenage stepdaughters straightaway. Others – per-

haps the majority – will have time to tune in to the stepfather–stepdaughter relationship before the onset of puberty. But
whatever the timing, in terms of sexual potential it is a totally
different scenario from the intact nuclear family. Although sexual
relationships between men and their biological daughters are
commoner than is generally realized, and surely less rare than
between mothers and sons, there are powerful inhibitions at
work where parents and children have grown up together. And
whilst incest is illegal, intercourse with a stepdaughter over
the age of consent (in Britain and most of the western world)
constitutes adultery rather than incest. The 12-year-old nymphet
of Nabokov's novel *Lolita* (1955) was of course well below the age
of consent, and her notorious stepfather Humbert Humbert's de-
fence was that she had seduced him. She was fictional, but she
stands as a lasting symbol of pervasive sexual anxieties between
the two generations within families created by remarriage. In
families created by adoption or fostering, sexuality across the
generation gap seems to be less of a problem. Where adoption has
taken place in early infancy, according to the traditional model,
one would expect the hazards to be no greater than in ordinary
families. Specialized foster care for adolescents is a growing trend,
as indicated in Chapter 2, but still too recent to allow evaluation
of the sexual implications. And although post-infancy adoption
has become commonplace, in 1984 (the latest year for which
figures were available at the time of writing) only 6 per cent of
orders granted to non-parents were in respect of children over
the age of 10.

Several writers have commented on the sexual rejuvenation
that is often a bonus of remarriage even in late middle age. This
will make a strong impact on teenagers of the family where the
physical restraint of the parents who had been drifting apart for
years is suddenly replaced by a warm and sensuous contact
during daylight hours and not just at night. Children who had
been inclined to view their parents as asexual will have ample
stimulus to rethink their attitudes as they grapple with their
own burgeoning sexuality. As yet, however, there have been
few if any empirical studies of how families handle this forcible
reminder that sexual interest and activity is by no means a pre-
rogative of the young.

THE ROLE OF THE NON-CUSTODIAL PARENT

When a parent has left home for the sake of a new liaison, there may be more pressing considerations than the need to maintain close links with the children of the marriage. And yet what happens in the early stages after separation may have a bearing on the shape of things to come. Mitchell (1985) has some telling comments on the failure of Scottish courts to make even the most elementary enquiries into arrangements for the children where there is no dispute over access. Her follow-up study revealed that if contact with the non-custodial parent was not kept alive from the start, it could quickly lapse. From the children's standpoint this is often one of the more pathetic consequences of divorce, all the more so as it ought to be avoidable. Alienation from their children is for most parents of either sex a heavy price to pay for the excitement of a new partnership.

And new partnerships are not guaranteed to last. Indeed, Mitchell found that most parents, custodial or not, had acquired new partners in the interim period, but first ventures of this kind were notably unstable – rapid cohabitation was almost bound to fail. In an evocative play for television, *Access to the Children*,[6] William Trevor depicted the husband as thoroughly miserable after the collapse of his new relationship. He took his children to the zoo, and the camera switched from his forlorn expression as he nibbled a monkey nut to the vacant stare of an ape similarly engaged. Such cheerless outings are the common coin of regular access, and the ingenuity of the average father is sorely taxed by the need to improvise week after week. Moreover the children's hopes of a meaningful relationship are seldom gratified under these circumstances, and the provision of Marmite sandwiches in large quantities is not the complete answer to their need for love.[7] The artificiality of the situation is seldom lost upon them. In those rarer instances where it is the mother who has left home, the upsurge of parental guilt feelings may be greater still. It does not take long to discover that affection cannot be bought with tawdry gifts. Divided loyalty is a common problem for the children, who may be more bewildered than censorious. However, rejection of the erring partner is not uncommon either, especially when they can agree on who is to blame. The child of divorced or separated parents will lack the cool objectivity of the lawyer, and is more likely to interpret the failure of the parents' marriage in terms of his or her own pre-existing feelings for each of them. But the pattern is unpredictable and can fluctuate over time. All that can be said with confidence is that the yearning for marital reconciliation dies hard. Quite clearly, some of the same emotional backlash can intrude into foster care, which again may be an outcome of parental discord. Yet if the foster parents have been well chosen and tactfully supported at least in the early stages, then the children may be partially protected against some of the more traumatic features of step-family life. Those with a vocation for surrogate parenthood (rather than having been pitchforked into it) will be better equipped to withstand the strain.

COUNSELLING AND SUPPORTIVE SERVICES

What happens when a malfunctioning step-family is in need of help? It has been reported that children of divorced parents are referred to psychiatric services with twice the frequency of those from intact families (Kalter 1977; Black 1982). It would be rash to dispute such a plausible observation, even if there is not the same consensus about stepchildren as there is about adopted children (see Chapter 3: 42–6). It seems unlikely that step-families would be less visible in the community, since there is no obvious reason why adoptive families should be more prone to draw attention to themselves. Child therapists interviewed informally by Maddox (1980) seem to have begun by denying that they were unduly familiar with stepchildren, and then gone on to demonstrate vivid recall of individual cases. One would hardly expect the status of stepchild (any more than that of adopted child) to remain undeclared in a clinical setting, but the psychiatric literature is still comparatively meagre. A tendency to antisocial conduct among the children of divorced parents has long been suspected (Wardle 1961; McDermott 1970), and it is now fairly well established that boys are not only harder to discipline but also more sensitive to the effects of marital discord (Rutter 1981). However, it is by no means clear that parental remarriage and the influence of a step-parent are protective factors (Richards and Dyson 1982). Indeed, the contrary may be true. Suffice it to say that in this complex area of human relationships it is particularly unsafe to generalize.

Visher and Visher (1979), convinced from both personal and professional experience that step-families are inherently vulnerable, have played a leading role in launching support groups in California and elsewhere in the USA. There can be no doubting the need for such initiatives, especially where they can be backed by the monitoring and evaluation that have become almost mandatory in new developments of this kind. Family therapy is complicated enough without taking remarried couples on board, which may help to explain why standard textbooks (for example, Minuchin 1974; Satir 1978) have little to say about step-families. Clinical research focused on the family unit is even more daunting. Empirical studies of interaction within step-families have been few and far between, though one or two brave attempts have been reported in the last few years (Clingempeel, Ievoli, and Brand 1984; Anderson and White 1986). It is too early to judge how far such clinically relevant research can be expected to promote the welfare of step-families in trouble, but it is a move in the right direction. The founding of a new British organization, 'Step-Family', in 1983 has led to many applications for membership (Mitchell 1985).

POSTSCRIPT: LOOSE ENDS AND CONFLICTING VALUES

Divorce is a messy business. As Maddox (1980: 144) remarks, 'What step-parents learn is that any marriage that has produced a child is never extinguished. One psychiatrist told me he defines divorce as "marriage carried on by other means, with a bond of hostility replacing the erotic bond".' The bond can remain unruptured even after the divorced partner's death, for memories linger on, aptly symbolized by the golf-clubs in the attic.

Visher and Visher (1979: 122), despite their transatlantic slant, are worth quoting on the problems of divergent tastes: 'An antique grandfather clock bumps the low ceiling as it stands awkwardly beside a modern plastic and aluminium chair. A standard VW and a Chrysler Imperial park together in the garage with great discomfort.' These perpetual reminders of past relationships – past but by no means extinguished – can generate inordinate tension during the bad patches experienced by all families. Small wonder that the seemingly innocuous discussions between step-family members can rapidly escalate into 'continuous group therapy', as one of the Vishers' couples expressed it. But it would be misleading to suggest that the tensions of couples with children from previous marriages are unique. Enough has already been said about fostering and adoption to demarcate some of the common ground, at least where the children bring ghosts from their past.

An important difference not so far acknowledged is that adoptive and foster parents have usually either completed their families or been diagnosed as infertile. Rarely are they faced with the dilemma of whether to add to their family through sexual intercourse. Maddox, who finally produced a second liveborn child, was convinced that children of the marriage could act as family therapists. It would be heartening to think so, and we know of no compelling evidence to the contrary. She also quotes several instances of infertility amongst stepmothers, hinting that it may have been psychosomatic. The case for psychosomatic infertility is largely unproven (Edelmann and Connolly 1986) though individual case studies can be persuasive (Humphrey and Humphrey in press). There will always be some women with stepchildren for whom it is important to bear a child of their own, and some step-couples (if the term be permitted) with a need for one another's children. Where family relationships are basically sound they are unlikely to be impaired by a child of the marriage and may be improved; where they are poor, we doubt whether the newcomer will have any therapeutic value. The role of step-mother is in many ways unenviable, comparing unfavourably with that of stepfather especially where the children are in their teens (Bowerman and Irish 1962; Bernard 1971; Duberman 1973; 1975). She may be too old even at the outset to contemplate having children of her own, or her realistic hopes may remain unfulfilled. In either case she may feel no less sad than the wife in a childless home, and possibly more so if her partner's children are a constant reminder of what she is missing. If she can manage to sublimate her own maternal needs in the care of another woman's children who are also her partner's, she deserves to be canonized.

7 Parenthood by donor insemination

Snowden and Snowden (1984) open their guidebook for couples contemplating donor insemination with an estimate of the number of marriages contracted annually which are rendered childless by male infertility. Lacking data from the general population they cannot offer a precise figure but suggest that it would lie between 16,000 and 24,000. We were able to check this calculation against data given in a more recently published study by Hull *et al* (1985), who estimated that at least one couple in six living in a defined geographical area (Avon) would need specialist advice for infertility at some time in their lives, or one in eight if couples with children already are excluded. The authors state in their summary that 'sperm defects or dysfunction were the commonest defined cause of infertility (24 per cent) and led to a poor chance of pregnancy (0–27 per cent) without donor insemination'. Applying these figures to the annual total of about 400,000 marriages would reduce the Snowdens' estimate to 12,000, which is still a far from negligible total. Some readers may be surprised that sub-fertility or indeed infertility should be so common, but the study has made a wide impact in following so closely after the Warnock Report (1984).

We have come a long way since the first recorded case of donor insemination in humans, with which Snowden and Mitchell (1981) introduced their preliminary account. A Philadelphian merchant and his wife were childless, and when his sterility was diagnosed she was inseminated under general anaesthetic with sperm supplied by the best-looking student from a class at Jefferson Medical College. This was said to have happened in 1884, initially without the knowledge of either partner; when the husband was subsequently informed he raised no objection, asking only that his wife should not be told. It was another twenty-five years before Hard (1909a; 1909b) broadcast the news of this bold experiment after visiting the merchant's son.

Snowden and Mitchell speculate that Hard himself may have been the donor.

In Britain interest in donor insemination was first aroused at the end of World War II by a comprehensive report in the *British Medical Journal* (Barton, Walker, and Weisner 1945). This led to a commission chaired by the Archbishop of Canterbury (1948) which recommended that the practice be made a criminal offence. Such a view was not endorsed by the Feversham Committee (1960), despite its strong disapproval on social and moral grounds. In the ensuing decade public attitudes began moving towards greater permissiveness as improved contraception made it easier to separate sexual pleasure from procreation. The Peel Committee (1973) took an altogether more benign view, even going so far as to recommend that donor insemination (DI) be made available under the National Health Service. Slowly the facilities have become more widespread, although at the time of writing they remain patchily distributed (Dobson and Mathieson 1986).

Regrettably there is still no reliable information on the frequency of resort to a sperm donor. The Warnock Committee, in quoting an annual figure of at least 780 live births achieved by this method (Royal College of Obstetricians and Gynaecologists 1982), recognized that this was 'undoubtedly an underestimate' (1984: 19). Snowden and Snowden (1984) from their enquiries among DI practitioners concluded that by the end of the 1970s some 2,000 children were being born annually in Britain alone, as compared with an estimated 15,000 in the USA. This would mean that the Peel Committee were perhaps unduly conservative in supposing that only 10 per cent of couples would even consider this solution to the problem of male infertility at some stage of married life, although genetic defects (rarely) and irreversible vasectomy (more commonly in recent years) might be expected to swell the numbers. Since there is no legal requirement to register a donor birth as such – understandably in that it would be so hard to enforce – there will always be a large element of guesswork unless the Warnock Committee's plea for a licensing authority to monitor specialized infertility services is honoured by new legislation. Meanwhile the supply of suitable donors will remain a limiting factor, especially in view of recent DHSS guidelines (1986) on testing semen for the presence of antibodies to the AIDS virus. Medical students are not the only source, as will be explained later in the chapter, although they offer certain advantages as a semi-captive population where fresh specimens are preferred. A conservatively estimated pregnancy rate of 50–60 per cent (for example, Dixon and Buttram 1976) leaves room for improvement and may already have improved with better methods of determining ovulation; however, if use of frozen sperm for prophylactic reasons is to become *de rigueur* in future, then something will have to be done to counteract its reduced efficacy as compared with fresh sperm. Better freezing and thawing techniques along with more accurate pin-pointing of ovulation might help to raise the conception rate to a more acceptable level, say at least 70–80 per cent. But with some 10–15 per cent of pregnancies aborting, as in normal conception, live births are what ultimately count.

Another factor with a bearing on ease of conception by donor is the degree of emotional stress experienced. Snowden, Mitchell, and Snowden (1983: 137) from a rare interview study of DI families found that where the procedure was still recalled as stressful, even after an interval of up to five years, twice as many inseminations had been required (on average twelve as against six). Possibly there is scope for anxiety management in this context using the techniques increasingly practised by clinical psychologists among others. At the time of writing such a study is about to begin at St George's Hospital.

SOCIAL AND PSYCHOLOGICAL CONSIDERATIONS

Who are the couples able to reconcile themselves – comfortably or otherwise – to the involvement of an unknown third party in their quest for a child? Legally DI is not adultery,[1] and psychologically it must be in a different world. Yet letters from members of the National Association for the Childless make it abundantly clear that wives as well as husbands are capable of rejecting this solution outright, as if from a 'gut feeling'. As yet there has been no systematic study of factors discriminating between couples who react positively and negatively, but it is known that manual workers are under-represented among those who actively proceed. Thus even in the period 1971–80, when the practice was fast becoming socially approved, half the women attending a private practitioner in Devon had husbands in non-manual occupations (Snowden, Mitchell, and Snowden 1983). Doubtless the private sector has always attracted the more affluent members of the community, and health insurance schemes do not normally cover this form of treatment. Even so our own ongoing series of couples referred for counselling from an NHS clinic has a perceptible middle-class bias, with something like a third of the husbands in non-manual occupations as against a national average of about 20 per cent. Education, sophistication, and ability to 'work the system' are probably less crucial today than they were at one time, but perhaps they still count for something.[2]

The impact of male infertility when first diagnosed can be quite devastating. Most of the husbands we have seen had learnt of their disability less than five years earlier; a fair number could still vividly recall the shock of the discovery, sometimes compounded by lack of sensitivity on the doctor's part. Some wives had been called upon to convey the shattering news to their husbands, which may have made matters worse. The absence of effective treatment merely reinforces the air of finality, so that the hapless couple may see themselves as condemned to an eternity of childlessness. Gone is the era when adoption could provide a way out, or rather a way forward. Interestingly, whereas follow-up studies of couples seen at infertility clinics have usually focused on pregnancy and childbirth (or sometimes pregnancy alone) as the only relevant outcome, a more comprehensive enquiry revealed a significant link between male infertility and the decision to adopt in an era when this could be implemented without difficulty (Humphrey and Mackenzie 1967; Humphrey 1969). Although this was not confirmed by Bohman (1970), who indeed found an opposite trend in a larger group of adoptions arranged by a Stockholm agency, the essential point is that DI has become a much more realistic alternative for couples whose infertility stems from the male partner. It would therefore be a major advantage if we could learn to identify couples with the appropriate attitudes to this form of surrogacy. Currently there is still a dearth of evidence, and no follow-up information on a worthwhile scale. In our own work (Humphrey and Humphrey 1987) we have described some of the social characteristics of couples seeking DI, but we know nothing about those who have either ignored or rejected this apparently simple solution to their problem. Furthermore we have been unable to follow up these couples for even a limited period, although some have remained in touch with us of their own accord.

Some practitioners (for example, Banks 1968; Jackson 1976; Joyce 1984) have been impressed by the degree of marital stability in their couples. We ourselves, whilst acknowledging that a strong sense of commitment to the marriage is not only required but often observed, would doubt whether this claim is based on sound evidence. We have made a practice of seeing couples twice (at an interval of up to three months) before treatment is begun, and two of the first 80–90 couples seen had separated before they could be re-assessed. In a third case the husband was all set to leave his wife when the donor child was only 6 months old. Infertility is always potentially a marital crisis (Humphrey 1986), and one would expect acute breakdown to occur sooner rather than later. Nothing is known about the long-term outcome, although Snowden, Mitchell, and Snowden (1983) refer explicitly to two divorces among their fifteen couples whose children had come of age. They also know of three couples from their sample of fifty-seven with pre-school children who within a few years of the interview were living apart (personal communication, 1986). Such findings are enough to query whether those who have to grapple with the consequences of male infertility are really such paragons of mutual devotion. In resorting to a sperm donor they are declaring an overwhelming need for a child, which could be taken to imply that they are not sufficient unto each other. Like any other unforeseen crisis, infertility can as easily drive couples apart as bring them closer together. Much will depend on the inherent strength of their relationship, or absence of serious flaws within it.

In a postal follow-up study of 843 couples who had attended an infertility clinic in Sheffield, Connolly, Edelmann, and Cooke (1987) attempted to quantify the emotional distress involved, and found that this was greater (with corresponding effects on the marriage) where the cause of the problem lay with the man. Depression and a sense of isolation were reported by the husbands and guilt feelings by both partners. There was no enquiry into the use of DI, possibly because local facilities were lacking or very limited during the survey period (1965–76).[3] Provided they are not allowed to persist for too long, any such adverse psychological effects are presumably mitigated by the birth of a healthy child even where a husband has no valid grounds for believing that he is the genetic father. Interviews with parents of pre-school children led Snowden, Mitchell, and Snowden (1983) to conclude that the role of the donor was often minimized or even denied, and who can be sure that this is a maladaptive response? Desirable as it might be for the promotion of knowledge to keep such families under long-term surveillance, we need also to consider the effects of undue vigilance upon family relationships.

Whenever we have asked a couple if either partner had needed to persuade the other to accept the idea of DI, we have been assured that the decision was entirely mutual. Usually we accept such an answer at its face value in the belief that no useful purpose would be served by trying to undermine a couple's defences or casting doubt on their honesty. Nothing short of a prospective study could hope to expose all the underlying conflicts which this deceptively easy solution to the problem of male infertility may engender, although obviously they will come to light in individual cases. We know of no plans for such a study, but from available indications it would be mistaken to assume that the major resistance comes typically from the male partner. Some of the earlier literature reviewed by Schellen (1957) suggested that he was not uncommonly the prime mover, sometimes after broaching the question of divorce. He may then find that his wife rejects the notion of a sperm donor as vigorously as she rejects divorce. His response may then range from disappointment to relief, but at least the way has been opened to further discussion. Where a couple wish to be sure of their options a laparoscopy[4] may be advised, but this is not to be recommended except where there is a real possibility of pursuing DI. Unfortunately the stigma attaching to male infertility still persists, probably by reason of its hidden connotation of sexual inadequacy, so that some women may prefer to share if not shoulder the blame for their childlessness. But where a husband is confident of his ability to accept a donated child as his own, and provided that the wife has no inhibitions about her capacity to carry and nurture the seed of an unknown volunteer, we can think of no sufficient reason for wanting to discourage them. The psychological problems are likely to be minor as compared with extra-marital pregnancy, which itself is not necessarily a complete bar to successful parenthood.

Men vary in their capacity to handle the news of their infertility, some responding with detachment and others with anger or pain. We have argued elsewhere (Humphrey and Humphrey 1987) that a crucial factor is the implied threat to the man's self-esteem, which we have investigated with the Marital Patterns Test (Ryle 1966). This self-report questionnaire comprises twenty-four paired items which measure exchange of affection between partners and dominance/submission in their relationship. As Birtchnell (1985) has pointed out, Ryle took a broad view of affection by incorporating items such as being patient with, giving time to, and not finding fault with one's partner, being considerate of their feelings and making them feel more confident. Thus giving and receiving affection in marriage is largely a matter of being supportive and well-disposed towards one another. The men in our series of couples seeking DI appeared to feel less well-supported by their wives, in terms of their scores for affection received, than a group of would-be adoptive fathers tested at an earlier period (Humphrey 1975). Most of the latter had been given to understand that their own fertility was unimpaired, and where this was not the case they too were apt to report less affection from their wives. As will be seen from Table 7.1, our husbands in the DI group scored somewhat lower on this

Table 7.1   *Scores on the Marital Patterns Test*

	n	Affection given		Affection received		Dominance	
		mean	s.d.	mean	s.d.	mean	s.d.
DI husbands	50	8.9	1.97	9.0	1.98	10.6	2.15
Fathers	40	9.3	2.12	10.2	2.47	10.3	1.94
Adopting husbands	50	10.7	2.17	11.7	1.75	10.9	2.22
DI wives	50	10.7	1.64	11.1	1.83	10.5	2.29
Mothers	40	9.4	2.81	10.8	2.06	11.7	2.31
Adopting wives	50	12.0	2.04	12.3	1.97	11.1	1.59

Source: Humphrey and Humphrey (1987: 215)

measure than ordinary fathers recruited through GPs, who themselves were significantly lower than the adopting husbands. Differences between the three groups of wives were less clear-cut, as
were inter-group differences in dominance scores for both husbands and wives.

The interpretation of this finding is still not entirely clear, and
we need more data. Elsewhere (Humphrey and Humphrey, in
press) we have speculated as follows:

> A man with shattered self-esteem, or temporarily mortified
> by the knowledge that he cannot hope to gratify his wife's
> maternal needs, may look to her for emotional support. At this
> stage of the marriage she may be too upset to provide it, or he
> may be inordinate in his demands (sometimes both). Hence
> we are concerned with the ratio of his AR (affection received)
> to her AG (affection given) score. Less than 5 per cent of our
> couples seemed to agree that he was receiving too little af-
> fection from her, and we think it more likely that the infertile
> husband goes through a phase of requiring enhanced proof of
> his wife's enduring love.

This would suggest that the moratorium imposed by long
waiting lists at many NHS clinics might have certain advantages.
At all events this aspect of a marriage needs careful appraisal
before DI is offered as a facile remedy. Doctors faced with an
intractable disability can be forgiven for wanting to circumvent it
if they can, but they should allow couples to proceed at their own
pace. Transition to parenthood is a taxing phase of almost any
marriage, and a number of studies have shown that marital satisfaction can be compromised by the presence of children, especially with regard to companionship (Rollins and Feldman 1970;
Rollins and Cannon 1974; Lupri and Frideres 1981). If the pre-
school period is particularly challenging for many couples, as the
evidence from such studies clearly indicates, this is all the more
reason for giving men and women time to come to terms with
their infertility rather than letting them plunge headlong into an
'artificial family' (Snowden and Mitchell 1981).

Another look at Table 7.1 may serve to bring home this
message. The group of ordinary mothers, most of whom had pre-
school children, saw themselves as giving less affection to their
husbands than either group of childless wives. Whether this was

a true reflection of their emotional state or whether they were over-sensitive to their maternal role must remain uncertain, but family therapists are well aware that fatherhood calls for a degree of maturity that is beyond many men whose fertility has never been questioned. It is therefore just as well that the average surrogate father has had rather more time in which to mature before taking on this commitment.

DI VERSUS ADOPTION

In an earlier follow-up study of forty childless and forty adopting couples traced through an infertility clinic (Humphrey 1969), it was found that all but four of the seventeen infertile husbands belonged to the adopting group. Children had been placed for adoption by a variety of agencies or in some cases privately, and in only one instance had the delay been longer than twelve months. Moreover, apart from 3-year-old twins who were adopted under pressure from a minister, none were placed after the age of 6 months. These couples, who lived in a predominantly rural area of the home counties, could afford to dwell on the disadvantages of DI, which would have entailed at least an hour's journey to London every month to visit one of the few private practitioners offering the facility at that time. Nevertheless four couples had actively considered it, including two who were still interested. One of the latter had already adopted two children but the wife was still frankly envious of pregnant women, having lost her original fiancé in a road accident. The second couple had seen themselves as debarred from adopting by a difference of age and religion. The husband was twelve years older and had a child by his first marriage before losing his fertility through illness. Thus in each case there was a specific reason for the wife's sense of emotional deprivation in being unable to conceive by her husband.

Many of the childless couples in the earlier study had outwardly accommodated well enough to their sense of loss even if few could recognize any benefits from the child-free state. Only five of the wives were under 30, and twelve were over 40, so that few could realistically hope for a belated child of their marriage. A minority had thought of adopting but none seriously, apart from four couples whose application had been rejected. But at least

this form of surrogate parenthood was available to those who
found it acceptable, and were capable of the necessary persistence
in their quest for a child. In contrast, most of the couples we have
counselled in more recent years about DI have been only too
aware of the obstacles to adoption in its traditional form. About
one in eight of the first 100 couples seen had taken the trouble to
make enquiries, only to be disheartened by the long wait and
uncertain outcome. Most couples in the previous series had
received their first child a good twenty years earlier, when 'blue
ribband' babies were not in short supply. Had adoption been
equally straightforward in the 1980s more of our couples would
have been interested, and even so about half of the wives said
they would be prepared to reconsider it if unable to conceive by
donor.

Often enough the couple pursuing DI seemed intent on making
a virtue of necessity. Not only the wives but the husbands too
would stress the psychological advantages of experiencing pregnancy and childbirth, albeit in circumstances quite different
from what was normal for a married couple. This way they could
be sure of a genetic link on at least one side of the family, and the
wife would not feel cheated of that fundamental human experience which the majority of adoptive mothers must forgo. And
the benefits to a husband of seeing his wife through a pregnancy,
even where this has been artificially contrived, are not to be dis-
counted. Rather more husbands in our series have been found on
semen analysis to be producing *some* sperm than none at all,
which gave them the option of clinging to the belief that a child
born after DI could be genetically their own after all.[5] Otherwise
there is an element of asymmetry in parent-child relationships,
which may be troublesome in the event of congenital abnormality, retarded development, difficult temperament, or other mis-
fortunes. (Since donors are drawn from the healthier members of
the population and then carefully screened, it must be tempting
to think of children thus conceived as having an immaculate set
of genes. In reality their developmental hazards are no greater
but also no less than in the normal course of events).

The predominantly optimistic picture conveyed by Snowden
and his colleagues was drawn from a single research interview,
with relatively superficial analysis of data. Of the eighty-one
couples with pre-school children contacted through a single-

handed practitioner, fifty-seven were actually interviewed, although a few others had expressed willingness – a participation rate of 70 per cent, which for a study of this nature is quite reasonably acceptable. A total of eighty-two children had been achieved by this means. Whilst difficulties were acknowledged, some of which may have arisen from the resort to a donor (we are not told), all the husbands and wives

> appeared to have accepted the children willingly and happily; indeed some of the fathers had a particularly close relationship with their children and appeared to be deeply involved in child care and family life. Because their children had been achieved after considerable heartache, and after much effort, they were particularly valued and loved and the couples tended to find parenting particularly rewarding and satisfying.
>
> (Snowden, Mitchell, and Snowden 1983: 81)

Exactly the same impression has been gained from follow-up studies of adoptive families, even where the circumstances giving rise to adoption were grossly unfavourable (Kadushin 1970). However, it must be borne in mind that all these fifty-seven families had been created within the previous five years, so that it was still early days. Contact was established with ten of the nineteen parents with grown-up children who had remained in touch with the practitioner, but even tentative conclusions can hardly be drawn from such a small number. Only three individuals could be contacted who knew of their unorthodox conception, and we still have little idea of what it means to grow up with this uneasy knowledge.

As already indicated, we are not planning to monitor the performance of our own couples as parents, which would be no easy task even in the short term. To follow the children through to adulthood would be a prohibitive undertaking and would be unlikely to demonstrate more than a range of possible outcomes, with no control over a welter of intervening variables. In so far as intelligence (and hence occupational achievement) is genetically determined, one might expect them to do rather well in life. In general they get off to a better start than adoptees, with a tendency towards more promising genes, and can count on parental care that is no less devoted. A Japanese follow-up study of fifty-four children aged up to 11 (Iizuka *et al* 1968) gave evidence of healthy development on the more obvious criteria of height, weight, and developmental or intelligence quotients.[6] Paternal rejection has been a hypothetical cause for concern all along, but we do not know that it occurs more frequently than in natural families. Our own casual experience of couples who have remained in touch has reinforced the impression of closeness between surrogate father and child (with the single exception already mentioned), but it would be useful to employ measures of parent-child interaction in order to put the matter on a more scientific basis. A marked lack of physical resemblance between father and son might prove to be an embarrassment in some cases, but we have seen some astonishingly good matches. One man, for example, produced a snapshot of himself at the age of 4 which appeared to cast his toddler in the role of younger sibling.

An issue we feel bound to discuss with all our clients is the need for secrecy. Whereas few adoptive parents nowadays are tempted to engage in make-believe, couples whose children were born after DI can all too easily succumb to this temptation. Given what is politely termed 'access' at the time of the inseminations, a man is both legally and in most cases also psychologically the father of any child who was in fact conceived by donor sperm. But much as it might suit the woman who carries that child and brings it into the world, or the man who takes on the nurturant role expected of any other husband and father, to pretend that they have produced a child of the marriage, there are usually long odds against such an eventuality. It would be a strange coincidence if a woman who had failed to conceive by her sexual partner during years of unprotected intercourse, were to do so within a short period of exposure to donated semen. Clearly this *could* happen, but after more than one negative semen test it is only a theoretical possibility. We look for a degree of self-honesty in the couples who come to us for counselling, and we are faintly perturbed when an infertile husband seems intent on denying the relevance of the donor even at this stage.

Nevertheless we can appreciate some of the barriers to greater openness, which we have discussed briefly elsewhere (Humphrey and Humphrey 1986). The Snowdens (1984) in their otherwise admirable guidebook seem determined to brush these aside, whilst those whose professional experience is largely or wholly confined to adoption (Brandon and Warner 1977; McWhinnie

1984) may be at risk of pressing the analogy too far. Benefits to be expected from confiding in relatives and close friends at the outset are not hard to envisage, and at least a third of our couples had already done so. They include moral support, relief from the discomforts of evasiveness, and better prospects of discovering others in the same predicament.[7] But when it comes to being completely open with the much-wanted child, different considerations arise. How can the parents begin to communicate such an awkward fact? How can the growing child begin to get to grips with the concept of an anonymous donor, especially during adolescence? And – perhaps the most daunting hurdle in the early years of parenthood – how can the couple reconcile themselves to the inevitable loss of control over their privacy? For to explain the role of the donor to the child must mean that the surrogate father's infertility is liable to become public knowledge, since children are not much good at keeping a secret. True, there is nothing inherently shameful about male infertility; but whilst it is not to be construed as a sexual problem, despite one report of temporary impotence following the diagnosis (Berger 1980), it is for most men invested with the same degree of intimacy. Why should they be expected not to care who knows? This is where adoptive parents have a distinct edge. Where neither parent is biologically related to the child, they can declare their true status without fear or favour; and what is more, they can choose how much to reveal about the nature of their infertility (whether within or outside the family) if there are no children of the marriage.

It is our experience that couples will sometimes blind themselves to the hazards of being open with selected others whilst insisting on a policy of saying nothing to their future child. Fortunately such a dilemma may resolve spontaneously in the course of family life if the child's sexual curiosity is strong enough to prevail over parental reticence. But where questions from the child are consistently parried by the parents they will have made themselves vulnerable to disclosure from another source, which is probably the last thing they would want. A more flexible attitude is what we have found ourselves advocating, if only to anticipate the unguarded moment experienced by one of the Snowdens' older couples. Their 14-year-old, after learning about dominant and recessive genes in an O level biology lesson, had asked why his eye colour did not match that of his parents, who were persuaded to confide in him a few years later (Snowden, Mitchell, and Snowden 1983: 96). Other examples are given by these authors of couples who felt impelled to abandon their stance of secrecy in order to allay possible genetic anxiety in their children, as where the surrogate father had become physically handicapped or was known to be promiscuous. In yet another case a younger son was told after dropping out of university, in the hope that knowledge of his true ancestry (that the male genes had been contributed by a professional person rather than a manual worker) would inspire him to greater effort.[8] Even Sandler (1979), whilst extolling the virtues of secrecy, has acknowledged that different considerations arise where DI has been used as a means of bypassing transmissible defects. However, even in the standard situation of male infertility we can begin to appreciate the value of parental open-mindedness.

WHAT OF THE DONORS?

If one advantage of DI over adoption is that at least one side of the child's pedigree is well known, another might be that the donors are likely to come of healthier stock than the male parents of children who are parted from their family of origin (see Chapter 3). For this appears to be a plausible assumption despite the paucity of detailed information about the kind of men who agree to donate their sperm.

In commenting on the difficulties of recruitment Snowden and Snowden (1984: 55) point out that 'it is no small thing to ask a man to donate semen which may be used to procreate new life – a child, or children, who will be his genetic offspring, but about whom he will remain completely ignorant and for whom he can fulfill no responsibility'. So how are such men to be found? Medical schools are a convenient source, particularly as many clinics with a DI service are located in or near teaching hospitals. Modern methods of semen analysis can largely take care of the objection that mature men of proven fertility are conspicuous by their rarity among medical students, though possibly more numerous in other faculties. Another drawback is that students of any kind are a heavily pre-selected group, especially in terms of intelligence and social class. This could become problematical where both partners of a recipient couple are of limited endowment, even if in our own experience such couples are rarely deterred by the prospect of a more gifted child than their own might have been. Men visiting maternity wards, or having cause to be grateful for the successful treatment of their sub-fertile wives, have been known to volunteer; similarly those about to undergo vasectomy may be open to persuasion, especially if at the same time they are allowed to store a frozen sample as an insurance against altered circumstances in their own lives. A broader cross-section of the community is embraced by all three categories. The enterprising French system of asking each recipient couple to recruit a volunteer from married couples among their own friends who will contribute to a semen bank (Le Lannon, Lobel, and Chambon 1980) seems eminently practicable, and far less hazardous than allowing a man to call upon his own brother to donate to his wife (as has been reported occasionally).

A pioneering study in New South Wales looked at the personal qualities of sperm donors as compared with male blood donors in the same age range (Nicholas and Tyler 1983). Both groups emerged as moderately extraverted on the Eysenck Personality Inventory or EPI (Eysenck and Eysenck 1964), whereas the sperm donors were significantly more stable ($p < 0.01$). Interestingly, the sole potential sperm donor to register an extreme deviation on the neuroticism scale (with a score of 23/24) did not reappear after the exploratory discussion. Men responding to the advertisement for the DI programme were mostly in their late twenties or early thirties (range 20–50), with a variety of occupations. All but eleven out of fifty returned after the preliminary interview, and apart from the man already mentioned there was nothing to distinguish between those willing to proceed and those who may have had second thoughts. Altruism and curiosity were seen as the prime motives, but with six to ten donations required of each man there was also the factor of convenience, for example, in terms of distance. Should these findings be replicated we can rest assured that cranks and misfits are not alarmingly over-represented in the donor population.

Nicholas and Tyler end their paper by observing that their data 'should be encouraging to potential semen recipients, although the degree of heritability of such characteristics is uncertain (Shields 1973)'. Doubt can be cast on almost any statement about

the inheritance of personality traits, especially in the light of complex findings from a more recent study (Scarr *et al* 1981) which
also used the EPI; yet Eysenck himself was convinced that the ex-
travert-introvert dimension was a basic property of the central nervous system and hence liable to genetic transmission. He argues,
for instance, that

> primary traits such as sociability, impulsivity, ascendancy,
> optimism, and so on, which combine to make up our pheno-
> typic concept of extraversion, arise through the confluence of a
> person's genotype, i.e. his excitation-inhibition balance, with
> a variety of environmental influences.
>
> (Eysenck 1967: 220)

Apart from the evidence from earlier twin studies, reviewed by
Mittler (1971), longitudinal studies have shown that sociability –
one of the hallmarks of a true extravert – remains fairly consistent in the same individual from infancy to adolescence (Scarr
1969). And one certainly would expect sperm donors, or indeed
any other public-spirited volunteers, to be anything but socially
withdrawn.

We ourselves have had no access to our medical student
donors, but we have used the later and better-standardized
version of the same test, the Eysenck Personality Questionnaire
(Eysenck and Eysenck 1975), with sixty-four out of the first
seventy-five couples referred for counselling. These husbands
and wives were close to the population mean on extraversion
and relatively low on neuroticism. The frequency of grossly ele-
vated lie scores in both men and women was what prompted us
to abandon the test, in view of the well-established negative
correlation between the lie score and neuroticism. A group of
fifty prospective adopters tested in an earlier study (Humphrey
1973b) were less extraverted on the EPI, but the use of a different
test means that the findings are not strictly comparable. Sybil
Eysenck (1961) found that her unmarried mothers were predominantly extraverted, but their sexual partners were not
tested. A more searching comparison of DI couples and adoptive
parents from a personality standpoint would be interesting but
scarcely practicable at the present time.

WHO SHOULD BE ELIGIBLE FOR DI?

DI is intended for couples whose infertility is due to factors in the male partner, whether of known or unknown origin, or who are at risk of passing on genetic disease or handicap through children of the marriage. In the USA it is said to have been tried also with couples whose infertility remains unexplained after full investigation, and there is no reason why it should not succeed in a proportion of such cases; however, we have not heard of this usage in the UK. The recipient couple are expected to provide evidence of a stable partnership, and the consent form is signed by both. Some clinics restrict the service to married couples, apparently on the principle that marriage symbolizes a public commitment. All of the 150 couples sent to us so far have in fact been married, apart from a few stably cohabiting couples who were planning to marry in the near future. It seems to us unrealistic to insist on a legal endorsement at a time when marriage as an institution has become more fragile, and when some manifestly devoted couples may be legally debarred from marrying.

The question of whether the service should be extended to homosexual and unsupported heterosexual women has not been widely debated, nor has it arisen more than once in our own experience.[9] Some doctors reserve the right to treat any woman who comes to them for this purpose, others make their own rules. In an unusual and first-time British study, Golombok, Spencer, and Rutter (1983) reported on a group of thirty-seven children aged 5–17 whose mothers were homosexual and mostly living in a stable partnership. They were at no disadvantage socially or emotionally as compared with a control group of children reared by unsupported heterosexual mothers, nor (with one possible exception) was there any sign of a homosexual orientation among the nine post-pubertal children of the experimental group. Admittedly a longer follow-up would be needed to assess psychosexual development; and whilst reasons were given for the choice of control group, there can be no certainty that it was appropriate. Nevertheless anybody is entitled to challenge the all too easy assumption that growing up in a fatherless household – whatever the nuances of adult sexuality therein contained – is inevitably detrimental to either boys or girls. At the same time it might be instructive to ask a group of donors whether they would have reservations about their semen being used to help women who were sexually or otherwise disposed to reject social norms.

At present we have no grounds for suggesting that more than a tiny minority of doctors (if any) behave irresponsibly in the service they offer to deprived human beings in this context. Whether a more judicious selection of applicants would be warranted is another question, but only rarely have we felt bound to advise rejection of a couple with overt marital problems or psychiatric disturbance (Humphrey and Humphrey 1987). In this sense the adoption worker has an altogether different frame of reference, with couples having to compete nowadays even for children who a decade or two ago would have been regarded as hard to place.

8 New trends in human reproduction

In an evocative and not entirely whimsical prologue to their lively book, Australian authors Singer and Wells (1984) describe a twenty-first century dinner party. The host and hostess, recently appointed to the staff of an unspecified school, have invited the Principal and his wife, together with another couple and a single woman from among their new colleagues. They are somewhat nervous in anticipation, for the greater diversity of life styles sixty to seventy years hence makes it even harder to predict whether those from the same work-place will find it easy to relate socially. At first it seems that they need not have worried, since conversation flows smoothly over the cleverly pre-programmed meal. It was only in what ought to have been a more relaxed post-prandial atmosphere that tensions began to surface. And this was after the hostess happened to mention that she was pregnant.

Why should such an innocent revelation have led to an embarrassing interchange? There was nothing unusual about such an event even in the mid-twenty-first century; and the fact that it had taken the couple some years to achieve with the help of *in vitro* fertilization would be no cause for untoward reactions even today, with more than ten years of the twentieth century still to run. As it happened donor insemination had also been on the cards, but the host's jocular explanation that 'with a little help from the doctors I managed to deliver the necessary goods' was received with appropriate laughter. So far so good. It was the husband's warning of a request for paternity leave that produced an unexpected turn in the conversation. There was already ample precedent for such an arrangement, now that a woman's need for continuity in her career and a man's yen for parenting were fully endorsed by society. The Principal, who was a conventional patriarch, recognized that his lingering uneasiness over the question of role reversal was quite irrational. But when it came to the other young couple expressing a similar intention, there was a surprise in store for the assembled company. They were expecting quadruplets, but not until the year after next. Parenthood called for careful planning if their individual careers were not to be jeopardized. Moreover children stood to benefit from growing up with several siblings, and with pre-selection of gender there was no obstacle to a balanced as well as a ready-made family.

It was perfectly simple. The couple had arranged to have their genetic material frozen and then stored for a year or more with a view to ectogenesis:

> It had to be ectogenesis. No one *chose* to be quadruply pregnant. The practice of ectogenesis was comparatively recent, but no longer rare. Like David and Angela, modern-minded couples were avoiding pregnancy by arranging for their future family to spend its first nine months in a laboratory.
>
> (Singer and Wells 1984: 4)

The news came as a shock not merely to the old-fashioned patriarch but to the host and hostess, who clung to the traditional view of pregnancy as a unique opportunity for emotional bonding between mother and foetus. But Angela was ready with her answer:

> 'If there is anything in bonding, it cuts two ways. We will be going to the laboratory to see them every day. David will actually feel closer to them than he would otherwise. In a pregnancy a woman can't see her baby but she can feel it. A man can't do either. David will actually see our children developing day by day.'

Whereupon David added:

> 'Apart from all that, it's in the children's interests to have a happy and fulfilled mother, just as it's in my interests to have a happy and fulfilled wife. Angela now has a brilliant scientific career ahead of her, and it wouldn't help if she was estranged from it for ten years having four babies successively. This way we can each take a year off, one after the other, and give the children our full attention in their formative years, without disrupting our careers.'
>
> (1984: 5–6)

A convincing *riposte*? Possibly, although nothing is said about the strain of raising quadruplets even with such a reciprocal arrangement, nor are the penalties of two partially interrupted careers weighed against the injustice of one career severely threatened. However, there is worse to come. Christine, the seemingly unattached female guest, takes a mischievous delight in announcing that she too is pregnant; and when asked to declare the father (a more personal question than the Principal would normally have risked), she replies that there isn't one. Strictly according to plan, she would be giving birth to her own clone. Again we must allow the authors to spell out their fantasy:

> Cloning had been possible for a few years, but was hardly ever practised. Any woman could do it, providing she didn't want a male child. She would herself supply the necessary egg, and the egg could be fertilized with material taken from any cell of her body. Her child would then have exactly her physical constitution, and would literally have no father. It was now the standard way of producing dairy cattle, of course, and one heard that women did it occasionally; but actually knowing someone who was doing it reduced all the diners to a state of shock.
>
> (1984: 6–7)

Yet it did not render them speechless, and Christine was at once called upon to defend herself against a charge of monstrous egotism. This left her undismayed. Was it any less selfish for a couple to insist upon reproducing one another's genetic codes, especially where it was against all the odds, as with their host and hostess? And as a teacher of sociology, she was well able to counter the argument that a child needed two parents. Had not the experience of the last hundred years given the lie to any such notion, at least where poverty was not a consequence of single parenthood? The others knew better than to challenge her on this, seeing that she was so much more familiar with the literature.

In vitro fertilization, ectogenesis, sex determination, cloning – what next? And yet Singer and Wells (1984) make it abundantly clear that they have not taken off wildly into the realm of science fiction. The first of these developments had arrived a few years earlier in Britain, though much more recently in Australia. As for the others, why, they could be just round the corner – or on the other hand it might take many years of further experimentation. What could be clearly envisaged meanwhile was the need for ethical guidelines, and hence this preliminary exploration of a complex and largely uncharted field. We ourselves are writing three years after the publication of the Warnock Report (1984), which examined some of the same issues before making recommendations to the British government. We would not claim to have anything novel to say about the dawning of a new era in human reproduction, but equally we were reluctant to limit our discussion of surrogate families to what was already standard practice. Let us set off on what has only recently begun to look like familiar territory.

IN VITRO FERTILIZATION (IVF)

Louise Brown was born in July 1978. There was nothing unusual in the manner of her birth, which took place at a cottage hospital in Oldham, Lancashire. Nor was there anything odd about her appearance, and she has continued to develop quite normally up to the age of 8. What made history was the manner of her conception, which was the product of nearly ten years research in both clinic and laboratory. As is now widely known, the clinician was Patrick Steptoe, the scientist Robert Edwards; their collaboration stemmed from a journal article by Steptoe which came to Edwards' attention as he browsed in a Cambridge library. It described the novel technique of laparoscopy, already mentioned in the previous chapter, which allowed a close examination of the inside of the abdomen without having to perform major surgery. The two men joined forces in 1968, and published a preliminary account of their work the following year (Edwards, Bavister, and Steptoe 1969).

Occlusion of the fallopian tubes had up to that time been hard to treat surgically, and it was not until more recently that advances in electron microscopy led to improvement in the success rate. Even so there was much to be said for bypassing the tubes altogether if fertilization could be achieved in the laboratory, followed by uterine implantation in the clinic. First it was a matter of developing the right culture fluid, in which the egg would continue to ripen for a few hours prior to fertilization. This took less than a year – if only the process of implanting the nuclear embryo could have been as simple! But it had long been known – or at least suspected – that one of the commoner hidden

causes of sub-fertility in couples with apparently normal reproductive physiology was failure of implantation. This could be
regarded as an example of early miscarriage, so early in fact that
the woman would remain unaware of it. Thus it was perhaps not
entirely unexpected that implantation rather than extra-cor-
poreal fertilization[1] would prove the major stumbling block. One
way of trying to overcome this was by implanting two or more
embryos simultaneously, but this was a later development and
still not the complete answer. In the event it took Edwards and
Steptoe several years of hormonal manipulation to bring about
the first pregnancy by this method, having initially satisfied
themselves that the artificially contrived embryo was capable of
normal growth. Most unfortunately this pregnancy was ectopic
and had to be terminated. A second pregnancy aborted spontaneously in the first few weeks, and it was not until December 1977
that the successful transfer of an embryo to Louise's mother.
Lesley Brown, was confirmed. The story of this brilliant innovat-
ion has been told by Edwards and Steptoe (1980). A more technical account of the latest developments was published after the
first international meeting at Bourn Hall, near Cambridge, where
the work continues (Edwards and Purdy, 1982).

As Singer and Wells point out, within five years of this major
breakthrough IVF was being used to treat various forms of
infertility throughout the world. Under the leadership of Carl
Wood a rival centre of excellence has been established at Melbourne (Wood and Westmore 1983; Wood and Trounson 1984).
Work is also proceeding in several other European countries as
well as in Israel and the USA. Whilst tubal damage or dysfunction
is still the prime indication, new hope has also been offered to
couples with oligospermia or unexplained infertility. There is no
reason why the scope of the treatment should not be extended,
although it remains prohibitively expensive for the average
couple and at the time of writing there is said to be only one NHS
centre where it is available entirely free of charge. Moreover, the
success rate is still disappointingly low as compared with the
much less demanding procedure of DI.[2]

By now the reader may be wondering why we have gone into
such detail over a procedure which, fascinating as it may be in its
own right, does not appear to fall within the scope of this book.
For at first sight a family created by this method is no different

from any other family. The children are genetically related to their parents in exactly the same way as children who owe their origins to an unguarded moment of copulation. It is therefore entirely up to the parents whether they tell their children of the obstacles that had to be overcome before they were conceived. Probably many if not most children conceived after a period of infertility get to know about it sooner or later, at least in this day and age (though we have no evidence on which to draw). Equally, we can assume that few couples involved in IVF would feel any need to keep it a closely guarded secret. It seems reasonable also to assume that a child's sense of security would be enhanced rather than diminished by learning that he or she was very much wanted, and not born through an act of fate to which the parents had to adapt. So what is the significance of IVF in the context of surrogate families? Simply that it opens the way to departures from the genetic norm.

Occasionally the husband of a woman accepted for IVF may find himself unable to masturbate to order, but rarely is this an insuperable problem. Less rarely a more fertile donor may be sought after the husband's sperm have proved ineffective even under the controlled conditions of the laboratory. Here the chances of success would be the same as where the husband is of normal fertility, and the child's situation would be complicated only by ignorance of his genetic father (as discussed in the previous chapter). It is where ovulation is incurably deficient (not a common picture, since anovular cycles are usually treatable), or where the woman is at risk of passing on a serious disorder, that new considerations arise. Here donation of an egg, or even an embryo, may be required. And although this may appear to be no different in principle from donating sperm, we do need to consider the implications rather carefully.

First, let us make clear that we are no longer in the realm of sheer fantasy. As Singer and Wells (1984) point out, Carl Wood's team had already achieved at least one pregnancy by donor egg and another by donor embryo at the time of writing. Although the collection of an egg entails laparoscopy (or as a more recent alternative, the use of ultrasound techniques) and is thus less simple than the collection of semen, this poses no problem at the present time or in the immediately forseeable future. As long as drugs are used to promote ovarian hyperactivity in women undergoing IVF, there will always be eggs to spare – and such women are unlikely to hold out against donating to their fellow sufferers. It is then simply a question of synchronizing the two cycles, at least until the technical difficulties of freezing and thawing embryos have been resolved. And even if for some unpredictable reason this source were to be drastically curtailed, women undergoing tubal sterilization can be (and indeed have been) called upon as an alternative source of supply. By suitable timing of the operation they can agree to part with a single egg at no personal inconvenience, or if willing to accept an ovarian stimulant they can donate several eggs without added risk.

So what is the problem, if any? Perhaps it is a case of needing more time to get used to the idea. If insemination with donated sperm is seen by some as a form of licensed adultery, we have to acknowledge that society has long been forced to accept the occurrence of extra-marital conception as a fact of life – common enough even if at times embarrassing, and not automatically a ground for abortion let alone divorce. Hence knowledge of paternity has always called for a wise child. Yet barring the increasingly rare phenomenon of concealed adoption, has there ever been any doubt about the genetic link between mother and child? Hitherto the answer is no, but if in future there is to be a significant demand for donated ova and no shortage of volunteers, then assumptions of this kind will no longer be tenable. However, there is no reason why appropriate safeguards should not be employed by professionals offering a service; the value of honesty in parent-child relationships can continue to be stressed, and with luck even the law can be changed so as to confer legitimate status on the children whose *de facto* parents have freely consented to their conception.

If use of donor sperm has become almost respectable over a span of forty years, and if donation of ova poses questions of practice rather than principle, then it is hard to see why donated embryos should introduce a new set of problems. If each is separately acceptable, why not the two in conjunction? Ironically the first pregnancy, reported in the *British Medical Journal* (Trounson *et al* 1983), was more controversial than it need have been, since the egg was supplied by a 42-year-old woman undergoing IVF and then fertilized by an anonymous sperm donor. This could be seen as an odd choice of female donor, and indeed the

Australian team were roundly attacked by Edwards and Steptoe in the correspondence columns of the same journal after the foetus had spontaneously aborted as a result of a chromosomal abnormality. In view of the known adverse effects of ageing on the female reproductive system it would clearly have been more sensible to look for a younger egg donor, but it would appear that none was available. It is worth noting that virtually no IVF programme in Britain today will accept a woman of over 40, and a lower age-limit is not uncommon.

Regardless of this ill-fated venture, there can be little doubt that the way is now open to a form of surrogacy which only ten years ago would have been hard to envisage. Just as two individuals who are unaware of one another's existence can donate their genetic material for the benefit of an unknown couple who would otherwise be fated to remain childless, so that couple can raise a child who is not genetically theirs although apparently a product of the marriage. It is perhaps not too fanciful to describe this as a form of pre-natal adoption, and it certainly carries some of the possible disadvantages of adoption in terms of parent-child discrepancies in physical or other characteristics (common enough in ordinary families but readily exaggerated in the absence of a genetic link). At the same time it confers the obvious advantage of a normal gestation period when all goes well, enabling the host couple to prepare themselves emotionally for the birth of their child in a way that is denied to prospective adopters. And in view of the trend in recent years towards placement of older children who import a variety of longstanding problems into the adoptive relationship, we can appreciate that pre-natal adoption would for those few eligible couples be a move in the right direction.

SURROGACY

From pre-natal adoption as a curious form of surrogacy we can move on to surrogacy as it is understood by the general public. This is where a fertile woman volunteers to conceive and carry a child for the benefit of an infertile couple who intend to bring it up as their own. This may be undertaken either for profit or for altruistic reasons, as where a close friend or relative is moved by compassion to make a gift of her own fertility. Normally it is the wife who is the infertile partner of the childless marriage, since the much simpler remedy of DI is available to couples whose problem lies in the husband. When the latter is believed to be fertile (usually on the basis of semen analysis, though he may have children from a previous marriage) the proposed surrogate mother can choose between sexual intercourse and artificial insemination (AI). For obvious reasons the latter is usually preferred by all parties, but a detailed account of surrogacy resulting from a sexual relationship with the commissioning father has been reported (Stevens and Dally 1985). If this particular experience is anything to go by we can believe that the elimination of any sexual component has much to commend it. Doing 'what comes naturally' in these unnatural circumstances has little in common with a love affair, whilst AI with the husband as donor may even be more efficient.

There are a number of situations where surrogacy might be worth considering as a possible solution to an infertility problem, especially with so few infants available for adoption. DI or more particularly IVF may have been attempted without success. The woman with a diseased or absent uterus would of course be debarred from either of these methods, and premature hysterectomy is sometimes unavoidable even where the woman is desperate for a child. There are also certain conditions, such as diabetes, hypertension, or renal disease, that would make pregnancy inadvisable but would not rule out motherhood altogether. In addition to such purely medical reasons for resorting to a surrogate mother, it is theoretically possible that a woman might see it as a means of safeguarding her career prospects (like Angela in the futuristic scenario) or even of avoiding the more unpleasant features of normal pregnancy. In practice we doubt whether such luxurious reasons will ever become socially acceptable unless the supply of potential surrogates begins to compare with that of adoptable infants in a bygone era, and probably not even then. After all, it has never been all that easy for a healthy woman to adopt a child merely as a means of escape from childbirth.

The Warnock Committee, whilst not wishing to invoke the criminal law in respect of private arrangements, came down heavily against commercial surrogacy. It pointed out that the contribution of the gestating woman was 'more intimate and personal' than that of the semen or ovum donor; and furthermore that it was 'inconsistent with human dignity that a woman should use her uterus for financial profit and treat it as an incubator for someone else's child' (1984: 45). Whereas it is any woman's right in law (with her husband's consent if she is married) to offer her child for adoption, it would be most unusual to find that the child was conceived for this express purpose.[3] It seems likely that there would be strong public support for the Committee's attitude to commercial surrogacy, which swiftly became the subject of a Surrogacy Arrangements Bill announced by the Secretary of State for Social Services in March 1985. Interestingly only three of the Committee's sixty-three recommendations relate to surrogacy, yet none of the other sixty look like being implemented during the lifetime of the present parliament.

Although there could hardly be a more time-honoured practice than surrogacy, with two vivid examples given in the Book of Genesis, remarkably little was known of the emotional impact on either the mother or the commissioning couple until a few years ago. A Michigan lawyer, Noel Keane, has been running a sort of one-man crusade to iron out the many legal difficulties besetting both parties to the agreement. Nine of his early cases have been enshrined in a book (Keane and Breo 1981), and some of them are truly awe-inspiring. The fundamental problem is that there is no basis for a satisfactory contract in the law as it stands, nor is it likely that any court would be willing to enforce the kind of contract that a lawyer might wish to draw up on behalf of his client.[4] For it is expecting a lot of any woman volunteering to act as a surrogate, no matter how enthusiastic at the outset, to bind herself to persevering with a pregnancy that might cause her unforeseen distress; and it is expecting even more of her that she should commit herself well in advance to parting with a child which she might in the event wish to keep. The emotional ambiguities of the post-natal period have long been recognized in adoption law, which lays down that the natural mother cannot sign a consent form before six weeks have elapsed, even where the baby has been placed with the adopters at birth. So whilst Keane has argued that an irrevocable agreement prior to conception is essential for the peace of mind of any commissioning couple, he does not make clear precisely how this is to be achieved.

A British case hit the headlines only six months after publication of the Warnock Report. At the start of 1985 Kim Cotton gave birth to her third child, a daughter. She was 28, and for the relief of financial difficulties of the kind that can befall any young couple on moving to a larger house, she had agreed through an agency to carry this child for an affluent childless couple who lived abroad. With a son and a daughter of their own, she and her husband Geoff had already decided that their family was complete, and had agreed on a vasectomy. Geoff was totally unfamiliar with the notion of surrogacy when it was first put to him, but rallied to her support when she proposed AI by the commissioning husband whom she had never met. The emotional ups and downs of her pregnancy are clearly conveyed in her book (Cotton and Winn 1985), but there was no way that either couple could have anticipated the furore that broke loose after the baby was born. Social workers from Barnet Social Services Department intervened on hearing of her intention to hand it over to an unknown couple, and a 'place of safety' order meant that no action could be taken until the baby's future was resolved. Because the genetic father had no rights over his illegitimate child, it had to be established whether he and his wife would make suitable parents or whether the child should be taken into care. In the event baby Cotton was made a ward of the High Court after the father had applied for custody, and then released with minimal delay. The eminent judge was able to find in favour of the recipient couple, who have remained anonymous to this day. So despite a period of acute turmoil the story had a happy ending. It repays careful reading if only because it brings home both the realities and the unrealities of this hazardous adventure. Doubtless there will always be people willing to embark on it, but let no one suppose that surrogacy is easy for either the carrying mother or the commissioning couple.

The future of this once newsworthy child is now presumably secured by an adoption order, but it seems doubtful whether follow-up studies will be conducted on any sizeable group of children launched upon family life in such a dramatic fashion. The stresses have something in common with step-parent adoption, except that this typically occurs later in the child's life when a parent marries or remarries. As in the case of more orthodox arrangements it takes a genuinely maternal woman to see another woman's child through to maturity, but surely not more so when the child is genetically her husband's? In the same way we might question whether it is necessarily any harder for a man to love a child who carries his wife's genes but not his own, which is the essential requirement if DI is to provide a long-term solution to the problem of his infertility.

Before leaving surrogacy we need to consider a possible new variant which may be with us sooner than we expect. Singer and Wells refer to this as 'full' surrogacy, in contrast to the 'partial' version so far discussed. Unlike pre-natal adoption, where a woman receives a donated embryo which (God willing) will grow into a child with neither her own nor her husband's genes, full surrogacy means that she and her husband provide the embryo through IVF which is then implanted in the uterus of a host mother who has agreed to carry it to term on their behalf. Bizarre as this procedure may appear, it is now technically possible. Already it has given rise to the concept of 'womb leasing'; and whilst some would regard this as degrading to the dignity of womanhood, there is no real reason why it should be. Although calling for high technology in the way that DI does not, once pregnancy has been achieved the emotional demands upon the host mother are certainly no greater and possibly less than where she herself has supplied half the genes. And from the child's viewpoint it is likely to be more satisfactory in that it avoids the spectre of unknown ancestry.

However, this intriguing possibility remains unrealized. As yet there has been only one pregnancy, brief in duration, from a donated embryo, but if it can happen once it can no doubt happen again. Singer and Wells have argued convincingly that it can make no difference to the chances of implantation whether the woman intends to rear the child herself or to surrender it to its genetic parents (1984: 112). Evidently several women in Victoria have volunteered to act as surrogates in this way, and it is probably only a question of time before one of the leading IVF teams will be ready to take up the challenge. Meanwhile neither the Australian National Health and Medical Research Council (1982) nor a British Medical Association working party (1983) in their ethical guidelines on IVF were willing to come off the fence. The caution of the British medical establishment was expressed in the following words:

The working group has yet to be satisfied that to undertake *in vitro* fertilization with the sperm and the ova of a couple and to transfer the embryo to the uterus of another woman who might carry the embryo to term on behalf of the couple will ever be acceptable.

(see Singer and Wells 1984: 111)

One need merely add that men who sit on committees are often more concerned to prevent things from happening than to promote startling innovations!

It seems fitting to end this section by harking back to the Warnock Committee's opening recommendation, which was to establish a new statutory licensing authority under lay chairmanship (and with substantial lay representation) for the purpose of regulating both research and infertility services of a kind that might benefit from being subject to control, such as IVF and DI. Even if there are good grounds for banning commercial surrogacy, might there not be a case for bringing private arrangements within the purview of such a body? Two of the Committee's sixteen members, in a commendably restrained expression of dissent, argued that there were 'rare occasions when surrogacy could be beneficial to couples as a last resort' (Warnock Committee 1984: 87), in which case the new licensing authority would need to include surrogacy within its terms of reference. Any non-profit making agency involved in surrogacy arrangements would then have to be licensed by the authority. If some of the worst pitfalls of adoption have been gradually eliminated by the cumulative legislation of the past sixty years, perhaps it is not too much to hope for similar progress with both full and partial surrogacy. Difficult decisions and complex evaluations abound, errors will be made; but this goes for almost any far-reaching human enterprise.

ECTOGENESIS, CLONING, AND PRE-DETERMINATION OF SEX

The use of ectogenesis to suit the convenience of a dual-career couple who wanted their family at one fell swoop was introduced earlier in the guise of a harmless fantasy. If babies of ever diminishing birthweight can be saved without inevitable handicap, thanks to clinical skills, and if the life of a human embryo can be extended day by day and then week by week in the laboratory, thanks to scientific expertise – given that these are realistic postulates, the evolution of a fully paid up infant outside the womb (ectogenesis) is already on the horizon. At one time a foetus weighing less than 1,000 grammes at delivery would have been considered non-viable, yet today in a special care baby unit it is expected to survive. How long before this optimism will stretch to the foetus of barely 500 grammes? In 1975, under the vigilant eye of Robert Edwards, a surplus embryo went on growing for nine days until his courage ran out. The embryo at this stage was still an almost invisible speck, and he has been unable to repeat his early success in keeping one alive for almost a week beyond the usual time limit; however, he remained convinced that this particular embryo would have developed further if left to its own devices (Edwards 1982). With the period of extra-uterine growth prolonged, and that of intra-uterine growth curtailed, there may indeed ultimately come a time when the special environment of the womb *can* be dispensed with.

Does this mean that we should be plunged willy-nilly into the extravaganza of Aldous Huxley's brave new world? We think not. Like any other major advance it would be open to abuse; ethical objections might be raised, for example, to the use of fully-formed embryos as a source of spare organs and tissues for transplantation. But among the more innocent developments would be ectogenesis as an alternative to surrogacy. This would have the merit of avoiding ownership disputes with the host mother, or behaviour on her part that might prove harmful to the foetus such as smoking or drug taking during pregnancy, even if there were no difficulty in balancing supply and demand. Extra-uterine preservation of the foetus would also dispose of the case against abortion, since a woman could then opt to have a pregnancy terminated without inevitably sacrificing a potential life. So there could be benefits enough without needing to be persuaded by the arguments once used by Firestone (1971), that women would thereby be freed from the 'tyranny of their reproductive biology'. (We are not rejecting this line of approach, but would see it as generally carrying more weight with ardent feminists than with most members of medical ethics committees. One would not in any case expect women of normal health and fertility to opt out of pregnancy in large numbers, or at least not until it had been shown that such children were at no biological disadvantage).

Once again any such revolutionary measure would need to be kept under stringent control, lest confusion were allowed to run riot over the genetic basis of subsequent family relationships. It may occasionally happen that babies are swapped on a maternity ward, but the risk of inadvertent or even deliberate substitution might be greater in a laboratory. In so far as it would become easier for any married or cohabiting couple to reach beyond the bounds of their own genetic material, without being accountable to society for their actions, there would need to be sufficient assurance that the welfare of the children was paramount. And even more crucially, if there are problems in allowing women to use their wombs for incubating other people's children (commercially or otherwise), such problems are not easily resolved by entrusting the major responsibility for human reproduction to scientists, clinicians, and laboratory attendants.

Cloning and pre-determination of sex have even less claim on our attention in the present context. Whilst aptly featuring among new trends in human reproduction, they are less obviously relevant to the management of infertility and the creation of surrogate families. Here the point is simply that each has been facilitated by the technical developments arising from IVF, so that what began as a highly specific treatment for a small sub-group of infertile women has opened up new possibilities of great moment for society. Possibly it was anxiety over this limitless vista, rather than respect for the sanctity of embryonic life, that prompted Enoch Powell and his successor Kenneth Hargreaves to introduce their Private Member's Bills aimed at restricting the scope of research focused on surplus or discarded human embryos.

The simplest form of cloning is already well within our capacity. All the biological scientist need do is to wait briefly for the newly fertilized ovum to undergo its first division and then separate the two cells under a microscope, allowing each to develop independently. This mimics what happens spontaneously every two or three hundred conceptions to produce identical twins, who share a common genetic constitution. This form of cloning has already proved successful in dairy farming, and there is no reason why it should not work equally well with humans. It is feasible because the cells of an early embryo have no specialized function, whereas later ones are earmarked for particular purposes such as blood, nerve, or bone marrow. These cloned individuals are necessarily of the same age, unless one embryo is implanted immediately whilst the other is frozen and stored for future implantation, a process which has yet to be accomplished.[5] In the popular imagination, however, cloning involves taking a cell from a living person and using it to produce one or more offspring genetically identical to the person from whom it was taken. This is not such a novel idea as it may sound, for it happens every time a gardening enthusiast or professional food grower takes a cutting. But to clone from a living creature, or at least from a mammal as opposed to an amphibian, is no easy matter. It calls for replacing the nucleus of one egg with the nucleus extracted from another one, so that the egg responds as if it had been fertilized. There is an unconfirmed report of a successful experiment with a mouse some years ago, but it does not look to be around the corner for humans.

To increase the proportion of genetically identical individuals within a population on any substantial scale might have unforeseen consequences, yet it is hard to envisage such an occurrence. As an insurance against foetal loss it might have something to commend it, but we doubt whether it would appeal to many women except after prolonged infertility.[6] The use of a spare embryo as a source of spare parts would be one thing, assuming that the technical difficulties could be overcome; the hoarding of spare human beings, with infant mortality at its present low level in the western world, is mind-boggling. Multiple pregnancies are no longer a foetal death sentence (even sextuplets have been known to survive apparently intact), whereas multiple parenthood must be something of a nightmare.

The opportunity to pre-select children by sex is one of the few advantages enjoyed by adoptive parents, or it used to be until amniocentesis and ultrasound scanning created an advanced warning system for pregnant women. Except in the case of sex-linked hereditary disease, however, the use of abortion to regulate family composition would be unacceptable not only to the medical profession but to most couples already grateful enough for their mastery of family size. Couples seeking a child through IVF might be given the option of discarding an embryo of the non-preferred sex, since by cloning and dissecting one member of the pair it is already possible to determine what is on offer. Again, though, one has to ask whether it would be fair to add a gratuitous dilemma to an emotionally fraught situation. If a simpler method of regulating choice of sex could be devised, as by separating the heavier female-producing X chromosome from the male-producing Y chromosome sperm and then artificially inseminating, as required, there might be considerable demand from some couples under certain circumstances. Since this could serve as an additional means of controlling population growth it is to be hoped that research along these lines will continue. The debate itself will surely continue, following useful leads from Etzioni (1968) and from several authors contributing to the volume edited by Holmes, Hoskins, and Gross (1981).

The social consequences of this ever increasing control over the technical aspects of human reproduction are hard to project. To picture in detail the impact on human happiness and family life calls for the vision of an Aldous Huxley or an H.G. Wells, who were fortunate in combining biological knowledge with a creative imagination. We have been concerned throughout this book to explore the known stresses in child development and family relationships where the normal genetic linkage is absent or attenuated. Yet had we confined ourselves to what is clearly known, or at least widely held on the basis of reasonable evidence, we would have found much less to say. In some areas of discourse, notably assisted reproduction, we can but speculate. It is sobering to reflect that even on more heavily-trodden ground, such as the adoptive family, there is still much to discover. The social scientist of the twenty-first century will not lack for material, with permutation of marriage partners likely to escalate and the frequency of reconstituted families unlikely to diminish. Surrogacy in the strictest sense may loom larger in the popular press if not in official statistics; surrogate families in the wider sense may become a growing preoccupation at many levels.

As to human sexuality, time will tell. We are not persuaded by the contemporary AIDS scare that sexual relationships will become any less fluid over the next hundred years – why should they? A massive boost in the sale of condoms is perhaps safer to anticipate than a return to some mythical era of chastity, even within marriage. But whatever the restrictions on sexual activity, we can assume that children will continue to be born. Veevers

(1980), a leading authority on voluntary childlessness, has always seen it as a minority cult, and our own up-to-date review of the literature (Humphrey 1987) does not suggest otherwise. What matters in the long run is that, regardless of family circumstances, children should not have too much cause to regret their existence. Here, as elsewhere, we are in full agreement with Singer and Wells (1984). In passing judgement on new variants of human reproduction, and the novel basis of family life to which they may give rise, we need look for no other criteria.

9 Epilogue: will the nuclear family survive?

In our opening chapter we put forward two major reasons for looking upon the nuclear family as an endangered species. The first is that if annual divorce rates are to continue at their present level, let alone increase, then one in three of today's marriages will come to grief. Those of us who remain committed to the ideal of monogamy, or have reason to recoil from the miseries of divorce, will find this a disquieting prospect. The second reason is that contraception is both more efficient and less intrusive than it used to be. Short of sterilization it can never approach perfect reliability, depending as it does on human caprice; but with the recent trend towards cohabitation as a prelude to marriage (not necessarily with the same partner), and thus greater incentive to avoid premature parenthood, postponement of a first child can all too easily become transformed into voluntary childlessness.

THE FLIGHT FROM PARENTHOOD

Even since the first chapter was drafted, a new survey has appeared, indicating that women born in 1950 are apparently several times more likely to opt out of motherhood than those born in 1935 (Johnson *et al* 1987). Admittedly this inference was drawn from routine case notes rather than from a more focused enquiry, and the study was confined to a single southern county. But women of 35 are rapidly becoming less fertile even granted a possible change of heart, and are less likely nowadays to have reached this age without seeking advice for inability to conceive. So if the authors' figure of one in nine voluntarily childless (as against fewer than one in thirty of those born fifteen years earlier) is a true index of a social trend, this must be food for thought. We are all uneasily aware that the human race may succumb to a sudden holocaust, but this is not to deny the value of life. If it were to die out from sheer inertia or from universal self-indulgence – what Lasch (1979) has dubbed 'the culture of narcissism' – then some of us may start wondering why we took the trouble to be born!

At this stage we can only speculate about patterns of fertility over the next few decades. Flight from parenthood, on the part of those who would rather gain their long-term satisfactions in other ways, is already a reality. Yet neither Veevers (1980) from a series of studies in Canada, nor Campbell (1985) from a limited enquiry in Scotland, was prompted to regard voluntary childlessness as a harbinger of doom. Both these authors, and others whose work they review, seem to perceive it as a welcome sign of personal autonomy amongst married women. If future generations are to be less readily influenced by social pressures in deciding to have children, this is surely all to the good. The costs of raising children are heavy, and are not bound in every single instance to be outweighed by the benefits (Group for the Advancement of Psychiatry 1973). If there is such a thing as a vocation for parenthood, it could with advantage be harnessed to reproductive behaviour.

The characteristics of voluntarily childless couples are beyond the scope of this chapter, and suffice it to say here that a number of typologies have been proposed.[1] What *does* concern us is the possible relationship between these two major threats to the family and its future. As already noted in Chapter 1, the statistical link between childlessness and marital breakdown has long been known. We quoted Chester (1985) as our authority for the statement that one in three divorcing couples are without children, but the latest figures suggest that this is now a conservative estimate. Between 1970 and 1981 the proportion of childless couples among those divorcing annually ranged from 38–44 per cent, with a mean of just over 40 per cent (Haskey 1983a). This is partly because the incidence of divorce reaches a peak within the first five years of marriage (Haskey 1982), during which any couple uncertain of the stability of their relationship are more likely to refrain from having children. To argue that prolonged childlessness is more stressful than precipitate parenthood would hardly carry conviction. The really intriguing question is whether cohabitation, as a means of postponing the commitment of marriage and parenthood, may lay the foundation for more permanent avoidance in a substantial minority of couples.

We have no data of our own that bear on this question, nor are we familiar with any published work of immediate relevance. Unlike the involuntarily childless, many of whom seek medical advice, the child-free are a non-captive population – Veevers has written of 'stalking an invisible minority' (1980: 171). Hence the almost exclusive reliance on volunteers for research, some of whom may not have been married long enough to test either the constancy of their attitudes to parenthood or the stability of their partnership. A selective summary of empirical work published between 1975–82 specified five years of marriage as the minimum period for inclusion in several studies (Veevers 1983). However, a significant proportion of more recently married couples have participated in other studies, including a British postal survey which stipulated no more than a year of marriage as an entry criterion (Baum and Cope 1980). So as yet there is no warrant for supposing that couples who are content to remain sufficient unto each other will share with conscientious parents the same sense of commitment to a life-long partnership. They may, but equally they may not. As Veevers (1980) has pointed out, they are quite likely to be tied by mortgages and monogamous marriages, which will set limits to their capacity for adventure; but should either or both partners seek an escape route, it can be contrived more readily.

The case *against* having children can be put quite persuasively, as Silverman and Silverman (1971) – a paediatrician married to a psychologist – have demonstrated. But in this book our target population has been mainly couples who, denied by natural process, would go to almost any lengths to achieve a surrogate family. To the child-free couple, glorying in their adult-centred lifestyle, the decision to resort to a sperm donor must seem little short of bizarre. Again, the barriers to acquiring an unblemished infant for adoption are enough to deter all but the most dedicated parents *manqués*. And the veritable obstacle course of *in vitro* fertilization calls for a high degree of emotional resilience as well as unflinching determination in any *bona fide* candidates. As for the surrogacy that would qualify for headlines in the *News of the World*, one might wonder whether sheer lunacy is the mainstay of those who either offer or ask for it. Only in the case of step-parenthood are we dealing with individuals who have children thrust upon them. If marriage is the price men pay for sexual intercourse, and sexual intercourse the price women pay for marriage (as Brigid Brophy was once said to have remarked), then stepchildren are the price sometimes to be paid by either sex for love.

THE ROLE OF THE FAMILY

We are not going to ask why some couples find it so important to have children, any more than we were diverted by the question of why some recoil from the idea. Partly it is a matter of whether other options are seen to exist and have sufficient appeal. Yet it may nevertheless be appropriate to consider – or rather reconsider, since the question is far from novel – what sort of functions the nuclear family is expected to serve. Murdock (1949) in the light of his transglobal survey took the view that its four cardinal functions (not necessarily in order of priority) were sexual, economic, reproductive, and educational. Somewhat surprisingly he went on record as stating that 'Agencies or relationships outside of the family may, to be sure, share in the fulfilment of any of these functions, but they never supplant the family' (Murdock 1949: 10). Writing nearly forty years later we can see that this is palpably untrue. Educational and economic functions can be – and often are – taken over by the state, whilst sexual and reproductive activities are not unknown outside a family context. Therefore the question is whether the family has any unique contribution to make in any or all of these areas. And the answer is maybe, or – at least in respect of sexuality and parenthood – that is what most Christians and not a few humanists would like to believe.

Talcott Parsons, writing at the same time as Murdock (Parsons 1949; see also Parsons and Bales 1955) laid more stress on the family as a source of social learning – indeed, he described it as a 'factory' for human personality. Fletcher (1966) took up this theme with enthusiasm, construing one of its major roles as follows:

> The family provides, in a continuing and detailed fashion, the earliest and most impressive education for the young. In so doing, it introduces the child to those values and modes of behaviour which are appropriate to all kinds of social activity both within and beyond the family. It accomplishes what is

usually called the 'socialization' of the child. Thus it serves as an important agency in the perpetuation of 'social traditions'.

(Fletcher 1966: 32)

More modern writers have tended to go along with this view. Let us now look in more detail, and from a developmental perspective, at what child-rearing involves. For convenience the tasks of ordinary parents can be seen as extending over three phases: the pre-school years, middle childhood, and adolescence. A prime requirement of the earliest phase is to inculcate a sense of trust (Erikson 1963), or in other words to learn how to handle the child's need for dependence. Serious mistakes at this stage can prove costly, if not irretrievable. Then in the early school years, and more especially during the pre-adolescent phase, the parent is expected to assume the role of guide and mentor. Formal teaching may be the responsibility of the school, yet an orientation towards learning for its own sake is something that parents are in a unique position to impart. The principles of algebra and the rules of cricket may have to be taught,[2] whereas social skills such as the management of anxiety and aggression are either absorbed more or less spontaneously through family example (older siblings can play a crucial part here) or allowed to go by default. Pointing young minds in the direction of worldly knowledge, emotional maturity, and good citizenship is a profoundly rewarding enterprise. But the biggest challenge is still to come, when the adolescent is torn between wanting to remain dependent on the parents and yet desperately needing to escape from their guardianship. If he is academically marginal as well as socially and sexually adrift, so much the worse for him (girls tend to grow up faster). Truly it is a testing time for every member of the family, although the degree of turmoil is easily exaggerated (Coleman 1980).

Applying this broad framework to the varieties of surrogate parenthood under consideration, we need hardly point out that couples blessed with a new-born infant (whether through fostering, adoption, or donor insemination) are in almost exactly the same position as ordinary parents. There are still important differences, of course, which led Kirk (1964) to postulate that adopters with a blind eye to these were putting themselves at an extra disadvantage. In similar vein Snowden, Mitchell, and

Snowden (1983) commented on a tendency to deny or minimize the role of the donor among some of the couples they interviewed up to five years after the birth of a child. Thus one husband confidently informed them that the inseminations were 'just a medical treatment the same as an operation is a medical treatment. It's the medical treatment for the medical problem, just the same as you take aspirins for a headache.' (1983: 140) The very anonymity of the donor can be used to diminish the significance of his role, in that 'there is no identifiable third party who may one day turn up on the doorstep and cause embarrassment or make demands' (142). Self-deception of this kind might constitute something of a handicap in the parental role; however, in terms of actual role performance over the years, the surrogate parent in these circumstances must cultivate the same repertoire of skills as any other parent. Nor need we anticipate that the relationship between parent and child will be qualitatively different, or the bond any less close.

Where the child has known and continues to keep in touch with other parents, the surrogate parents are faced with a set of tasks that may be outwardly similar. In crucial respects, however, they may be radically different. In previous chapters we have discussed some of the ambiguities of the quasi-parental role under these conditions, which we shall not recapitulate. Here we are concerned more explicitly with the developmental stages that may have been missed, to the possible detriment of family relationships at their best. The child of school age is usually a party to any adoption proceedings, being required indeed to consent to the application before an order can be granted. The legal aspects of the case may be a great deal more straightforward than the emotional aspects, of which the adopters will need to acquire a sound grasp in the early stages of the relationship. Group meetings have been found helpful for this purpose, especially where more experienced foster parents have been available to tell newcomers what to expect. As Trasler (1960) pointed out many years ago, the success of the venture may largely depend on narrowing the gulf between expectations and reality.

It is a recurring problem that so few social workers have studied child development in any depth, so that most have to learn by listening. To take upon oneself the social education of a school-aged child, without having first helped the same child through the period of maximum dependency, is not the task of an ordinary parent. It calls for special qualities in the surrogate parents if not also a measure of professional support, and a minor miracle is that such qualities are so often elicited from those willing to invest time and energy for as long as the task requires. Such couples are a far cry from those epitomized by Peck (1973), who in her own child-free marriage relished the opportunity to seduce her husband when the spirit moved her, and to be taken out to dinner when the spirit moved him!

There is nothing wrong with the cult of narcissism, except that it may pall and become self-defeating with the passage of time. Eating out can be one of the more reliable pleasures of the post-parental years, even if seduction by then has lost some of its savour. But if there is any category of parent who is entitled to feel cheated of life's simple pleasures, and at times frankly envious of the child- free couple, it is the step-parent. Foster parents, like adoptive parents with a disadvantaged child, share the same rights and obligations towards that child. Not so the stepmother or stepfather, who is not only in an inferior position to the child's true parent but is legally in limbo, unless adoptive status has been conferred.[3] It is high time that more attention was paid to the psychological problems of women in particular as they find themselves abruptly confronted with the step-maternal role, and burdened additionally with all the negative imagery of folklore. Obviously it is much easier to take over the care of an infant, whatever has befallen its true parent. We know a psychologist to whom this happened in her early twenties, giving her ample time to produce two of her own. But by the nature of custody arrangements this relatively easy introduction to step-parenthood is more likely to favour men, as in the two cases quoted in Chapter 4. Maddox (1980), who was cited repeatedly in Chapter 6, encountered strong resistance from her two school-age stepchildren, and regrettably this is what so often lies in wait for the unwary second wife.

In concluding this section we can but observe that many foster children and stepchildren are luckier than they realize. Single parenthood is all very well, but it exposes a child to the hazard of further loss. A second parent-figure ought to be welcome if only as a form of insurance policy. Our review of the literature on step-families, while admittedly selective, suggests that there is no shortage of potentially devoted care-takers ready to pick up the pieces after a child's world has been cruelly shattered. Whether or not they feel well-equipped for the task, it has been thrust upon them and cannot be side-stepped. The selfless devotion of many foster parents may be harder for most of us to understand, especially if we are intent on making life comfortable for ourselves. But possibly herein lies the key. Is it a worthy aim in life to devote one's best efforts to smoothing over or avoiding its recurring difficulties?

OTHER OPTIONS FOR WOMEN

A stable marriage, a comfortable home, two children who are not visibly handicapped, and a quiet life in store for the ageing couple whose children have made their getaway. Is this ultimately all that our 70–80 years on this earth have to offer us? The era of large families and early death is far behind us. We want fewer children and have fewer children. In her survey of more than 5,000 first marriages Dunnell (1979: 86) was prompted to suggest that couples' control over their fertility had gone almost too far, so that 'the problems of under-achievement of fertility ideals may become as important as those of over-achievement to those personally involved, with all the implications for provision of services'.

And so for all except the severely underprivileged, life has ceased to be a struggle for survival. We can choose to live well within ourselves, or we can stretch ourselves to the utmost by taking on a variety of extra challenges whilst we are still young enough to enjoy them. Among highly-educated couples a source of satisfaction from challenges well met is the dual-career family, in which the wife has no intention of subordinating her career to that of her husband (Fogarty, Rapoport, and Rapoport 1971; Rapoport and Rapoport 1971; 1976). For such couples it is usually demanding enough to raise two or at most three children, whilst the harassed parents juggle with their conflicting priorities. It sounds competitive, and the Rapoports and others who have written about dual-career families make no effort to disguise the strain.

Couples with this chosen lifestyle are unlikely to find themselves acting as surrogate parents unless it be through remarriage, and they are probably too well organized to tangle with divorce. But this mode of compensation for the small family of the past two decades is unacceptable or more often impracticable for more than a small minority of couples, those with the necessary combination of ability, enterprise, and stamina. And there are not too many women with a penchant for the line of greatest resistance, which is what the mother with an uninterrupted career has to pursue. There may be many more women who would rather forgo motherhood for the sake of a demanding and fulfilling career; this will partly depend on the attitude of any long-term sexual partner, in that some men are keen on father-hood. And a woman's career aspirations may be all too easily abandoned when a loving partnership is finally achieved after a series of abortive relationships.

MOTHERS AND DAUGHTERS, FATHERS AND SONS

An issue seldom addressed, whether in relation to surrogate families or in any other context, is that of sex differences in atti-tude to parenthood. As it happens the writer has been involved in two enquiries of this nature. In the first of these (Humphrey 1977) personal construct theory was used to explore the ideas of men and women, some of whom already had young children whilst others were waiting to adopt a child. It was found, predict-ably, that motherhood was more likely to be viewed as a source of contentment for women than was fatherhood for men; and a second finding, though undeniably weaker, was that fatherhood was more of a sexual identity symbol for men than motherhood was for women. That the need for children may be stronger in women remains a distinct possibility, but the study was not de-signed to answer this question.

More recently Humphrey and Lenham (1984) employed a sim-ple but apparently effective technique to bring out the contrasted life expectations of boys and girls at two senior independent schools in south London. They were asked to write a brief essay with the opening sentence: 'Today is my eightieth birthday and I look back to the day I left school. . . .' Predictably, again, the major finding was that girls were strongly orientated towards family life whereas boys were essentially career-minded. Table 9.1 is one way of illustrating the consistency of the difference in

Table 9.1   *Projections of parenthood (%)*

	Girls *n* = 120	Boys *n* = 120
Number of children	78	29
Sex of children	53	23
Names of children	26	7
Age gaps between children	22	3
Future life pattern of children	41	10
Grand/great-grandchildren	33	7

Source: Humphrey and Lenham (1984: 300)

regard to parenthood. It was already conspicuous in the third year (mean age 13.9) and became even more so at the sixth-form level (mean age 16.9). Taken in conjunction these two studies serve to reinforce an incidental message from the enquiry reported in Chapter 5. This set out to study sex differences within the wider context of adoptees in search of their origins, but ended by highlighting women's more intense concern with personal relationships.

It is entirely possible that sex differences in attitude to parenthood may hold the key to the survival of the nuclear family. Although it might be said that the role of the father in child development has been unjustly neglected until recently (Lamb 1981), it remains true that the mother is normally the lynchpin of the family. And like it or not, many women are still brought up to expect that marriage and motherhood will be their major role in adult life. As Rapoport *et al* (1977) have pointed out, the *mater-familias* is often constantly available as a role model; daughters know what to expect from life, whereas sons may have only the vaguest idea of what their fathers do for a living. So although it is still possible for a son to follow in father's footsteps by becoming a butcher, a baker, or a candlestick maker, he ought to enjoy greater psychological freedom than his sister when the time comes to choose a career. A daughter on the other hand, provided that she enjoys a close relationship with her mother, may well find it harder to strike out on her own.[4] History will repeat itself, the wheel will come full circle, and by the time she is 30 (or probably a little older if she has all the makings of a promising career) she will have completed her family. Her first marriage may not last, but is there any reason to anticipate that the cycle will ever be reversed?

With this rhetorical question we end our disquisition on surrogate families. By the time our grand-daughter comes of age the era of the commune may have arrived for good, but we shall be too old to care. We cannot be wholly sanguine that the nuclear family will survive, nor even that in its present form it deserves to do so. As a social institution it undoubtedly has its faults, and children as well as parents would benefit from a more flourishing kinship network. If it *does* survive, we trust that this is because children really do need parents. And for our purposes a parent may be defined as a caring adult who is dedicated to the child's welfare, both immediately and in the long term. Where parents and children are genetically related, so much the better; where they are not, this is no reason why the reconstituted family should not still provide the foundations for healthy living.

Notes

PROLOGUE

1 Enshrined by the Institute of Community Studies, the source of such classical enquiries as Townsend (1957), and Young and Willmott (1957).

1 THE NUCLEAR FAMILY AS AN ENDANGERED SPECIES

1 A surprisingly high proportion of children born between 3rd and 9th March of that year have remained under surveillance to this day. In the process some of the earlier calculations have been revised, so that Ferri (1984: 129) gives the proportion of 7 year-olds living with both natural parents as 92 per cent – which is still quite impressive. At ages 11 and 16 the figures were 89 and 85 per cent respectively.
2 The parents would have been a whole generation younger than Sir Edmund, who wrote: 'In our runaway world, no one much over the age of 45 is really fit to teach anybody anything. And that includes me. I am 57. It is hard to accept but that's just the point.' (Leach 1968: 74)
3 For the sake of continuity in her career she had made do with annual leave in place of maternity leave.
4 A full discussion of varying cohabitation rates in different countries would need to take account of fiscal and other administrative considerations which are beyond the scope of this chapter.
5 This collaborative study was organized by CECOS (the Fédération des Centres d'Etude et de Conservation du Sperme Humain). The authors concede that the success rate of artificial insemination may differ from that of normal reproduction, but give no reasons for thinking so. Sexual arousal is a possible factor, although whether it can increase the chances of conception remains unclear.

2 FOSTER CARE

1 The original Adoption Act of 1926 had been introduced twenty years earlier.
2 Such posts were created in response to the Seebohm Committee (1968), which advocated a more generic style of social work. Fostering

and adoption have tended to remain a specialized branch of the social services, and they are often combined within the same unit.

3 Gordon Trasler is now firmly accepted as a psychologist, but graduated in sociology and economics immediately before embarking on his doctoral research.

4 This can happen in adoption too, although placements of this nature are more readily avoided with adoptive families. Conception within the first year of adoption or foster placement could have the same effect, but the adopted child's reputation as a fertility charm is exaggerated if not wholly undeserved (Humphrey 1969).

5 Space does not allow detailed discussion of these predominantly successful placements. Three times as many children were still in touch with their parents, who were apt to feel excluded although there was no question of permanent transfer. Social workers rated these homes highly and were understandably inclined to let events take their course.

6 The National Foster Care Association was set up in 1974 to monitor existing practices and to press for improvements of this nature.

7 They are not completely silent. Thus Wolff (1981: 255), a distinguished child psychiatrist, has written as follows: 'Foster children are always emotionally disturbed to a greater or lesser degree, and fostering itself must be looked on as a therapeutic undertaking.'

3 ADOPTION (1): INHERENT STRESSES

1 There were two families where both adopted boys attended.

2 This proportion of 27 per cent corresponds closely to the proportion of all out-patients admitted during the study (30 per cent).

3 Other published studies are based on considerably smaller numbers.

4 On the other hand Kirk, Jonassohn, and Fish (1966) have reminded us that some figures may be inflated by the inclusion of children not legally adopted. Thus one worker contributing to their own study defined as adopted 'anyone not born into the family'.

5 Recent leaflets for adoptive parents have happily struck a more realistic note.

6 This has led to a blurring of the boundaries between adoption and fostering, as noted in chapter 2.

7 None of the biological fathers were known to have a psychiatric hospital record, although a degree of assortative mating could not be ruled out.

8 A history of freedom from crime over the past five years only was stipulated.

9 At the time this chapter was completed, Jeremy Bamber, aged 25, was found guilty of murdering his adoptive parents, his older sister (also adopted), and her twin sons. The offspring of a city accountant

and a future nurse, he was placed by an adoption society in early infancy. There is some evidence that he had rejected his adoptive father, a man of high principles, but no grounds for questioning his natural background. Had his plan succeeded he would have stood to inherit almost half a million pounds, and perhaps been able to draw on inherited skills. However, the typical accountant is supposed to be obsessional rather than psychopathic.

10 Since this chapter was completed our attention has been drawn to a pioneering study of adoptees and their half-siblings by Schiff and Lewontin (1986). The authors argue fiercely for a non-genetic interpretation of their data, and their book is sympathetically reviewed by Rutter (1987). However, as the age-range of the adoptees was 6–13 it would appear that the findings do not seriously challenge Scarr and Weinberg's conclusion.

11 The exclusion of children with severe congenital handicap (for example, birth injury, Down's syndrome) from an adopted group would inflate the mean IQ by only one or two points. Munsinger (1975) has argued that the prompt release of children for adoption by the more intelligent mothers might be expected to introduce a more perceptible bias in the same direction, and for obvious reasons early placement has been the norm in most nature-nurture studies of adoptive families.

4 ADOPTION (2): THE NEED FOR IDENTITY

1 We have been unable to obtain a copy of Paton's book and must therefore rely on this secondary source. We do not know whether she is still alive, but if so she would be in her eighties.

2 Private adoptions have since been outlawed by the 1975 Children Act, although there has never been any satisfactory evidence that they work out less favourably. Prior to the Act agency adoptions accounted for about 85 per cent.

3 The Act proposed that in such circumstances the child's interests would often be better served by some form of guardianship, aimed at conferring a measure of legal security without excluding the other natural parent (usually the father) or other members of the original family. The Masson, Norbury, and Chatterton study was commissioned by the DHSS to monitor the effects on step-parent adoption of changes brought about by the Act. The authors reported wide variation in the practices of different courts, but we have come across no evidence of the extent to which guardianship is being offered instead of adoption.

4 We are grateful to Brian Southam of Athlone Press for this suggestion.

6 STEP-PARENTHOOD

1 Even older children who have flown the nest can be slow to accept a newly acquired step-parent. By a curious coincidence, two secretaries who offered to put this chapter through a word processor were each in this situation and confessed to a strong antipathy towards their stepmother.

2 She cites only Bowerman and Irish (1962). A much more recent British study (Ferri 1984) found that step-family relationships were easier after bereavement, but the evidence was far from conclusive.

3 An equally important study by Hetherington, Cox, and Cox (1982) in Virginia has been excluded from consideration here because it was mainly concerned with the more immediate consequences of divorce, that is, during the first two years when step-families were less likely to be formed. In the event three-quarters of the divorced parents in this study remarried within six years, and a separate report on these re-constituted families was promised. However, at the time of writing we could find no detailed reference to this.

4 There was no information on alimony payments, but family size was well above average with almost 20 per cent of stepchildren having five or more siblings (Ferri 1984, Table A 3.22).

5 For an extension of the Californian study see Wallerstein (1983; 1985).

6 Adapted from a short story published in *The Ballroom of Romance* (Trevor 1972).

7 In contrast, custodial fathers have also been known to discover nurturant qualities that had lain dormant, with marked benefit to their relationships with their children.

7 PARENTHOOD BY DONOR INSEMINATION

1 MacLennan v MacLennan 1958, S.C. 105.

2 There is an obvious parallel with adoption.

3 Fostering and adoption were mentioned in the questionnaire but no data were reported.

4 This is a technique for visualizing the ovaries and fallopian tubes through an illuminated telescope inserted in the abdomen.

5 Even the sterile husband can readily engage in make-believe, as was brought home to us when a man whose absence of sperm had been diagnosed in a previous marriage could recognize his own features in the child just born to his second wife. Almost in the same breath he added, 'Brilliant matching of the donor!'

6 The use of frozen sperm was in no way associated with inferior

development, but there were only nine children in this category. Donors were all medical students.

7 Members of the National Association for the Childless can reap some of these benefits without having to confide in their nearest and dearest.

8 We are not told whether this was effective, merely that the parents' honesty was then extended to the older son.

9 A young homosexual woman without a current partner was referred for counselling but needed gynaecological treatment before she could be seen, and we have not heard from her again.

8 NEW TRENDS IN HUMAN REPRODUCTION

1 This is not the most elegant term imaginable but has some advantages over IVF, which has led to the notion of test-tube babies. In practice a glass dish rather than a test-tube is used to achieve fertilization.

2 Direct comparison is made harder by alternative approaches to the calculation of successful IVF. Singer and Wells (1984: 24) quote a pregnancy-per-laparoscopy rate of 15−25 per cent, which is much lower than the conservative estimate of 50−60 per cent quoted in the previous chapter for DI.

3 Equally, the argument that a woman should be persuaded to carry her unwanted child to term with a view to adoption rather than be offered an abortion, seems to have been little used even by the most ardent pro-life campaigners.

4 Since this chapter was written the case of baby M has received enormous publicity. Here the host mother's right of access was suspended by a stern judge whose own four children were possibly a blessing to be taken for granted. The commissioning couple were both aged 41, he a biochemist seemingly obsessed with the urge to perpetuate his name, she a paediatrician who had put off motherhood in order to qualify and then found that she was suffering from a mild form of mutliple sclerosis − scarcely the ideal basis for adopting a child that was genetically her husband's yet brought into the world by another woman.

5 A unique case has since been reported in the national press. A woman who had been sterilized in her first marriage went to Patrick Steptoe for help in conceiving by her second husband. IVF was used to produce several embryos, one of which was implanted immediately whilst the rest were frozen. Some nine months after the birth of a healthy daughter one of the frozen embryos was successfully thawed then implanted to produce a second daughter. The children are thus eighteen months apart in age, and though simultaneously conceived are no more alike than dizygotic twins.

6 Couples seen prior to DI seem to welcome the prospect of twins as a

possible consequence of the use of fertility drugs, and the same may apply to IVF couples offered the choice between one or more than one embryo for implantation.

9 EPILOGUE: WILL THE NUCLEAR FAMILY SURVIVE?

1 One such is *rejectors*, who avoid parenthood on account of its many negative aspects, and *aficionados*, who do so because of a preference for investing their time and energy in other pursuits (Veevers 1980).

2 This should not be attempted too soon. We well recall a friendly cricket match in which a 2-year-old visiting our own family refused to be given out leg-before-wicket. A neighbour acting as umpire subsequently lamented the 'lack of discipline in today's young people'!

3 In practice this would hardly arise for a stepmother, who cannot expect to bestow her surname on a man's child. What is not generally appreciated is that, on a strict interpretation, the step-relationship ends with the marriage that gave rise to it. Thus step-parents who are divorced or widowed can remain in touch with their stepchildren only by invitation.

4 For a psychoanalytic account of parent–child relationships as a basis for woman's drive towards mothering see Chodorow (1978).

References

Adamson, G. (1973) *The Care-Takers*, London: Bookstall Publications.

Addis, R.S., Salzberger, F., and Rabl, E. (1954) *A Survey Based on Adoption Case Records*, London: National Association for Mental Health.

Anderson, J.Z. and White, G.D. (1986) 'Dysfunctional intact families and step families', *Family Process* 25: 407–22.

Archbishop of Canterbury (1948) *Report of a Commission Appointed by His Grace the Archbishop of Canterbury. Artificial Human Insemination*, London: SPCK.

Bane, M.J. (1976) 'Marital disruption and the lives of children', *Journal of Social Issues* 32: 103–17.

Banks, A.L. (1968) 'Aspects of adoption and artificial insemination', in S.J. Behrman and R.W. Kistner (eds) *Progress in Infertility*, Boston Mass: Little-Brown.

Barton, M., Walker, K., and Weisner, B.P. (1945) 'Artificial insemination', *British Medical Journal* i: 40–3.

Baum, F. and Cope, D.R. (1980) 'Some characteristics of intentionally childless wives in Britain', *Journal of Biosocial Science* 16: 501–9.

Bentovim, A. (1980) 'Psychiatric issues', in M. Adcock and R. White (eds) *Terminating Parental Contact: An Exploration of the Issues Relating to Children in Care*, London: Association of British Adoption and Fostering Agencies.

Berger, D.M. (1980) 'Couples' reactions to male infertility and donor insemination', *American Journal of Psychiatry* 137: 1047–9.

Bernard, J. (1971) *Remarriage: A Study of Marriage* (2nd edn), New York: Russell & Russell.

—— (1976) *The Future of Marriage*, Harmondsworth: Penguin.

Birtchnell, J. (1985) 'The relationship between scores on Ryle's Marital Patterns Test and independent ratings of marital quality', *British Journal of Psychiatry* 146: 638–44.

Black, D. (1982) 'Custody and access: a literary lesson', *Journal of Family Therapy* 4: 247–56.

Bohman, M. (1970) *Adopted Children and Their Families: A Follow-up Study of Adopted Children, Their Background, Environment, and Adjustment*. Stockholm: Proprius.

—— (1971) 'A comparative study of adopted children, foster children, and children in their biological environment born after undesired pregnancies', *Acta Paediatrica Scandinavica* Supplement 221.

—— (1978) 'Some genetic aspects of alcoholism and criminality',

Archives of General Psychiatry 35: 269—76.

Bohman, M. and von Knorring, A.L. (1979) 'Psychiatric illness among adults adopted as infants', *Acta Psychiatrica Scandinavica* 60: 106—12.

Bowerman, C.E. and Irish, D.P. (1962) 'Some relationships of stepchildren to their parents', *Marriage and Family Living* 24: 113—21.

Bowlby, J. (1951) *Maternal Care and Mental Health*, Geneva: WHO.

Brandon, J. and Warner, J. (1977) 'AID and adoption: some comparisons', *British Journal of Social Work* 7: 335—42.

Bratfos, O., Eitinger, L., and Tau, T. (1968) 'Mental illness and crime in adopted children and adoptive parents', *Acta Psychiatrica Scandinavica* 44: 376—84.

British Medical Association (1983) 'Interim report on human *in vitro* fertilization and embryo replacement and transfer', *British Medical Journal* 286: 1594—5.

Bumpass, L. and Rindfuss, R. (1978) *Children's Experience of Marital Disruption*, University of Wisconsin, Madison: Institute for Research on Poverty.

Burgoyne, J. and Clark, D. (1982) 'Reconstituted families', in R.N. Rapoport, M.P. Fogarty, and R. Rapoport (eds) *Families in Britain*, London: Routledge & Kegan Paul.

——— (1984) *Making a Go of it: A Study of Step-Families in Sheffield*, London: Routledge & Kegan Paul.

Cadoret, R.J. and Gath, A. (1978) 'Inheritance of alcoholism in adoptees', *British Journal of Psychiatry* 132: 252—8.

Cadoret, R.J., Cain, C.A., and Grove, W.M. (1980) 'Development of alcoholism in adoptees raised apart from alcoholic biological relatives', *Archives of General Psychiatry* 37: 561—3.

Camberwell Council on Alcoholism (1980) *Women and Alcohol*, London: Tavistock.

Campbell, E. (1985) *The Childless Marriage: An Exploratory Study of Couples Who Do Not Want Children*, London: Tavistock.

Chester, R. (1985) 'The rise of the neo-conventional family', *New Society* 72: 185—8.

Chodorow, N. (1978) *The Reproduction of Mothering: Psychoanalysis and the Sociology of Gender*, Berkeley: University of California Press.

Clarke, A.D.B. (1968) 'Learning and human development', *British Journal of Psychiatry* 114: 1061—77.

Clarke, A.M. and Clarke, A.D.B. (eds) (1976) *Early Experience: Myth and Evidence*, London: Open Books.

Clingempeel, W.G., Ievoli, R., and Brand, E. (1984) 'Structural complexity and the quality of stepfather-stepchild relationships', *Family Process* 23: 547—59.

Cobb, J.P. (ed.) (1980) *Babyshock: A Mother's First Five Years*, London: Hutchinson.

Coleman, J.C. (1980) *The Nature of Adolescence*, London: Methuen.

Coleman, J.C., Herzberg, J., and Morris, M. (1977) 'Identity in adolescence: present and future self-concepts', *Journal of Youth and Adolescence* 6: 63–75.

Connolly, K.J., Edelmann, R.J., and Cooke, I.D. (1987) 'Distress and marital problems associated with infertility', *Journal of Reproductive and Infant Psychology* 5: 49–57.

Cooper, D.G. (1970) *The Death of the Family*, New York: Pantheon.

Cotton, K. and Winn, D. (1985) *Baby Cotton: For Love and Money*, London: Dorling Kindersley.

Crowe, R.R. (1974) 'An adoption study of antisocial personality', *Archives of General Psychiatry* 31: 785–91.

—— (1975) 'Adoption studies in psychiatry', *Biological Psychiatry* 10: 353–71.

Cunningham, L., Cadoret, R.J., Loftus, L., and Edwards, J.E. (1975) 'Studies of adoptees from psychiatrically disturbed biological parents: psychiatric conditions in childhood and adolescence', *British Journal of Psychiatry* 126: 534–49.

Curtis Report (1946) *Report of the Care of Children Committee*, London: HMSO.

Day, C. and Leeding, A. (1980) *Access to Birth Records*, London: The Association of British Adoption and Fostering Agencies (ABAFA).

Department of Health and Social Security (1976) *Guide to Fostering Practice*, London: HMSO.

Dixon, R.E. and Buttram, V.C. (1976) 'Artificial insemination using donor semen: a review of 171 cases', *Fertility and Sterility* 27: 130–4.

Dobson, F. and Mathieson, D. (1986) 'Infertility services in the NHS: what's going on?' A report prepared for Frank Dobson, MP, Shadow Health Minister. Unpublished but obtainable from House of Commons.

Douvan, E. and Adelson, J. (1966) *The Adolescent Experience*, New York: Wiley.

Duberman, L. (1973) 'Step-kin relationships', *Journal of Marriage and the Family* 35: 283–92.

—— (1975) *The Reconstituted Family*, Chicago: Nelson Hall.

du Maurier, D. (1938) *Rebecca*, London: Gollancz.

Dunnell, K. (1979) *Family Formation 1976: A Survey Carried Out on Behalf of the OPCS*, London: HMSO.

Edelmann, R.J. and Connolly, K.J. (1986) 'Psychological aspects of infertility', *British Journal of Medical Psychology* 59: 209–19.

Edwards, R.G. (1982) 'The case for studying human embryos and their constituent tissues *in vitro*', in R.G. Edwards and J.M. Purdy (eds) *Human Conception In Vitro*, London: Academic Press.

Edwards, R.G. and Purdy, J.M. (1982) *Human Conception In Vitro*, London: Academic Press.

Edwards, R.G. and Steptoe, P.C. (1980) *A Matter of Life*, London: Hutchinson.

Edwards, R.G., Bavister, B.D., and Steptoe, P.C. (1969) 'Early stages of fertilization *in vitro* of human oocytes matured *in vitro*', *Nature* 211: 632–5.

Elliott, S.A. and Watson, J.P. (1985) 'Sex during pregnancy and the first postnatal year', *Journal of Psychosomatic Research* 29: 541–8.

Erikson, E. (1963) *Childhood and Society* (rev. edn), New York: Norton.

———— (1968) *Identity, Youth, and Crisis*, New York: Norton.

Etzioni, A. (1968) 'Sex control, science, and society', *Science* 161: 1107–12.

Eysenck, H.J. (1967) *The Biological Basis of Personality*, Springfield, Illinois: Thomas.

Eysenck, H.J. and Eysenck, S.B.G. (1964) *Manual of the Eysenck Personality Inventory*, London: Hodder & Stoughton.

———— (1975) *Manual of the Eysenck Personality Questionnaire*, London: Hodder & Stoughton.

Eysenck, S.B.G. (1961) 'Personality and pain assessment in childbirth of married and unmarried mothers', *Journal of Mental Science* 107: 417–30.

Fanshel, D. and Shinn, E.B. (1978) *Children in Foster Care: A Longitudinal Investigation*, New York: Columbia University Press.

Ferguson, T. (1966) *Children in Care – and After*, London: Oxford University Press.

Ferri, E. (1976) *Growing Up in a One-Parent Family: A Long-Term Study of Child Development*, Windsor: National Foundation for Educational Research.

———— (1984) *Stepchildren: A National Study*, Windsor: NFER-Nelson.

Feversham Committee (1960) *Report of the Departmental Committee on Human Artificial Insemination*, London: HMSO.

Finer Committee (1974) *Report of the Committee on One-Parent Families* (2 vols), London: HMSO.

Firestone, S. (1971) *The Dialectic of Sex*, New York: Bantam.

Fisher, F. (1973) *The Search for Anna Fisher*, Greenwich, Conn.: Fawcett.

Fletcher, R. (1966) *The Family and Marriage in Britain: An Analysis and Moral Assessment*, Harmondsworth: Penguin.

Fogarty, M., Rapoport, R., and Rapoport, R.N. (1971) *Sex, Career, and Family*, London: Allen & Unwin.

Garnett, A. (1984) *Deceived with Kindness: A Bloomsbury Childhood*, London: Chatto & Windus.

Gavron, H. (1966) *The Captive Wife: Conflicts of Housebound Mothers*, London: Routledge & Kegan Paul.

George, V. (1970) *Foster Care: Theory and Practice*, London: Routledge & Kegan Paul.

George, V. and Wilding, P. (1972) *Motherless Families*, London: Routledge & Kegan Paul.

Goldstein, J., Freud, A., and Solnit, A. (1973) *Beyond the Best Interests of the Child*, New York: Free Press.

Golombok, S., Spencer, A., and Rutter, M. (1983) 'Children in lesbian and single-parent households: psychiatric and psychosexual appraisal', *Journal of Child Psychology and Psychiatry* 24: 551–72.

Goodacre, I. (1966) *Adoption Policy and Practice*, London: Allen & Unwin.

Goodman, J.D., Silberstein, R.M., and Mandell, W. (1963) 'Adopted children brought to child psychiatric clinic', *Archives of General Psychiatry* 9: 451–6.

Goodwin, D.W., Schulsinger, F., Hermansen, L., Guze, S.B., and Winokur, G. (1973) 'Alcohol problems in adoptees raised apart from alcoholic biological parents', *Archives of General Psychiatry* 28: 238–43.

—— (1975) 'Alcoholism and the hyperactive child syndrome', *Journal of Nervous and Mental Disease* 160: 349–53.

Goodwin, D.W., Schulsinger, F., Moller, N., Hermansen, L., Winokur, G., and Guze S.B. (1974) 'Drinking problems in adopted and non-adopted sons of alcoholics', *Archives of General Psychiatry* 31: 164–9.

Goody, E.N. (1971) 'Forms of pro-parenthood: the sharing and substitution of parental roles', in J. Goody (ed.) *Kinship: Selected Readings*, Harmondsworth: Penguin.

Gray, P.G. and Parr, E.A. (1957) *Children in Care and the Recruitment of Foster Parents*, London: Social Survey.

Grey, E. and Blunden, R.M. (1971) 'A survey of adoption in Great Britain', *Home Office Research Studies* 10, London: HMSO.

Group for the Advancement of Psychiatry (1973) *Joys and Sorrows of Parenthood*, New York: Scribner.

Gunderson, E.K. (1956) 'Body size, self-evaluation, and military effectiveness', *Journal of Personality and Social Psychology* 2: 902–6.

Haimes, E.V. and Timms, N.W. (1983) 'Access to birth records and counselling of adopted persons under Section 26 of the Children Act 1975', Final Report to the DHSS (unpublished).

—— (1985) *Adoption, Identity and Social Policy: The Search for Distant Relatives*, Aldershot: Gower.

Hard, A.D. (1909a) 'Artificial impregnation', *Medical World* 27: 163.

—— (1909b) 'Letters', *Medical World* 27: 306.

Harris, C. (1983) *The Family and Industrial Society*, London: Allen & Unwin.

Haskey, J. (1982) 'The proportion of marriages ending in divorce', *OPCS Population Trends* 27, London: HMSO.

—— (1983a) 'Children of divorcing couples', *OPCS Population Trends* 31, London: HMSO.

—— (1983b) 'Marital status before marriage and age at marriage: their influence on the chance of divorce', *OPCS Population Trends* 32, London: HMSO.

Hazel, N. (1980) 'Normalization or segregation in the care of adolescents', in J. Triseliotis (ed.) *New Developments in Foster Care and Adoption*, London: Routledge & Kegan Paul.

—— (1981) *A Bridge to Independence*, Oxford: Blackwell.

Heim, A. (1983) *Thicker than Water? Adoption: Its Loyalties, Pitfalls, and Joys*, London: Secker & Warburg.

Hersov. L. (1985) 'Adoption and fostering', in M. Rutter and L. Hersov (eds) *Child and Adolescent Psychiatry: Modern Approaches* (2nd edn), Oxford: Blackwell.

Heston, L.L. (1966) 'Psychiatric disorders in foster home reared children of schizophrenic mothers', *British Journal of Psychiatry* 112: 819–25.

Heston, L.L. and Denney, D.D. (1968) 'Interactions between early life experience and biological factors in schizophrenia', in D. Rosenthal and S.S. Kety (eds) *The Transmission of Schizophrenia*, Oxford: Pergamon.

Hetherington, E.M., Cox, M., and Cox, R. (1982) 'Effects of divorce on parents and children', in M.E. Lamb (ed.) *Non-Traditional Families*, Hillside, NJ: Erlbaum.

Holman, R. (1973) *Trading in Children: A Study of Private Fostering*, London: Routledge & Kegan Paul.

—— (1980) 'Exclusive and inclusive concepts of fostering', in J. Triseliotis (ed.) *New Developments in Foster Care and Adoption*, London: Routledge & Kegan Paul.

Holmes, H.B., Hoskins, B.B., and Gross, M. (eds) (1981) *The Custom-Made Child*, Clifton, NJ: Humana Press.

Horn, J.M. (1983) 'The Texas adoption project: adopted children and their intellectual resemblance to biological and adoptive parents', *Child Development* 54: 268–75.

Houghton Committee (1972) *Report of the Departmental Committee on the Adoption of Children*, London: HMSO.

Hull, M.G.R. *et al.* (1985) 'Population study of causes, treatment, and outcome of infertility', *British Medical Journal* 291: 1693–7.

Humphrey, M. (1969) *The Hostage Seekers: A Study of Childless and Adopting Couples*, London: Longman.

—— (1973a) 'The adopted child at school', in V.P. Varma (ed.) *Stresses in Children*, London: London University Press.

—— (1973b) 'Childless marriage as a basis for adoptive parenthood', Unpublished Ph.D. thesis: University of London.

—— (1975) 'The effect of children upon the marriage relationship', *British Journal of Medical Psychology* 48: 273–9.

—— (1977) 'Sex differences in attitude to parenthood', *Human Relations* 30: 737–49.

—— (1984) 'Are criminal tendencies inherited?', *Adoption and Fostering* 8(4): 42–3.

—— (1986) 'Infertility as a marital crisis', *Stress Medicine* 2: 221–4.

—— (in press) 'Voluntary childlessness: the problem of long-range prediction', in H.G. Moors and J.J. Schoorl (eds) *Proceedings of Workshop on Lifestyle, Contraception, and Parenthood*, Amsterdam: September 1986.

Humphrey, M. and Humphrey, H. (1986) 'A fresh look at genealogical bewilderment', *British Journal of Medical Psychology* 59: 133–40.

—— (1987) 'Marital relationships in couples seeking donor insemination', *Journal of Biosocial Science* 19: 209–19.

———— (in press) 'Infertility', in T.P. Burns and J.H. Lacey (eds) *The Psychological Management of the Physically Ill*, Edinburgh: Churchill-Livingstone.

Humphrey, M. and Lenham, C. (1984) 'Adolescent fantasy and self-fulfilment: the problem of female passivity', *Journal of Adolescence* 7: 295–304.

Humphrey, M. and Mackenzie, K.M. (1967) 'Infertility and adoption: follow-up of 216 couples attending a hospital clinic', *British Journal of Preventive and Social Medicine* 21: 90–6.

Humphrey, M. and Ounsted, C. (1963) 'Adoptive families referred for psychiatric advice: (I) The children', *British Journal of Psychiatry* 109: 599–608.

———— (1964) 'Adoptive families referred for psychiatric advice: (II) The parents', *British Journal of Psychiatry* 110: 549–55.

Hurst Committee (1954) *Report of the Departmental Committee on the Adoption of Children*, London: HMSO.

Hutchings, B. and Mednick, S.A. (1975) 'Registered criminality in the adoptive and biological parents of registered male criminal adoptees', in R.R. Fieve, H. Brill, and D. Rosenthal (eds) *Genetic Research in Psychiatry*, Baltimore: Johns Hopkins University Press.

Hutchinson, D. (1943) *In Quest of Foster Parents*, New York: Columbia University Press.

Huxley, A. (1932) *Brave New World*, London: Chatto & Windus.

Iizuka, R., Sawada, Y., Nishina, N. and Ohi, M. (1968) 'The physical and mental development of children born following artificial insemination', *International Journal of Fertility* 13: 24–32.

Ineichen, B. (1977) 'Youthful marriage: the vortex of disadvantage', in J. Peel and R. Chester (eds) *Equalities and Inequalities in Family Life*, London: Academic Press.

Jackson, B. (1983) *Fatherhood*, London: Allen & Unwin.

Jackson, L. (1968) 'Unsuccessful adoptions: a study of forty cases who attended a child guidance clinic', *British Journal of Medical Psychology* 41: 389–98.

Jackson, M. (1976) in M. Brudenell, A. McLaren, R. Short, and M. Symonds (eds) *Proceedings of the Fourth Study Group of the Royal College of Obstetricians and Gynaecologists*, London: Royal College of Obstetricians and Gynaecologists.

Jaffee, B. and Fanshel, D. (1970) *How they Fared in Adoption: A Follow-up Study*, New York: Columbia University Press.

James, P.D. (1980) *Innocent Blood*, London: Faber & Faber.

Jenkins, R. (1965) 'The needs of foster parents', *Case Conference* 11: 211–19.

Jensen, A.R. (1969) 'How much can we boost IQ and scholastic achievement?', *Harvard Educational Review* 39: 1–123.

Johnson, G. *et al.* (1987) 'Infertile or childless by choice? A multipractice survey of women aged 35 and 50', *British Medical Journal* 294: 804–6.

Jourard, S.M. and Secord, P.F. (1955) 'Body-cathexis and the ideal female figure', *Journal of Abnormal and Social Psychology* 50: 243–6.

Joyce, D.N. (1984) 'The implications of greater openness concerning AID', in *AID and After*, London: Association of British Adoption and Fostering Agencies.

Kadushin, A. (1966) 'Adoptive parenthood: a hazardous adventure?', *Social Work* 11: 30–9.

—— (1970) *Adopting Older Children*, New York: Columbia University Press.

Kalter, N. (1977) 'Children of divorce in an out-patient psychiatric population', *American Journal of Orthopsychiatry* 47: 40–51.

Kamin, L.J. (1974) *The Science and Politics of IQ*, Hillsdale, NJ: Erlbaum.

—— (1981) 'Studies of adopted children', in H.J. Eysenck versus Leon Kamin *Intelligence: The Battle for the Mind*, London: Pan Books.

Karlsson, J.L. (1970) 'The rate of schizophrenia in foster-reared close relatives of schizophrenic index cases', *Biological Psychiatry* 2: 285–90.

Keane, N. and Breo, D. (1981) *The Surrogate Mother*, New York: Everett House.

Kety, S.S., Rosenthal, D., Wender, P.H., and Schulsinger, F. (1968) 'The types and prevalence of mental illness in the biological and adopted families of adopted schizophrenics', in D. Rosenthal and S.S. Kety (eds) *The Transmission of Schizophrenia*, Oxford: Pergamon.

—— (1971) 'Mental illness in the biological and adoptive families of adopted schizophrenics', *American Journal of Psychiatry* 128: 302–6.

Kiernan, K. (1983) 'The structure of families today: continuity or change?', *OPCS Occasional Paper* 31, London: OPCS.

Kirk, H.D. (1964) *Shared Fate: A Theory of Adoption and Mental Health*, Toronto: Collier-Macmillan.

Kirk, H.D., Jonassohn, K., and Fish, R.D. (1966) 'Are adopted children especially vulnerable to stress?', *Archives of General Psychiatry* 14: 291–8.

Kumar, R., Brant, H.A., and Robson, K.M. (1981) 'Childbearing and maternal sexuality: a prospective survey of 119 primiparae', *Journal of Psychosomatic Research* 25: 373–83.

Lamb, M.E. (ed.) (1981) *The Role of the Father in Child Development* (rev. edn), New York: Wiley.

Lambert, L. and Streather, J. (1980) *Children in Changing Families: A Study of Adoption and Illegitimacy*, London: Macmillan.

Lasch, C. (1979) *The Culture of Narcissism: American Life in an Age of Diminishing Expectations*, New York: Norton.

Laslett, P. (1972) *Family and Household in Past Time*, Harmondsworth: Penguin.

—— (1977) *Family Life and Illicit Love in Earlier Generations*, Cambridge: Cambridge University Press.

Leach, E. (1968) 'A Runaway World?', *The Reith Lectures 1967*, London: BBC.

Leahy, A.M. (1935) 'Nature, nurture, and intelligence', *Genetic Psychology Monographs* 17; 237–307.

Le Lannon, D., Lobel, B., and Chambon, Y. (1980) 'Sperm banks and donor recruitment in France', in G. David and W.S. Price (eds) *Human Artificial Insemination and Semen Preservation*, New York: Plenum.

Leete, R. and Anthony, S. (1979) 'Divorce and remarriage: a record linkage study', *Population Trends* 16, London: HMSO.

Leitch, D. (1973) *God Stand Up for Bastards*, London: Heinemann.

—— (1984) *Family Secrets*, London: Heinemann.

Levine, J.A. (1976) *Who Will Raise the Children? New Options for Fathers (and Mothers)*, New York: Lippincott.

Lupri, E. and Frideres, J. (1981) 'The quality of marriage and the passage of time: marital satisfactions over the family life cycle', *Canadian Journal of Sociology* 6: 283–305.

McDermott, J.F. (1970) 'Divorce and its psychiatric sequelae in children', *Archives of General Psychiatry* 23: 421–7.

McWhinnie, A.M. (1967) *Adopted Children, How They Grow Up: A Study of Their Adjustment as Adults*, London: Routledge & Kegan Paul.

—— (1984) 'The case for greater openness concerning AID', in *AID and After*, London: Association of British Adoption and Fostering Agencies.

Maddox, B. (1975) *The Half-Parent*, New York: Evans. Republished (1980) *Step-Parenting: How to Live with Other People's Children*, London: Allen & Unwin.

Marcia, J.E. (1980) 'Identity in adolescence', in J. Adelson (ed.) *Handbook of Adolescent Psychology*, New York: Wiley.

Marsden, D. (1969) *Mothers Alone*, London: Allen Lane.

Masson, J., Norbury, D., and Chatterton, S.G. (1983) *Mine, Yours, or Ours? A Study of Step-Parent Adoption*, London: HMSO.

Mead, G.H. (1934) *Mind, Self, and Society: From the Standpoint of a Social Behaviourist*, Chicago: Chicago University Press.

Mednick, S.A., Gabrielli, W.F., and Hutchings, B. (1984) 'Genetic influences in criminal convictions: evidence from an adoption cohort', *Science* 224: 891–4.

Menlove, F.L. (1965) 'Aggressive symptoms in emotionally disturbed adopted children', *Child Development* 36: 519–32.

Minuchin, S. (1974) *Families and Family Therapy*, Cambridge, Mass: Harvard University Press.

Mitchell, A. (1985) *Children in the Middle: Living Through Divorce*, London: Tavistock.

Mittler, P. (1971) *The Study of Twins*, Harmondsworth: Penguin.

Monckton Committee (1945) *Report on the Circumstances Which Led to the Boarding-Out of Dennis and Terence O'Neill at Bank Farm, Minsterley, and the Steps Taken to Supervise Their Welfare*, London: HMSO.

Morris, P. (1965) *Prisoners and Their Families*, London: Allen & Unwin.

Munsinger, H. (1975) 'The adopted child's IQ: a critical review',

Psychological Bulletin 82: 623–59.

Murdock, G.P. (1949) *Social Structure*, New York: MacMillan.

Murphy, M.J. (1984) 'Fertility, birth timing, and marital breakdown: a reinterpretation of the evidence', *Journal of Biosocial Science* 16: 487–500.

Nabokov, V. (1955) *Lolita*, Paris: Olympia.

Napier. H. (1972) 'Success and failure in foster care', *British Journal of Social Work* 2: 187–204.

Nicholas, M.K. and Tyler, J.P.P. (1983) 'Characteristics, attitudes, and personalities of AI donors', *Clinical Reproduction and Fertility* 2: 47–54.

Oakley, A. (1974) *Housewife*, London: Allen Lane.

Office of Population Census and Surveys (1983) *Marriage and Divorce Statistics (Annually from 1974)*, London: HMSO.

Offord, D.R., Aponte, J.F., and Cross, L.A. (1969) 'Presenting symptomatology of adopted children', *Archives of General Psychiatry* 20: 110–16.

Ounsted, C. (1955) 'The hyperkinetic syndrome in epileptic children', *Lancet* ii: 303–11.

Parker, R.A. (1966) *Decision in Child Care: A Study of Prediction in Fostering*, London: Allen & Unwin.

Parsons, T. (1949) 'The social structure of the family', in R.N. Anshen (ed.) *The Family: Its Function and Destiny*, New York: Harper & Row.

Parsons, T. and Bales, R.F. (1955) *Family, Socialization, and Interaction Process*, Chicago: Chicago Free Press.

Paton, J.M. (1954) *The Adopted Break Silence*, Acton, Calif.: Life History Study Center.

Peck, E. (1973) *The Baby Trap*, London: Hanau.

Peel, J. (1973) 'Report of the panel on human artificial insemination (Peel Report)', *British Medical Journal* ii: suppl. appendix V: 3.

Picton, C. (1982) 'Adoptees in search of origins', *Adoption and Fostering* 6(2): 49–52.

Pringle, M.L.K. (1961) 'The incidence of some supposedly adverse family conditions and of left-handedness in schools for maladjusted children', *British Journal of Educational Psychology* 31: 183–93.

—— (1967) *Adoption – Facts and Fallacies*, London: Longman.

Pringle, M.L.K. and Dinnage, R. (1967) *Foster Home Care: Facts and Fallacies*, London: Longman.

Pringle, M.L.K., Butler, N.R., and Davie, R. (1966) *11,000 7-Year-Olds. First Report of the National Child Development Study (1958 cohort)*, London: Longman.

Prosser, H. (1978) *Perspectives on Foster Care*, Windsor: NFER.

Rapoport, R. and Rapoport, R.N. (1971) *Dual-Career Families*, Harmondsworth: Penguin.

—— (1976) *Dual-Career Families Re-examined*, London: Martin Robertson.

Rapoport, R., Rapoport, R.N., and Strelitz, Z., with Kew, S. (1977)

Fathers, Mothers, and Others: Towards New Alliances, London: Routledge & Kegan Paul.

Raynor, L. (1980) *The Adopted Child Comes of Age*, London: Allen & Unwin.

Richards, M.P.M. and Dyson, M. (1982) *Separation, Divorce, and the Development of Children: A Review*, Cambridge: Child Care and Development Group.

Rimmer, L. (1981) *Families in Focus*, London: Study Commission on the Family.

Robinson, M. (1980) 'Stepfamilies: a reconstituted family system', *Journal of Family Therapy* 2: 45–69.

Rollins, B.C. and Cannon, K.L. (1974) 'Marital satisfaction over the family life cycle: a re-evaluation', *Journal of Marriage and the Family* 36: 271–82.

Rollins, B.C. and Feldman, H. (1970) 'Marital satisfaction over the family life cycle', *Journal of Marriage and the Family* 32: 20–8.

Roosevelt, R. and Lofas, J. (1976) *Living in Step*, New York: Stein & Day.

Rosenbaum, J. and Rosenbaum, V. (1977) *Step-Parenting*, Corte Madera, Calif: Chandler & Sharp.

Rosenberg, M. (1979) *Conceiving the Self*, New York: Basic Books.

Rosenthal, D., Wender, P.H., Kety, S.S., Welner, J., and Schulsinger, F. (1971) 'The adopted-away offspring of schizophrenics', in D. Rosenthal, and S.S. Kety (eds) *The Transmission of Schizophrenia*. Oxford: Pergamon.

Rosenthal, D., Wender, P.H., Kety, S.S., Schulsinger, F., Welner, J., and Ostergaard, L. (1968) 'Schizophrenics' offspring reared in adoptive homes', in D. Rosenthal and S.S. Kety (eds) *The Transmission of Schizophrenia*, Oxford: Pergamon.

Rowe, J. (1983) *Fostering in the Eighties*, London: Association of British Adoption and Fostering Agencies.

Rowe, J. and Lambert, L. (1973) *Children Who Wait: A Study of Children Needing Substitute Families*, London: Association of British Adoption Agencies.

Rowe, J., Cain, H., Hundleby, M., and Keane, A. (1984) *Long-Term Foster Care*, London: Batsford Academic.

Rowntree, G. and Carrier, N. (1958) 'The resort to divorce in England and Wales 1858–1957', *Population Studies* 11: 188–233.

Rutter, M. (1981) *Maternal Deprivation Reassessed* (2nd edn), Harmondsworth: Penguin.

——— (1982) 'Epidemiological-longitudinal approaches to the study of development', in W.A. Collins (ed.) *The Concept of Development (Minnesota Symposia on Child Psychology, vol. 15)*, Hillsdale, NJ: Erlbaum.

——— (1987) 'Review of Schiff and Lewontin (1986)', *Bulletin of the British Psychological Society* 40: 135.

Rutter, M., Tizard, J., and Whitmore, K. (1970) *Education, Health, and Behaviour*, London: Longman.

Rutter, M., Birch, H.G., Thomas, A., and Chess, S. (1964) 'Temperamental characteristics in infancy and the later development of behaviour disorders', *British Journal of Psychiatry* 110: 651–61.

Rutter, M., Graham, P., Chadwick, O., and Yule, W. (1976) 'Adolescent turmoil: fact or fiction?', *Journal of Child Psychology and Psychiatry* 17: 35–56.

Ryan, T. and Walker, R. (1985) *Making Life Story Books*, London: Association of British Adoption and Fostering Agencies.

Ryle, A. (1966) 'A marital patterns test for use in psychiatric research', *British Journal of Psychiatry* 112: 285–93.

Sandler, B. (1979) 'Artificial insemination by donor', in S. Wolkind (ed.) *Medical Aspects of Adoption and Foster Care*, London: Heinemann.

Sants, H.J. (1964) 'Genealogical bewilderment in children with substitute parents', *British Journal of Medical Psychology* 37: 133–41.

Satir, V. (1978) *Conjoint Family Therapy: A guide to Theory and Technique* (rev. edn), London: Souvenir Press.

Sawbridge, P. (1980) 'Seeking new parents: a decade of development', in J. Triseliotis (ed.) *New Developments in Foster Care and Adoption*, London: Routledge & Kegan Paul.

Scarr, S. (1969) 'Social introversion-extraversion as a heritable response', *Child Development* 40: 823–32.

Scarr, S. and Weinberg, R.A. (1978) 'The influence of "family background" on intellectual attainment', *American Sociological Review* 43: 674–92.

—— (1983) 'The Minnesota Adoption Studies: genetic differences and malleability', *Child Development* 54: 260–7.

Scarr, S., Webber, P.L., Weinberg, R.A., and Wittig, M.A. (1981) 'Personality resemblance among adolescents and their parents in biologically related and adoptive families', *Journal of Personality and Social Psychology* 40: 885–98.

Schaffer, H.R. and Emerson, P.E. (1964) 'The development of social attachments in infancy', *Monographs of the Society for Research in Child Development* 29: No.3.

Schaffer, H.R. and Schaffer, E.B. (1968) 'Child care and the family: a study of short-term admission to care', *Occasional Papers on Social Administration* 25, London: Bell.

Schechter, M.D. (1960) 'Observations on adopted children', *Archives of General Psychiatry* 3: 21–32.

Schechter, M.D., Carlson, P.V., Simmons, J.Q., and Work, H.H. (1964) 'Emotional problems in the adoptee', *Archives of General Psychiatry* 10: 109–18.

Schellen, A.M.C.M. (1957) *Artificial Insemination in the Human* (trans. A.M. Hollander), Amsterdam: Elsevier.

Schiff, M. and Lewontin, R. (1986) *Education and Class: The Irrelevance of IQ Genetic Studies*, Oxford: Clarendon Press.

Schroeder, H., Lightfoot, D., and Rees, S. (1985) 'Black applicants to Ealing recruitment campaign', *Adoption and Fostering* 9(2): 50–3.

Schuckit, M.A., Goodwin, D.W., and Winokur, G. (1972) 'A study of alcoholism in half siblings', *American Journal of Psychiatry* 128: 1132−6.

Schuckit. M., Rimmer, J., Reich, T., and Winokur, G. (1970) 'Alcoholism: antisocial traits in male alcoholics', *British Journal of Psychiatry* 117: 575−6.

Schulsinger, F. (1972) 'Psychopathy: heredity and environment', *International Journal of Mental Health* 1: 190−206.

Schwartz, D. and Mayaux, B.A. (1982) 'Female fecundity as a function of age: results of artificial insemination in 2193 nulliparous women with azoospermic husbands', *New England Journal of Medicine* 306: 404−6.

Seebohm Committee (1968) *Report of the Committee on Local Authority and Allied Personal Social Services*, London: HMSO.

Seglow, J., Pringle, M.L.K., and Wedge, P. (1972) *Growing Up Adopted: A Long-Term National Study of Adopted Children and Their Families*, Windsor: NFER.

Shaw, M. (1984) 'Growing up adopted', in P. Bean (ed.) *Adoption: Essays in Social Policy, Law, and Sociology*, London: Tavistock.

Shaw, M. and Hipgrave, T. (1983) *Specialist Fostering*, London: Batsford Academic.

Shields, J. (1973) 'Heredity and psychological abnormality', in H.J. Eysenck (ed.) *Handbook of Abnormal Psychology* (2nd edn.), London: Pitman.

Silverman, A. and Silverman, A. (1971) *The Case Against Having Children*, New York: McKay.

Simon, A.W. (1964) *Stepchild in the Family: A View of Children in Remarriage*, New York: Odyssey.

Simon, N.M. and Senturia, A.G. (1966) 'Adoption and psychiatric illness', *American Journal of Psychiatry* 122: 858−67.

Singer, P. and Wells, D. (1984) *The Reproduction Revolution: New Ways of Making Babies*, Melbourne: Oxford University Press.

Skinner, C. (1986) *Elusive Mr Right: The Social and Personal Context of a Young Woman's Use of Contraception*, London: Carolina Publications.

Skodak, M. and Skeels, H. (1949) 'A final follow-up of one hundred adopted children', *Journal of Genetic Psychology* 75: 85−125.

Snowden, R. and Mitchell, G.D. (1981) *The Artificial Family: A Consideration of Artificial Insemination by Donor*, London: Allen & Unwin.

Snowden, R. and Snowden, E. (1984) *The Gift of a Child*, London: Allen & Unwin.

Snowden, R., Mitchell, G.D., and Snowden, E.M. (1983) *Artificial Reproduction: A Social Investigation*, London: Allen & Unwin.

Sorosky, A.D., Baran, A., and Pannor, R. (1974) 'The reunion of adoptees and birth relatives', *Journal of Youth and Adolescence* 3: 195−206.

Spann, O. and Spann, N. (1977) *Your Child? I thought it was My Child!*, Pasadena, Calif.: Ward Ritchie.

Standing, L. and Mckelvie. S. (1986) 'Psychology journals: a case for treatment', *Bulletin of the British Psychological Society* 39: 445–50.

Stein, L.M. and Hoopes, J.L. (1985) *Identity Formation in the Adopted Adolescent: The Delaware Family Study*, New York: Child Welfare League of America.

Stevens, K. and Dally, E. (1985) *Surrogate Mother: One Woman's Story*, London: Century.

Stone, F.H. (1969) 'Adoption and identity', *Child Adoption* 58: 17–28.

Stone, L. (1977) *The Family, Sex, and Marriage in England 1500–1800*, London: Weidenfeld & Nicolson.

Storey, P. (1986) *Psychological Medicine* (10th edn), Edinburgh: Churchill-Livingstone.

Stott, D.H. (1966) *The Social Adjustment of Children: Manual for the Bristol Social Adjustment Guides* (3rd edn), London: London University Press.

Stroud, J. (1961) *On the Loose*, London: Longman.

———— (1965) *An Introduction to the Child-Care Service*, London: Longman.

Sullivan, H.S. (1953) *The Interpersonal Theory of Psychiatry*, New York: Norton.

Sweeny, D.M., Gasbarro, D.T., and Gluck, M.R. (1963) 'A descriptive study of adopted children seen in a child guidance centre', *Child Welfare* 42: 345–9.

Terman, L.M. and Wallin, P. (1949) 'Marriage prediction and marital adjustment tests', *American Sociological Review* 14: 497–504.

Thomson, H. (1966) *The Successful Step-Parent*, New York: Harper & Row.

Tienari, P. (1963) 'Psychiatric illness in identical twins', *Acta Psychiatrica Scandinavica* 39: 1–195 (Suppl. 171).

Tizard, B. (1977) *Adoption: A Second Chance*, London: Open Books.

Townsend, P. (1957) *The Family Life of Old People: An Inquiry in East London*, London: Routledge & Kegan Paul.

Toynbee, P. (1985) *Lost Children: The Story of Adopted Children Searching for Their Mothers*, London: Hutchinson.

Trasler, G. (1955) 'A study of success and failure of foster home placements', Unpublished Ph.D. thesis: University of London.

———— (1960) *In Place of Parents: A Study of Foster Care*, London: Routledge & Kegan Paul.

Trevor, W. (1972) *The Ballroom of Romance*, London: Bodley Head.

Triseliotis, J. (1973) *In Search of Origins: The Experiences of Adopted People*, London: Routledge & Kegan Paul.

———— (1980) 'Growing up in foster care and after', in J. Triseliotis (ed.) *New Developments in Foster Care and Adoption*, London: Routledge & Kegan Paul.

———— (1984) 'Obtaining birth certificates', In P. Bean (ed.) *Adoption: Essays in Social Policy, Law, and Sociology*, London: Tavistock.

Triseliotis, J. and Russell, J. (1984) *Hard to Place: The Outcome of Adoption and Residential Care*, London: Heinemann.

Trost, J. (in press) 'Cohabitation and marriage: transitional pattern, different lifestyle, or just another legal form', in H.G. Moors and J.J. Schoorl (eds) *Proceedings of Workship on Lifestyle, Contraception, and Parenthood*, Amsterdam: September 1986.

Trounson, A., Leeten, J. Besanko, M., Wood, C., and Conti, A. (1983) 'Pregnancy established in an infertile patient after transfer of a donated embryo fertilized *in vitro*', *British Medical Journal* 286: 835–8.

Veevers, J.E. (1980) *Childless by Choice*, Toronto: Butterworth.

—— (1983) 'Researching voluntary childlessness: a critical assessment of current strategies and findings', in E. Macklin and R. Rubin (eds) *Contemporary Families and Alternative Life Styles*, Beverly Hills, Calif.: Sage.

Visher, E.B. and Visher, J.S. (1979) *Step-Families : A Guide to Working with Step-Parents and Step-Children*, New York: Brunner/Mazel.

Wallerstein, J.S. (1983) 'Children of divorce: the psychological tasks of the child', *American Journal of Orthopsychiatry* 53: 240–53.

—— (1985) 'Children of divorce: preliminary report of a ten-year follow-up of older children and adolescents', *Journal of the American Academy of Child Psychiatry* 24: 545–53.

Wallerstein, J.S. and Kelly, J.B. (1980) *Surviving the Breakup*, New York: Basic Books.

Walsh, E.D. and Lewis, F.S. (1969) 'A study of adoptive mothers in a child guidance clinic', *Social Casework* 50: 587–94.

Wardle, C.J. (1961) 'Two generations of broken homes in the genesis of conduct and behaviour disorders in childhood', *British Medical Journal* ii: 349–54.

Warnock Committee (1984) *Report of the Committee of Inquiry into Human Fertilization and Embryology*, London: HMSO.

Waterman, A.S. (1982) 'Identity development from adolescence to adulthood: an extension of theory and a review of research', *Developmental Psychology* 3: 341–58.

Wedge, P. and Thoburn, J. (eds) (1986) *Finding Families for 'Hard-to-Place' Children: Evidence from Research*, London: Association of British Adoption and Fostering Agencies.

Weidell, R.C. (1980) 'Unsealing sealed birth certificates in Minnesota', *Child Welfare* 59: 113–19.

Weinstein, E.A. (1960) *The Self-Image of the Foster Child*, New York: Russell Sage Foundation.

Wellisch, E. (1952) 'Children without genealogy: a problem of adoption', *Mental Health* 15: No.1 (letter).

Wender, P.H., Rosenthal, D., Kety, S.S, Schulsinger, F., and Welner, J. (1974) 'Cross-fostering: a research strategy for clarifying the role of genetic and experiential factors in the etiology of schizophrenia', *Archives of General Psychiatry* 30: 121–8.

West, A. (1984) *Heritage*, London: Secker & Warburg. First published (1955) New York: Random House.

Wilson, A. (1985) *Family*, London: Tavistock.

Wolff, S. (1981) *Children under Stress* (2nd edn), Harmondsworth: Penguin.

Wolins, M. (1963) *Selecting Foster Parents: The Ideal and the Reality*, New York: Columbia University Press.

Wolkind, S. (1977) 'Women who have been in care: psychological and social status during pregnancy', *Journal of Child Psychology and Psychiatry* 18: 179–82.

Wood, C. and Trounson, A. (eds) (1984) *Clinical In Vitro Fertilization*, Berlin: Springer-Verlag.

Wood, C. and Westmore, A. (1983) *Test-Tube Conception*, Melbourne: Hill of Content.

Woolf, M. (1971) *Family Intentions*, London: HMSO.

Yelloly, M. (1965) 'Factors relating to an adoption decision by the mothers of illegitimate infants', *Sociological Review* 13: 6–13.

——— (1979) *Independent Evaluation of 25 Placements*, Maidstone: Kent Social Services Department.

Young, M. and Willmott, P. (1957) *Family and Kinship in East London*, London: Routledge & Kegan Paul.

Appendix I

Name (optional):   Date of birth: Sex (ring) M / F

Address (nearest town if preferred):

Occupation:

Marital status (tick): single / married / divorced / separated / widowed

Husband's occupation (married women):

Children (age and sex):

Adoptive family:

    Father: alive, aged   / died aged   in (year of death)
           Occupation:

    Mother: alive, aged   / died aged   in (year of death)
           Occupation:

    Siblings: (age. sex, whether also adopted, occupation)

Age at placement for adoption (if known):

Age at court order (if known):

Age at which first told of adoption (tick):

    Always knew

    Remember being told specifically: Before age 5
                                     5 - 10
                                     after age 10

Told by (tick):

    Adoptive mother / adoptive father / sibling / other relative (specify) /

    Discovered from outside source (specify)

Early knowledge of birth parents (age, location, work, marital status, etc.):

Do you know your birth father's name?   YES / NO

Were you told why you were offered for adoption?   YES / NO

    If 'Yes' please explain:

- 2 -

Were you told your original name?   YES / NO

    If 'Yes' how important was this for you?   very / fairly / not very

When and why did you first want to find out more about your background?

Did any particular event make you decide to join NORCAP

  e.g. Coming of age / marriage / pregnancy / death of adoptive mother or father, etc.

How far have you taken your enquiries to date?

    (a) Counselling   (b) inspection of birth certificate

    (c) search for natural mother / relatives

    (d) meeting with natural mother / relatives

        If not yet (d) do you intend to take the matter further?

                now / in future / not sure / no

        If 'Yes' to (d), how did you both feel when you first met?

        Outcome of meeting:

        Plans for maintaining contact:

- 3 -

Please underline your response to the following statements:

(1) I am sure of my place in the world .... TRUE   FALSE

(2) Friends who know I'm adopted have usually accepted
     the fact without comment .... TRUE   FALSE

(3) I've never felt comfortable about my adoptive status .... TRUE   FALSE

(4) My adoptive parents have always respected my
     individuality .... TRUE   FALSE

(5) I have often wondered who I really am .... TRUE   FALSE

(6) I've never felt that I was living under a bogus
     identity .... TRUE   FALSE

(7) Learning more about my background has helped (or would
     probably help) me to come to terms with myself .... TRUE   FALSE

(8) I find myself wishing I'd remained with
     my original family .... OFTEN / SOMETIMES / RARELY / NEVER

It has been suggested that preoccupation with one's origins may arise from an
unhappy experience of adoption.   We are not sure how far to believe this and
would ask you to forgive the following questions, which you must feel free to
ignore if they upset you:

(a) Were you happy, on the whole, in your adoptive family?   YES / NO

     Please amplify if you wish:

(b) Have you ever attended a child guidance or adult psychiatric clinic? YES / NO

     Please amplify if you wish:

Many thanks for your help.   Please add any comments of your own overleaf.

- 4 -

Additional comments:

Signature (optional): Date:

Appendix II

We have selected six cases from our NORCAP series (Chapter 5) to illustrate the extraordinary range of experiences that can befall those who grow up as adoptees. Each trio of women and men includes a success story as well as two less auspicious accounts. As partial validation of our adoption stress score we have recorded this for each case.

The two unhappy women were among the three respondents who were interviewed personally. Their stories were too vivid to be left out. Both had undergone intensive psychotherapy, as had one of the two unhappy men. There is nothing to indicate that either of the two happier individuals were unusually robust in personality, but they were certainly more fortunate in their family life. Even with the most scrupulously careful selection procedures adoption will always remain something of a lottery, as these brief case histories amply demonstrate.

(1) MARIA (STRESS SCORE = 9)

Maria is aged 38 and divorced. She was adopted at the age of 8 weeks. Her adoptive parents had two sons, ten and fourteen years older than her, but despite repeated miscarriages her adoptive mother still wanted a daughter. She became pregnant again before Maria was placed, and succeeded in giving birth to a daughter, one month premature, when Maria was 8 months old. Although her adoptive father had had reservations about adopting he became very fond of her and remained her only source of love and security until his untimely death in an accident when she was 8 years old. She was quite unable to mourn his loss and became very withdrawn and isolated. Her adoptive mother had never had much time for her, and with the change in circumstances which followed on her husband's death, lost patience with her entirely. She became the butt of the family's anger and was ill-treated by them all, including sexual abuse from the younger son. She was frequently taken to child guidance clinics by her mother, spent a short time at boarding school, and left home for good at the age of 18. She had often stayed with relatives of the family to get away from home, and had worked at weekends and holidays as soon as she was old enough for the same reason.

She came to London and trained as a nurse, and spent the next sixteen years in nursing. At the age of 24 she married, but could not sustain the relationship, and took flight from the marriage eighteen months later. The warmth with which her husband's family had welcomed her seemed attractive at first, but she was unable to respond to it or to cope with married life.

She first sought psychiatric help soon after the breakdown of her marriage, when she attempted to take an overdose. The first psychiatrist she saw gave her considerable support, but he was climbing the career ladder and moved to another part of the country on obtaining a consultant post. Thereafter she went to a series of therapists, all of whom she rejected. By the time she was 31 she was very depressed and desperate for help. Her first admission to hospital lasted only a month, though she was persuaded to continue as a day patient. It was at this stage that she was diagnosed as anorectic – a diagnosis she was totally unable to accept at the time. However, a subsequent admission to hospital did enable her to confront her problem. She had been a plump child and had begun to diet at about 14 years old. However, her weight had never fallen so low that her menstrual function ceased altogether. At 18 she developed ulcerative colitis. After treatment for this condition, excessive purgation became her form of weight control and over time she became dependent on laxatives. An attempt to solve this problem by a change of prescription was unsuccessful. Eventually with help she was able to shed her dependence on laxatives. She continued to receive support with weekly visits to a psychotherapist and monthly ones to the psychiatrist at the hospital.

For as long as she could remember, Maria had wanted to trace her natural mother. She had been given her adoption papers at the time of her marriage but had not made use of the information they contained. When Section 26 of the 1975 Children Act became law she received counselling and obtained her birth certificate. She made intermittent attempts to take the matter further for some years after that, but while recovering from her illness she met a man who was willing to help and support her in her search. They managed to trace her mother, and with the help of a NORCAP intermediary contact was made. Her family were welcoming and enthusiastic about getting to know her and she and her mother have now exchanged overnight visits and maintain regular contact by telephone. Her stepfather had known of her existence but her two half-brothers and half-sister had not. Although she was delighted to have found her family, she found the establishment of new relationships very difficult, and had to work hard to overcome her instinct to withdraw in the face of their exuberant insistence on her participation. In particular, she found it hard to tell her mother of her unhappy childhood, but she managed to do so, and in return learned of the circumstances of her own conception (her mother was raped by a convalescent serviceman in the grounds of the establishment where she was nursing). It is now two years since Maria found her family, and although they are keen for her to move to live near them she cannot yet commit herself to doing so. She has not seen her adoptive mother for a number of years, although she still occasionally meets her sister and one of her brothers.

Maria's unhappy experiences have made it extremely difficult for her to maintain relationships. She says she ran away from her marriage because she was frightened of the commitment, and she is sad that she also retreated from the relationship with the man who helped her to find her family. A few months ago she met a man who was very keen to settle in marriage and have a family, and after a short time she agreed to marry him. However, as she got to know him better she began to doubt the wisdom of this move, and after much agonizing she withdrew on the eve of the wedding. She has always wanted to have children, though has never felt secure enough in a relationship to risk this. Now, however, she is nearly 39 and desperate to have a child while she still can, having learnt that the women in her family are likely to have an early menopause. She plans to seek donor insemination and claims to be able to organize her life so as to succeed as a single parent.

(2) NICOLA (STRESS SCORE = 9)

Nicola is 35 years old and single. She appears to the outside world as an attractive successful business woman. She has a good-sized flat in a prestige block in a fashionable part of London. Outward appearances, however, are deceptive and she had a sad story to tell.

She was born in a Baptist mother-and-baby home in the west country and so far as she knows her mother was a telephonist. She was adopted soon after birth by a Baptist minister and his wife. Her adoptive father was then in his forties and mother in her late thirties. It was decided by her parents that she would go to Oxford and have a career, and she knew this from the age of 3. She was never allowed to meet other children, and by the time she went to school at 5 years old she could read and write and had started to learn Greek, but had no idea how to relate to her peers. She was never given dolls to play with or encouraged in any way to take a feminine view of life. At the age of about 4 her mother discovered that Nicola's father was having an incestuous relationship with her, whereupon she tried to kill her. (In later years she learnt that her mother was probably suffering from paranoid schizophrenia). Her father disappeared from the scene for several months with a nervous breakdown. He had apparently become ill earlier in his career, and Nicola remembers him disappearing for another spell when she was about 12.

Relations between her parents were very strained, and she remembers that for months at a time they would only communicate through her. Her mother was totally dominant, and her father appeared to be falling over backwards to compensate for something. She had been told of her adoption at about 3 years old, but when she remembered the incident later she was unsure if it was a fantasy, since it was never referred to again until she was 17. However, hints were dropped by her grandparents when she was 8 or 9 and she spent many hours searching the house for evidence, which she never found. At one stage her adoptive mother dyed Nicola's hair blond and curled it so that she would appear to take after her physically.

When she was 11, and had just started grammar school, her parents moved to the Midlands to a new parish, leaving behind many friends and a pleasant life in a country town. They disliked their new surroundings, and Nicola had to make a fresh start in another grammar school where there was little emphasis on academic achievement. However, she worked hard and in due course won the place at Oxford that her parents so coveted. During these years the problems at home increased. Her mother was very strict and would often beat her for asking permission to do something outside the home, let alone allow her to do it. Her father played a lesser role in this regime, but any attempts she made to develop her own individuality were stamped on. At 17, her parents found out that she was having an affair with a married man, and the fact of her adoption together with allegations about her natural mother were flung at her.

She spent four years at Oxford, doing modern languages for two years and then switching to PPE. She narrowly missed a first. Oxford had promised the answer to all her problems – the reality was very different and it became a test of endurance to finish her degree. She set to work systematically to eradicate her Midlands accent, and espoused a promiscuous lifestyle, but meaningful relationships eluded her and she remained as lonely and insecure as she had been in childhood. The strain of her years at Oxford nearly precipitated a breakdown, but she kept going partly through fear of parental rejection and partly through her determination to support herself in a career. She joined the world of business and became a planning executive.

There have been inconsistencies in her career pattern which she is anxiously aware do not look good on her curriculum vitae. At age 25 she was earning £20,000 a year and theoretically could be making £25,000 a year by now. She knows her capabilities and is prepared to work hard, but acknowledges that her aggressive self-confidence in this area tends to put colleagues off and she invariably finds herself an unpopular member of staff. In her most recent executive job she found herself in an uncongenially political environment where she felt she was being squeezed out as her prospects for advancement diminished, and this helped to precipitate a breakdown about nine months ago. She spent a month in hospital, resigned her job, and since then has been doing temporary work as a stopgap in jobs that are below her level of competence and aspiration. The most recent of these, however, had been offered to her on a permanent basis, and although at a far lower salary than she was used to she was hoping to continue in it at least for the time being.

Whilst in a private psychiatric unit last year she formed a relationship with a male patient, fourteen years her junior, and this has lasted until very recently, when he returned to his family home ostensibly for a brief respite. This was the longest relationship she had ever managed to sustain apart from her first at the age of 16. She said that she did not get on with men in her own age-group and had mostly been involved with those fifteen or more years older than herself. To live with a much younger partner was a new experience for her, and they had supported one another through recovery from breakdown. She was aware, however, that she may have been something of a mother-figure to him, especially as she bears some physical resemblance to his actual mother. She had contemplated having a child by this man and admitted that the need for a child with its biological link had assumed somewhat more importance recently. She had become pregnant whilst at Oxford and had felt that an abortion was unavoidable at that stage.

She had said that the only identity she had managed to build for herself was within the context of her intellectual and business capacity. During the last year this had been badly undermined, and at a personal level she has never been able to decide who she is. She has no close friends and feels that she is generally unpopular, but cannot stop herself rubbing people up the wrong way. She would like to find out about her background not from any need to look like someone else, but because she would like to know from whom she has inherited her talents (in addition to her intellectual ability she is a keen pianist). She would be more interested to meet her natural father than her mother, and thinks this might contribute to the search for her own identity. However, apart from obtaining her birth certificate, she has not pursued the search for either parent further since she is aware that she needs to be feeling confident and successful to cope with any meeting that might result. She is also concerned that her natural mother should not feel guilt about the events of her adoption.

She has always been inclined to depression when problems have got on top of her, and spent three years in analysis a few years ago. However, she was a somewhat intermittent attender who tended to drop out of treatment whenever she started to feel better. She made more than one suicide attempt in the months before her hospital admission last year, but after five weeks' inpatient care was told that she was not in fact depressed, and she admitted to us that she had been in a much worse state after she left university. From her earliest childhood she has always panicked when people have left her, feeling certain that she will never see them again, and her experiences in adult life have done nothing to help her overcome this fear. She acknowledges her tendency to cling to people who invariably let her down because they too have problems they cannot resolve.

(3) JULIE (STRESS SCORE = 3)

Julie is a journalist. She is 37 years old, married, with a 6-year-old son. She was adopted when she was 6 weeks old and recalls a happy childhood. She was an only child, however, as her adoptive mother developed diabetes shortly after she was placed and was advised against adopting more children.

Julie's parents were always very open with her about her adoption but had very little information to give her. However, they stressed the fact that Julie had not been rejected by her natural mother, but had been placed with them because she was loved and deserved a better life than would have been possible if she had stayed with her (then single) natural mother. Julie remembers that she did feel somewhat different from other children, and was shy and anxious to please. She used to wonder if her natural mother was all right and sometimes prayed for siblings (she later found eight!). She grew up wanting to find out about her background but was unable to do anything about it until Section 26 of the 1975 Children Act came into force.

At that stage she became involved in a television programme which debated the issues raised by the new law, and had difficulty in extricating herself from their manoeuvres to find her natural mother for her and then film the confrontation. However, another guest on the programme became a personal friend, who helped her to continue her search privately and acted as intermediary before she met her natural mother. Some years after she found her original family a television programme was made about it.

Julie found that her natural mother was married soon after she had been placed for adoption (though not to Julie's father), and had then had eight more children. The family all knew about Julie and welcomed her. She says it was very important to her to discover her physical resemblance to her natural mother and other members of the family, and to be able to compare temperaments and abilities. She had also felt a strong need for medical information since she had sometimes been embarrassed by questions of this nature which she was unable to answer. However, the discovery that her eldest half-sister had Down's syndrome led her to be rather anxious about the likelihood of having a handicapped child herself, and her fears were hardly dispelled by a totally unsympathetic gynaecologist when she became pregnant at the age of 30. Happily, her fears were groundless and she has a lively and enterprising son.

Julie says that she didn't quite know what she was looking for in seeking her natural mother and family, but she feels she has found whatever it was now that she knows them. She feels more 'settled and complete' now and has gained enormously in self-confidence. She stressed how important it had been for her to have her adoptive parents' love and support while she searched, and she said that it was only because she felt secure and happy with them that she was able to go ahead and meet her original family. At the end of the questionnaire she wrote:

> Adoptive parents fear they will lose the love and respect of their children if they start to search. Love is not like a cake that will only cut into eight slices and person number nine gets nothing.

(4) ALAN (STRESS SCORE = 5)

Alan is 35 years old and single. His story differs from that of the majority of our respondents in that most of his childhood was spent in care.

His mother was a single girl, living in London, and his father was a married Indian, who had come to this country in 1945 in order to earn a better living to support his family in India. Alan's mother turned to the local authority for help and they placed her in the care of a north London moral welfare agency, which was run by nuns. As a result Alan was placed in a children's home against her wishes. At that time the policy of the agency which ran the home was to discourage contact between a single parent and her illegitimate child, and although his mother wanted to remain in touch it was made difficult for her, particularly when he was moved to a home in the north of England, where he spent most of his childhood. He remembers being allowed to visit her in

London on one occasion when he was about 14, and thereafter
lost touch with her.

Alan says he had a very middle-class upbringing in the
children's home. When he was about 14 it was decided that he
should work for O levels and he needed somewhere to stay
during the week in order to attend an appropriate school.
Through contacts of the children's home he was invited to stay
with a family during this period. The father had four children by a
first marriage, and was starting a second family with his new
wife. The older children were away at boarding school and they
had a large house with plenty of room. Alan was the same age as
the eldest son and they got on well together. He gradually became part of the family, staying with them full-time instead of
returning to the children's home at weekends, and they suggested that they should adopt him. He was legally adopted at the age
of 16, and says he formed something of a bridge between the
older and younger children in the family. When a second boy was
adopted into the family nearly ten years later he admits that his
nose was put badly out of joint as he had always seen himself as a
'special' member of the family. However, he was gently chided
that at 25 this was rather an extreme reaction!

He enjoys being a member of his adoptive family and they
continue to give him support. However, since he moved to
London in 1976 and the family home is in the north he does not
have very much contact with them now – occasional visits have
to suffice. He passed his O levels but failed his A levels. At a much
later stage he studied as a mature student at a London poly-
technic. He started a degree in English but transferred to a full-
time diploma in acting which led to his present career.

In spite of his late and happy adoption, Alan reached adulthood
with many unresolved questions about his early life. It seemed
that nobody was willing to be open with him during his years in
care as to why he was there, and he grew up feeling rejected by
his natural mother and with a considerably dented self-image. In
1981, a friend who was training as a psychoanalyst suggested that
Alan might find this form of therapy helpful, and introduced him
to the analyst he is still seeing. In the course of analysis it became
apparent that finding out about his origins might be particularly
helpful in view of his feelings of rejection by his mother.

When he approached the agency which had been responsible

for him he found that policies had changed drastically since he was a child, and they gave him full access to his file, in which were a number of comments about the need to keep the child away from an unsuitable mother! He then turned to the social services department in the borough, whose staff were extremely co-operative in helping him to trace his mother. With further help from NORCAP he made contact, and first met her as an adult about two years ago. At a cerebral level he understands why things worked out the way they did, but says he finds himself still feeling that she is to blame for his blighted childhood. This makes it quite difficult for him to visit her, even though she lives within easy reach.

However, another social services department managed to locate his half-brother on his father's side, whom he had met briefly on a visit to London many years ago. He lives nearby, and meeting him again appears to have been quite a pleasure. This man, about ten years older than Alan, had joined his father in England to help support the family, and when his father returned to what had become Bangladesh, his brother remained in England. He married a charming Indian woman and was running a small business. Through him, Alan met his father on a visit to England, but found it somewhat frustrating as his father speaks no English and was temporarily blind. However, successful surgery has since restored his sight, and visual contact has made the relationship much fuller.

Alan says he feels he is still evolving as a person. Having roots in two different cultures complicates things, and he is slowly learning about the Indian side of his family with his brother's help. Although he feels he will continue to need the support of his analyst for some time yet, he says treatment has fundamentally changed him, enabling him to feel free to make his own choices in life for the first time. He is very grateful to his adoptive parents for making it financially possible for him to start treatment.

He says his relationships with women tend to be 'fairly shambolic'. He finds it difficult to sustain a relationship beyond the six month stage where sexual attraction starts to make room for getting to know someone. He thinks he tends to be attracted to people who also have problems about their identity. His feelings about the importance of having children of his own tend to vary and he is aware of other issues to resolve before he can deal with that one. His first reaction on being asked if he would want children was to say that he would want to adopt a child before having any of his own, so that the adopted child would have first place in the family.

(5) ERIC (STRESS SCORE = 4, INCOMPLETE)

Eric is a married man of 47, with two teenage daughters and a 5-year-old son. The first eight years of his life were spent in a children's home in north London. He remembers them as a time of great insecurity, with constant changes of staff and frequent punishments. He hated being part of such a group of children, often pretended he didn't belong to it, and invariably found himself cleaning all the shoes on his own as punishment. After several trial weekends with other prospective parents had come to nothing he was at last found a home.

His adoptive parents had been married for many years and his adoptive mother was 47 years old when Eric arrived in the family. She was totally dominant in the home, with a rigid Victorian outlook. Eric lived under constant threat of being returned to the children's home if he misbehaved, and adoption was a shameful, forbidden topic to which he must never refer. As he continued to attend the same school after his adoption it was decided that he should retain his original surname for school purposes, but the rest of the time his adoptive surname was used. This led to endless complications, including being bullied and beaten at school, but he was never allowed to complain or ask why the decision had been made. His father attempted to alleviate Eric's situation by buying comics, but when his mother found out she soon put a stop to it, and thereafter both he and his father had to toe the line. Eric had to join the church choir to satisfy his mother's religious zeal, and he was expected to achieve at school. He remembers fainting in exams under the pressure of it all.

When he was 18 years old, Eric left home to join the Army and his adoptive mother never forgave him. Despite constant efforts to please her with letters, cards, and presents which she never acknowledged, he could do nothing right. Although he did not live with his parents again after his spell in the Army, he regularly spent his holidays with them. His social life on these occasions, however, was very restricted since his mother never approved of his girlfriends and he was expected to be home by 10 p.m. Finally he decided on a career which would entail his living away from home permanently, but he was 28 years old by the time he escaped.

Whilst in the Army, Eric overheard another young man talking openly about his adoption, and fully expected him to be struck by lightning for mentioning such a taboo subject. When nothing disastrous happened he felt suddenly liberated and became able to discuss his own situation with other people at last. His wider experience of life gradually enabled him to put his own past into some sort of perspective, though he felt himself considerably hampered in his ability to make relationships with women until after he left home. Soon after this step had been taken his first steady girlfriend became his wife.

When his adoptive father died Eric found he had been left half his estate. However, his mother made such a fuss about it that he gave up his portion to her to avoid unpleasantness. Three years later his mother died, and he discovered that she had changed her solicitors, left her entire estate to other members of the family, and destroyed all evidence that he had ever existed. The cousin to whom most of the estate had been left urged Eric to contest the will, but he was too upset to do so. This cousin, however, was able to shed some light on his mother's actions. He told Eric that his adoptive parents had taken, in turn, two young boys who were relatives into their home. Both had been called Eric, and both had left to join the forces at the earliest possible age (then 14) and had never been heard of again. Later, his adoptive maternal grandmother had lived with them and been looked after until her death. It was following this event that Eric himself joined the family.

Despite the deprivations of his stony upbringing, Eric has been successful in his chosen career and enjoys his job. His own more emotional nature has found satisfaction in his wife and family. He said that it was very important for him to have children of his own, and particularly to have a son, but that he would have wanted to adopt if this had not been possible.

He has always been curious about his own origins but delayed any attempts to find out until after the death of both adoptive parents. Unfortunately, his adoptive mother had made it extremely difficult for him and the only record he had was his adoption certificate. He has experienced endless frustrations in trying to trace his origins, as even the records from the children's home had vanished. However, at the time of our conversation a glimmer of light had appeared at last as the children's home records had been tracked down and a social worker with his interests at heart had found some information for him. Eric says that with this lack of background he still does not know who he is. Sometimes he feels that he shouldn't really exist at all. He thinks it would help to know he took after someone else, and would want to meet any relatives he managed to trace. He is well aware that his natural mother would be getting on in years if she is still alive, and he would be anxious not to upset her, but he knows he would find rejection by her extremely hard to bear. He says he still can't get over being treated as 'just an object' by his adoptive mother. If there are half-siblings he would be hopeful about meeting them, and his wife fully supports his efforts to trace his family.

Looking back at his life, Eric thinks his childhood was the worst time, and that things have improved enormously in adult life, largely thanks to a good marriage.

(6) BARRY (STRESS SCORE = 1)

Barry is 41 years old and has recently married. He joined his adoptive family at the age of 12 weeks, and has an adopted sister who is five years younger. He feels very positive about having been adopted. He knew of his adoption from an early age but never felt it necessary to tell other children so was not made to feel different.

His parents were in their thirties when he came to them, and had discovered early in their marriage that they were unable to have children of their own. They appeared to have a very equal partnership, and he and his sister grew up in an open and happy atmosphere. He was just beginning to appreciate his father's company in a more adult way when he died when Barry was 19. He mourned his loss and became closer to his mother, who valued the support of his sister and himself through her widowhood.

It was not until after his adoptive mother's death ten years ago that he began to think of researching his origins. He harboured no strong doubts as to his identity and attached no particular importance to physical resemblance, but he found himself curious as to the circumstances which led to his adoption, and was interested to know what had happened to his natural mother and whether he had any half-siblings. In common with so many other adoptive parents of their time, his own had very little information to pass on about his origins.

It took him about four months to trace his natural mother, and he used NORCAP's intermediary service to establish contact with her. His reappearance came as a shock to her, to the extent that she became ill for a while and lost weight. Her husband and two sons had no knowledge of his existence. However, after the initial shock he was welcomed as a member of the family and is now in regular contact. He is aware of his good fortune in not finding any skeletons in the family cupboard, and in his mother's willingness to accept him and introduce him to the rest of the family.

Through his work with children, both able-bodied and handicapped, he met his wife, and he looks forward to having children of his own. He thinks the biological link would be important, but would certainly try to adopt if this were denied him. It took him some while to reach marriage, and he says that in common with a number of men he had some earlier problems in making relationships with women. However, he has always been able to talk to people and make friends.

His support for other adoptees who hope to trace their origins has involved him in meetings, seminars, and practical help. He has even taken part in seminars for prospective adopters to put the point of view of the adoptee who needs information about his original family.

Name index

Subject index

Families with a Difference ——

Families with a Difference
Varieties of surrogate parenthood

Michael *and* Heather Humphrey

Families other than those made up of the natural
mother, father, and siblings are increasing in number.
This book looks at these 'alternative' families and
considers the psychological and social consequences of
growing up in a family where the genetic link between
parents and children is missing or incomplete. The
authors discuss adoption, fostering, stepfamilies, and
parenthood by donor insemination, as well as such
controversial areas as 'womb-leasing' and homosexual
parenthood. A recurring theme is whether, when, and
what to tell children of their extrafamilial origins, and
how they and other family members react to the
knowledge.

Families with a Difference is a comprehensive new
analysis of the changing nature of family life in
western society which, in the aftermath of the
influential Warnock Report, will be important reading
for students and professionals in social policy, social
work, psychology, and the social aspects of medicine.

Michael Humphrey is Reader in Psychology, and
Heather Humphrey is a researcher in the Department
of Psychiatry at St George's Hospital Medical School,
University of London.